TRUTH COMMISSIONS
AND CRIMINAL COURTS

This detailed evaluation of the relationship between trials and truth commissions challenges their assumed compatibility through an analysis of their operational features at national, inter-state and international levels. Alison Bisset conducts case-study analyses of national practice in South Africa, East Timor and Sierra Leone, evaluates the problems posed by the International Criminal Court and considers the challenges presented by the possibility of bystander state prosecutions. At each level, she highlights potential operational conflicts and formulates targeted proposals to enable effective coexistence.

ALISON BISSET is a lecturer in law at the University of Reading.

TRUTH COMMISSIONS AND CRIMINAL COURTS

ALISON BISSET

CAMBRIDGE
UNIVERSITY PRESS

CAMBRIDGE UNIVERSITY PRESS
Cambridge, New York, Melbourne, Madrid, Cape Town,
Singapore, São Paulo, Delhi, Mexico City

Cambridge University Press
The Edinburgh Building, Cambridge CB2 8RU, UK

Published in the United States of America by Cambridge University Press, New York

www.cambridge.org
Information on this title: www.cambridge.org/9781107008038

© Alison Bisset 2012

This publication is in copyright. Subject to statutory exception
and to the provisions of relevant collective licensing agreements,
no reproduction of any part may take place without the written
permission of Cambridge University Press.

First published 2012

Printed and bound in the United States of America

A catalogue record for this publication is available from the British Library

Library of Congress Cataloging in Publication data
Bisset, Alison.
Truth commissions and criminal courts / Alison Bisset.
pages   cm
Includes index.
ISBN 978-1-107-00803-8 (hardback)
1. International criminal courts.   2. Truth commissions.   3. Jurisdiction
(International law)   4. Transitional justice.   I. Title.
KZ7230.B57 2012
345–dc23
2012002161

ISBN 978-1-107-00803-8 Hardback

Cambridge University Press has no responsibility for the persistence or
accuracy of URLs for external or third-party internet websites referred to in
this publication, and does not guarantee that any content on such websites is,
or will remain, accurate or appropriate.

CONTENTS

ACKNOWLEDGEMENTS

The research for this book began with my doctoral studies at the University of Dundee. My Ph.D. supervisors, Mark Mackarel and Elizabeth Kirk, provided me with invaluable guidance during that period. I hope they will enjoy reading the end result.

My colleagues at the University of Reading have offered me much encouragement and support as I have prepared this book. Heartfelt thanks are owed to my mentor, Professor Sandy Ghandhi, for his endless kindness, reassurance and sound advice. I am grateful to Thérèse Callus for her comments on various sections of the book and to Anne Thies for her helpful suggestions.

Thank you also to my friends and family who have tolerated with good grace the neglect I have shown them while this book has been completed. As ever, my mother has given me unfailing support. She, together with my father, laid the foundations for my interest in human rights through their sense of fairness, concern for others and readiness to transform it into action.

Last, and most of all, I would like to thank my husband, Barry Fenton, for his interest, willingness to listen and belief in my abilities. I could not have done this without his abundant patience and support.

TABLE OF CASES

Inter-American Court of Human Rights

International Criminal Court
Central African Republic, Situation in (Case No. ICC-01/05)

Democratic Republic of Congo, Situation in (Case No. ICC-01/04)

International Criminal Tribunal for the former Yugoslavia

Permanent Court of International Justice

Special Court for Sierra Leone

Special Panels for Serious Crimes (East Timor)

National Cases

Israel

South Africa

United Kingdom

United States

Denmark

ABBREVIATIONS

ANC	African National Congress
CAT	UN Convention against Torture and other Cruel, Inhuman and Degrading Treatment
CAVR	Commission for Reception, Truth and Reconciliation
CRP	Community Reconciliation Process
DRC	Democratic Republic of Congo
ECCC	Extraordinary Chambers in the Courts of Cambodia
ECHR	European Court of Human Rights
ECR	European Court Reports
EHRR	European Human Rights Reports
ETS	European Treaty Series
EU	European Union
GAOR	General Assembly Official Reports
HRC	Human Rights Committee
IACHR	Inter-American Court of Human Rights
ICC	International Criminal Court
ICCPR	International Covenant on Civil and Political Rights
ICJ	International Court of Justice
ICRC	International Committee for the Red Cross and Red Crescent
ICTJ	International Center for Transitional Justice
ICTR	International Criminal Tribunal for Rwanda
ICTY	International Criminal Tribunal for the former Yugoslavia
ILM	International Legal Materials
ILR	International Law Reports
LRA	Lord's Resistance Army
NGO	Non-governmental organisation
NISGUA	Network in Solidarity with Guatemala
OASTS	Organisation of American States Treaty Series
OGP	Office of the General Prosecutor
OJ	Official Journal
OTP	Office of the Prosecutor
RPE	Rules of Procedure and Evidence

RUF	Revolutionary United Front
SAARC	South Asian Association for Regional Cooperation
SADF	South African Defence Force
SALR	South African Law Reports
SCSL	Special Court for Sierra Leone
SCU	Serious Crimes Unit
SLTRC	Truth and Reconciliation Commission for Sierra Leone
TRC	Truth and Reconciliation Commission
UN	United Nations
UNMIK	United Nations Mission in Kosovo
UNTAET	United Nations Transitional Administration in East Timor
UNTS	United Nations Treaty Series
ZACC	South African Constitutional Court Cases

~

Introduction

Within the field of transitional justice, truth commissions and criminal prosecutions have emerged as the primary mechanisms for responding to a legacy of serious human rights violations. Discourse on the establishment of these bodies, their operation, strengths and weaknesses, and the merits of one over the other, has dominated the transitional justice literature,[1] as much as their use has monopolised transitional justice practice. Recent times have seen a move away from the traditional 'either/or' approach to the establishment of these bodies. Truth commissions have shaken off the perception that they are 'inferior substitutes for prosecution'[2] and are increasingly recognised as an important element of transitional justice strategies to address past abuses.[3] There is a growing consensus that truth commissions and criminal trials bring distinct

---

[1] M. Cherif Bassiouni (ed.), *Post-Conflict Justice* (New York: Transnational Publishers, 2002); Mark Freeman, *Truth Commissions and Procedural Fairness* (Cambridge University Press, 2006); Priscilla B. Hayner, *Unspeakable Truths. Facing the Challenge of Truth Commissions* (New York: Routledge, 2001); Priscilla B. Hayner, *Unspeakable Truths: Transitional Justice and the Challenge of Truth Commissions* (2nd edn) (London and New York: Routledge, 2010); Martha Minow, *From Vengeance to Forgiveness: Facing History after Genocide and Mass Violence* (Boston: Beacon Press, 1998); Robert I. Rotberg, and Dennis Thompson (eds.), *Truth v. Justice. The Morality of Truth Commissions* (Princeton University Press, 2000); Jane Stromseth, *Accountability for Atrocities: National and International Responses* (New York: Transnational Publishers, 2003); Eric Wiebelhaus-Brahm, *Truth Commissions and Transitional Societies: The Impact on Human Rights and Democracy* (London and New York: Routledge, 2010); Tristan Anne Borer (ed.), *Telling the Truths: Truth Telling and Peace Building in Post-Conflict Societies* (University of Notre Dame Press, 2006).

[2] Miriam Aukerman, 'Extraordinary Evil, Ordinary Crime: A Framework for Understanding Transitional Justice' (2002) 15 *Harvard Human Rights Journal* 39, 40.

[3] Wiebelhaus-Brahm, *Truth Commissions and Transitional Societies*, 5–6; Janet Cherry, 'Truth and Transitional Justice in South Africa', in Hugo Van der Merwe, Victoria Baxter and Audrey R. Chapman (eds.), *Assessing the Impact of Transitional Justice: Challenges for Empirical Research* (Washington DC: United States Institute of Peace Press, 2009), 249–65.

benefits to transitional states and that they ought to be viewed, not as mutually exclusive alternatives, but as contemporaneous complements.[4]

The theoretical compatibility and complementary nature of these mechanisms has been affirmed by the United Nations (UN), non-governmental organisations (NGOs) and academics alike.[5] However, the focus on the consistency of the benefits assumed to be delivered by truth commissions and criminal trials has resulted in a failure to assess whether their actual modes of operation are compatible. Despite overlapping subject matter mandates and requirements to access the same evidence and witnesses, studies on coordinating their proceedings are lacking, and policies and guidelines to enable their effective coexistence have not been forthcoming. The academic and NGO attention that has been directed towards the practical operations of these bodies has focused on cooperation arrangements between simultaneously operating truth commissions and criminal courts.[6] Proposals have typically centred upon the contribution that truth commissions might make to trials through the sharing of the information they may uncover during truth-seeking operations.[7] Little consideration has been given to the compatibility of such an arrangement with the non-judicial character of truth commissions. Beyond the possible inhibition of perpetrators,[8] the potential impact of information sharing on the wider truth-seeking process has not been addressed and the

---

[4] Naomi Roht-Arriaza and Javier Mariezcurrena (eds.), *Transitional Justice in the Twenty-First Century: Beyond Truth Versus Justice* (Cambridge University Press, 2006); Charles Villa-Vicencio, 'Why Perpetrators Should Not Always Be Prosecuted: Where the International Criminal Court and Truth Commissions Meet' (2000) 49 *Emory Law Journal* 205; Charles Villa-Vicencio, 'The Reek of Cruelty and the Quest for Healing: Where Retributive and Restorative Justice Meet' (1999–2000) 14 *Journal of Law and Religion* 165; UN Security Council, *Report of the Secretary General on the Rule of Law and Transitional Justice in Conflict and Post-Conflict Societies*, UN Doc. S/2004/616, 23 August 2004; Amnesty International, *Truth, Justice and Reparation: Establishing an Effective Truth Commission*, 11 June 2007.

[5] See all the works cited in note 4.

[6] Human Rights Watch, *Policy Paper on the Interrelationship between the Sierra Leone Special Court and Truth and Reconciliation Commission*, 18 April 2002; Marieke Wierda, Priscilla B. Hayner and Paul van Zyl, *Exploring the Relationship between the Special Court and the Truth and Reconciliation Commission of Sierra Leone*, International Center for Transitional Justice, June 2002; William A. Schabas, 'The Relationship between Truth Commissions and International Courts: The Case of Sierra Leone' (2003) 25 *Human Rights Quarterly* 1035; Patrick Burgess, 'Justice and Reconciliation in East Timor: The Relationship between the Commission for Reception, Truth and Reconciliation and the Courts' (2004) 15 *Criminal Law Forum* 135.

[7] Amnesty International, *Truth, Justice and Reparation*, Part V.

[8] PRIDE, *Ex-Combatant Views of the Truth and Reconciliation Commission and the Special Court for Sierra Leone*, A Study in Partnership with the International Center for Transitional Justice, Freetown, 12 September 2002.

compatibility of information sharing with the exercise of quasi-judicial powers by truth commissions has received scant examination. Proposals advanced to date have verged on the simplistic, arguing either that truth commission information ought to be available to prosecuting authorities[9] or that it ought to be protected from disclosure.[10]

The equilibrium in the relationship between truth commissions and trials faces new and additional challenges as a consequence of the renewed importance placed upon prosecution under the Rome Statute of the International Criminal Court.[11] As the operation of the International Criminal Court (ICC) moves transitional justice practice into a new era, there is a pressing need to thoroughly question afresh whether truth commissions and criminal trials are truly complementary and, if so, to identify conditions under which they can operate effectively together. The establishment of the ICC with its far-reaching powers to prosecute genocide, crimes against humanity and war crimes,[12] coupled with the founding principle of complementarity,[13] has prioritised prosecution as the primary response to the commission of the most serious human rights crimes, at national and international levels. The dynamics of the field of transitional justice have been altered by the creation of an international treaty regime which demands the prosecution of 'core' crimes and which elevates the pursuit of criminal trials over the successful operation of other transitional justice mechanisms where these crimes have been committed. The creation of this transitional justice hierarchy means that in investigating the most serious human rights crimes, future truth commissions will fulfil not only a complementary role to prosecutions, but a secondary one. Where core crimes have been committed, the relationship between truth commissions and prosecution can no longer be seen as one of equals: the truth commission has become subordinate.

The status of truth commissions under the ICC, an issue the Statute itself is silent upon, has attracted much scholarly debate.[14] Commentators

---

[9] Freeman, *Truth Commissions and Procedural Fairness*, 252; Human Rights Watch, *Policy Paper on the Interrelationship between the Sierra Leone Special Court and Truth and Reconciliation Commission*; Wierda *et al.*, *Exploring the Relationship between the Special Court and the Truth and Reconciliation Commission of Sierra Leone*.

[10] Schabas, 'The Relationship between Truth Commissions and International Courts'.

[11] Rome Statute of the International Criminal Court, A/Conf.183/9, 17 July 1998, (1998) 37 *International Legal Materials* 1002.

[12] Rome Statute, Art. 5.   [13] Rome Statute, Arts. 1 and 17.

[14] Carsten Stahn, 'Complementarity, Amnesties and Alternative Forms of Justice: Some Interpretative Guidelines for the International Criminal Court' (2005) 3 *Journal of International Criminal Justice* 695; Anja Seibert-Fohr, 'The Relevance of the Rome Statute of the International Criminal Court for Amnesties and Truth Commissions'

have sought to find loopholes within the Rome Statute that might allow for the establishment of truth commissions as alternatives to criminal trials. Discussion has centred on whether 'accountable' truth commission models might satisfy the complementarity criteria and prevent the ICC exercising jurisdiction.[15] It has been questioned whether the ICC might defer to truth commission initiatives where prosecution does not appear to be 'in the interests of justice'.[16] Others have considered whether the UN Security Council might use its powers to 'defer' prosecutions in favour of national truth commission proceedings.[17] Why the search for loopholes has been the main focus of scholarly attention on the relationship between truth commissions and the ICC remains unclear to this author. As the ICC Statute entered into force, transitional justice practice had already moved beyond this 'either/or' approach and truth commissions and prosecutions were being used as a multifaceted approach to past violations in East Timor and Sierra Leone. The pertinent question is not, therefore, whether there is still some back door through which to surreptitiously create a truth commission and avoid carrying out criminal trials where serious human rights crimes have been committed. The issue that warrants consideration is *how* truth commissions and prosecutorial institutions can operate effectively together in the ICC era. This is the question that this book seeks to answer.

(2003) 7 *Max Planck Yearbook of United Nations Law* 553; Michael P. Scharf, 'The Amnesty Exception to the Jurisdiction of the International Criminal Court' (1999) 32 *Cornell International Law Journal* 507; Declan Roche, 'Truth Commission Amnesties and the International Criminal Court' (2005) 45 *British Journal of Criminology* 565; Darryl Robinson, 'Serving the Interests of Justice: Amnesties, Truth Commissions and the International Criminal Court' (2003) 14 *European Journal of International Law* 481; Laura M. Olson, 'Provoking the Dragon on the Patio. Matters of Transitional Justice: Penal Repression v Amnesties' (2006) 88 *International Review of the Red Cross* 275; Jessica Gavron, 'Amnesties in the Light of Developments in International Law and the Establishment of the International Criminal Court' (2002) 51 *International and Comparative Law Quarterly* 91; John Dugard, 'Dealing with the Crimes of a Past Regime: Is Amnesty Still an Option?' (1999) 12 *Leiden Journal of International Law* 1003.

15 Dugard, 'Dealing with the Crimes of a Past Regime', 701–2; Stahn, 'Complementarity, Amnesties and Alternative Forms of Justice', 711–12; Seibert-Fohr, 'The Relevance of the Rome Statute of the International Criminal Court for Amnesties and Truth Commissions', 569; Robinson, 'Serving the Interests of Justice', 501–2.

16 Thomas Hethe Clark, 'The Prosecutor of the International Criminal Court, Amnesties and the "Interests of Justice": Striking a Delicate Balance' (2005) 4 *Washington University Global Studies Law Review* 389, 409–10; Villa-Vicencio, 'Why Perpetrators Should Not Always Be Prosecuted', 221.

17 Scharf, 'The Amnesty Exception to the Jurisdiction of the International Criminal Court', 522.

Consideration of the effective coexistence of truth commissions and prosecutions is not limited to the relationship between truth commissions and the ICC, and should not be dominated by it. That said, neither should the wider implications of the Rome Statute model be underestimated. The Rome Statute has not simply created a permanent International Criminal Court with the objective of prosecuting the most serious human rights crimes.[18] The complementarity regime, which underpins the Statute, ensures that prosecution for these crimes has become a national priority as states parties must carry out effective criminal trials if they are to avoid the assumption of jurisdiction by the Court.[19] Additionally, although perhaps an unintended consequence of the Statute, in passing national implementing legislation to ensure their ability to comply with Rome Statute obligations, a number of states have extended their own jurisdictional capabilities over core crimes, increasing the possibility of third-state prosecutions for such violations.[20] There is a sense that the quest for prosecution is gaining momentum, and as a result the role of the truth commission risks becoming marginalised.

Nevertheless, the ICC itself is only one example of the prosecutorial institutions alongside which future truth commissions may operate. Indeed, if the ICC complementarity regime functions as intended, even trials of ICC crimes will occur at the national level and the prosecutorial bodies with which future truth commissions will have to be coordinated will be domestic institutions. States may also hold trials in situations where the crimes concerned do not fall within the jurisdiction of the ICC but where prosecution is necessary to fulfil other treaty or customary international law obligations.[21] Again, truth commissions may be established to operate alongside these prosecutions. Truth commissions may additionally have to coexist with prosecutorial proceedings in different countries, should other states exercise jurisdiction in relation to the crimes being investigated by the truth commission, be these core ICC crimes or violations for which prosecution is required under treaty or customary law. There is, therefore, a broad spectrum across which truth commissions and prosecutorial institutions may coexist, with each situation likely to give rise to its own set of difficulties and challenges.

---

[18] Rome Statute, Art. 1.   [19] Rome Statute, Art. 17.

[20] See for example, New Zealand's International Crimes and International Criminal Court Act 2000 s. 8(1)(c); German Code of Crimes against International Law 2002, s. 1; Canada's Crimes against Humanity and War Crimes Act 2000, s. 8(b); South Africa's Rome Statute of the International Criminal Court Act 2002, s. 4(3)(iii).

[21] These obligations will be discussed in Chapter 2.

This book undertakes a broad analysis of the interrelationship between truth commissions and prosecutorial institutions at national and international levels, with a particular focus on the practical issues of coordination. The study is carried out on three levels and examines: (1) the relationship between truth commissions and prosecutorial institutions of the same state; (2) the relationship between truth commissions and the ICC; and (3) the relationship between truth commissions and prosecutorial institutions of different states. By analysing past practice and the relevant national and international legal instruments, this book identifies and evaluates the objectives, mandates, exercisable powers and operational procedures of truth commissions and considers them against those of criminal trials, in order to ascertain whether these mechanisms are capable of effective coexistence. This method is used to identify areas of potential difficulty between truth commissions and prosecutorial institutions, to examine the barriers that truth commissions pose to successful prosecution at national and international levels and to analyse the obstacles that the operation of prosecutorial institutions present to effective truth commission proceedings.

The analysis demonstrates that the overlapping investigations of truth commissions and prosecutorial institutions will create situations in which there will be tension surrounding access to information, the exchange and provision of evidence and the role of witnesses. It argues that despite the perceived compatibility of truth commissions and trials, there is a practical discord in their operations, which in some cases will result in conflict and make it impossible to achieve either full, effective truth seeking or successful prosecutions. The book argues that only through the development of guidelines regulating the relationship between truth commissions and prosecutorial institutions can they operate effectively together. Thus, the areas of difficulty uncovered through the analysis inform the formulation of proposals aimed at minimising the risk of conflict to enable truth commissions and prosecutorial institutions to coexist effectively in this new era of transitional justice.

Chapter 1 considers the place of truth commissions and criminal trials within the transitional justice framework. It examines their role in fulfilling the rights of victims of serious human rights crimes and considers the aims and objectives of both bodies. The chapter undertakes a critical analysis of the strengths and weaknesses of both institutions in responding to mass human rights violations in order to ascertain the contribution they make to transitional states and establish the validity of their dual use.

Chapter 2 examines the overlap between international law obligations to prosecute human rights violations and the investigatory mandates of truth commissions. It considers treaty and customary sources requiring the prosecution of serious human rights violations, their overlap with the subject matter mandates of truth commissions and the implications of these obligations for the establishment and operation of truth commissions. The overlap between truth commission mandates and the jurisdiction of the ICC is examined and the implications of the complementarity regime for truth commission operation considered. The specific areas of potential difficulty between truth commissions and prosecutorial institutions identified in this chapter form the subject of analysis in subsequent chapters.

Regardless of whether human rights violations require prosecution at the national level as a result of international treaty obligations, customary international law or in accordance with the complementarity regime of the ICC, questions arise as to whether and how successful prosecutions can be ensured and effective truth commission proceedings carried out. Coordination of these operations poses many practical difficulties. Chapter 3 concentrates on coordination at the national level. The chapter conducts case studies of the strong truth commission model implemented in South Africa, the equality model that was established in Sierra Leone and the weak truth commission model employed in East Timor. Analysis of the different models is carried out in order to ascertain in which situations their adoption might be appropriate or possible and whether there are general lessons to be drawn from all three on how operations can be coordinated optimally.

Chapter 4 undertakes a detailed analysis of the issues likely to create tension between truth commissions and the ICC. The status of truth commissions under the ICC regime is evaluated in light of the provisions of the Rome Statute and the objectives of the Court. The powers of the ICC and obligations imposed upon states parties under the Statute are identified. Analysis of the impact that the powers of the Court may have on the operation of future truth commissions is undertaken. Chapter 4 considers, in particular, the problems that may arise where truth commissions are in possession of confidential or self-incriminating evidence obtained under their powers to grant confidentiality or to compel the provision of self-incriminating information. Evaluation of the possibilities and practicalities of limiting the mandates of truth commissions to overcome potential tensions is carried out. Policy recommendations for coordinating the operations of truth commissions and the ICC are advanced.

Chapter 5 focuses on the difficulties that may occur where a third state exercises jurisdiction in relation to violations that are being/have been investigated by a truth commission in another state. The increased likelihood of overlapping prosecution and truth commission initiatives within different states as a result of the jurisdictional extensions under Rome Statute implementing legislation is analysed. The potential difficulties for national truth commissions and prosecutorial institutions where effective prosecutions are dependent on the exchange of information and transfer of suspects between states under existing mutual legal assistance and extradition arrangements are demonstrated. Analysis of the practical difficulties of operating each initiative effectively given the reliance on existing judicial cooperation agreements is carried out.

The final chapter draws together the findings in each of the three situations examined and again considers the key issue of coexistence in light of the qualitative information generated throughout the study. It demonstrates that in each of the situations investigated there is potential for tension and conflict between the operations of truth commissions and criminal trials, indicating a disharmony between these mechanisms and challenging the assumption that they are truly complementary. In light of these findings, this book calls for the development of targeted policies regulating the relationship between truth commissions and prosecutorial institutions at different levels. It develops multi-level proposals aimed at minimising the potential for conflict and maximising the possibilities for effective coexistence.

Truth commissions and trials within the transitional justice framework

1 Introduction

Truth commissions and criminal trials form two important components of the field of transitional justice. Along with lustration, public apologies, the erection of memorials to victims and the payment of reparations, both have frequently been utilised by states to respond to past human rights violations. While prosecution has perhaps the highest profile of the transitional justice mechanisms, truth commissions are more commonly used, and although the use of these bodies dominates transitional justice practice, the forms that they have taken have varied widely. Prosecution has occurred in international criminal tribunals, hybrid courts, domestic institutions and, more recently, has been pursued by the ICC. Likewise, truth commissions have been endowed with a diverse range of structures, objectives and mandates.

The establishment of these mechanisms follows no particular pattern. In some situations they have been employed as alternative solutions to past violations. In others, prosecutions have followed the operation of truth commissions, and in others still, they have been created simultaneously as part of a multifaceted approach to responding to the past. The lack of a uniform approach in establishing truth commissions and prosecutorial institutions reflects the variety of national contexts in which transitional justice mechanisms operate. While it is widely agreed that the past must be addressed,[1] there is also an increasing recognition of the need to consider each situation on its own merits and to develop tailored transitional justice policies accordingly.[2] This contextualisation of transitional justice

---

[1] Hugo Van der Merwe, Victoria Baxter and Audrey R. Chapman (eds.), *Assessing the Impact of Transitional Justice: Challenges for Empirical Research* (Washington DC: United States Institute of Peace Press, 2009), 2.

[2] Neil Kritz, 'Policy Implications of Empirical Research on Transitional Justice', in Hugo Van der Merwe, Victoria Baxter and Audrey R. Chapman (eds.), *Assessing the Impact of Transitional Justice: Challenges for Empirical Research* (Washington DC: United States Institute of Peace Press, 2009), 13–23, 13–14.

may go some way to explaining the absence of joined-up policy on coordinating the use and operations of truth commissions and criminal trials.

This chapter will consider the place of truth commissions and trials within the transitional justice framework. It will examine the mandates of both institutions and the aims and objectives assigned to them in order to develop an understanding of the purpose of their respective operations, ascertain their compatibility and establish a platform from which to formulate proposals to coordinate their effective coexistence. The chapter will also undertake an analysis of the strengths and weaknesses of both institutions in responding to mass human rights violations in order to ascertain the contribution they make to transitional states and determine the legitimacy of their contemporaneous establishment.

2   Truth commissions and trials as mechanisms of transitional justice

Truth commissions and criminal trials operate within the broad framework of transitional justice. Transitional justice is a multidisciplinary field of study and practice and is concerned with the strategies employed to deal with past human rights abuses in countries moving from conflict or repressive regime to democratic rule.[3] The measures implemented in these states may be judicial or non-judicial in nature and include, 'with differing levels of international involvement (or none at all) ... individual prosecutions, reparations, truth seeking, institutional reform, vetting and dismissals or a combination thereof'.[4] Transitional justice therefore 'comprises the full range of processes and mechanisms associated with a society's attempts to come to terms with a legacy of large-scale past abuses, in order to ensure accountability, serve justice and achieve reconciliation'.[5]

The term 'transitional justice' is in many ways misleading. It refers to 'justice during transition' rather than to any particular theory or form of modified or altered justice.[6] 'Justice' must be understood broadly and, in this context, has been described as:

---

[3] Mark Freeman, *Truth Commissions and Procedural Fairness* (Cambridge University Press, 2006), 4.

[4] UN Security Council, *Report of the Secretary General on the Rule of Law and Transitional Justice in Conflict and Post Conflict Societies*, S/2004/616, 23 August 2004, para. 8.

[5] *Ibid.* See also Louis Bickford, *The Encyclopaedia of Genocide and Crimes against Humanity*, 3 vols. (New York: Macmillan Reference, 2004), vol. 3, 1045.

[6] Bickford, *The Encyclopaedia of Genocide and Crimes against Humanity*.

an ideal of accountability and fairness in the protection and vindication of rights and the prevention and punishment of wrongs. Justice implies regard for the rights of the accused, for the interests of victims and for the well being of society at large. It is a concept rooted in all national cultures and traditions, and while its administration usually implies formal judicial mechanisms, traditional dispute resolution mechanisms are equally relevant.[7]

Prosecution can form an important element of transitional justice, but 'justice', as conceived here, extends beyond retributive criminal justice delivered through criminal trials,[8] and encompasses a theory of restorative justice.[9] The focus in transitional justice is on repairing past harm and the aim is to involve and bring about reconciliation among those most affected by that harm.[10] The transitional justice framework therefore utilises prosecutions, truth commissions and many other measures to meet the diverse needs of transitional states, contribute to a sustainable peace and bring about healing, repair and reconciliation.[11]

All transitional justice programmes seek to fulfil four main objectives: the determination of the truth through the establishment of a record of human rights abuses; the delivery of justice; the entrenchment of the rule of law and implementation of democratic reform; and the establishment of a durable peace.[12] These objectives reflect the influence of the human rights movement on the development of transitional justice. This influence explains the correlation between the objectives and mechanisms of

---

[7] UN Security Council, *Report of the Secretary General on the Rule of Law and Transitional Justice in Conflict and Post-Conflict Societies*, para. 7.

[8] Under retributive theory the aim of prosecution is to apportion blame and ensure that the wrongdoer is punished in proportion to the harm they have inflicted upon the victim. See Herbert L. A. Hart, *Punishment and Responsibility* (Oxford: Clarendon Press, 1968), 8–9; Immanuel Kant, 'Justice and Punishment', trans. W. Hastie, in Gertrude Ezorsky (ed.), *Philosophical Perspectives on Punishment* (Albany: State University of New York Press, 1972), 104; Chin Liew Ten, 'Crime and Punishment', in Peter Singer (ed.), *A Companion to Ethics* (Oxford: Blackwell Publishers, 1991), 38.

[9] Charles Villa-Vicencio and Erik Doxtader, *Pieces of the Puzzle: Keywords on Reconciliation and Transitional Justice* (Cape Town: Institute for Justice and Reconciliation, 2004), 68; Kai Ambos, 'The Legal Framework of Transitional Justice: A Systematic Study with a Special Focus on the ICC', in Kai Ambos *et al.* (eds.), *Building a Future on Peace and Justice: Studies on Transitional Justice, Peace and Development* (Heidelberg and Berlin: Springer-Verlag, 2009), 19–105, 23.

[10] Daniel Van Ness, 'Restorative Justice and International Human Rights', in Burt Galaway and Joe Hudson (eds.), *Restorative Justice: International Perspectives* (New York: Criminal Justice Press, 1996), 17–36, 23.

[11] Villa-Vicencio and Doxtader, *Pieces of the Puzzle*, 72.

[12] Kritz, 'Policy Implications of Empirical Research on Transitional Justice', 13.

transitional justice and the legal obligations possessed by states under international human rights law to address past violations.[13] Thus, transitional justice focuses on four main mechanisms, which correspond to the duties of states and rights of individuals under international human rights law: trials, truth seeking, reparations and justice reforms.[14] Trials enable states to fulfil their obligation to investigate and punish the perpetrators of human rights violations and provide victims with their right to justice and an effective remedy. Fact-finding investigations, which often take the form of truth commissions, are a means by which states implement their duty to investigate and identify perpetrators and their victims and thereby provide victims, their families and the wider society with the right to know or the right to truth. Through reparations states fulfil their obligation to provide restitution and compensation to victims and provide them with their right to reparation. Finally, justice reforms allow a state to implement its duty to take effective measures to prevent future violations and thereby guarantee the right of non-repetition.[15]

While these rights and obligations are separate and distinct,[16] this description fails to elucidate their interconnectedness and the overlapping contributions made by these transitional justice mechanisms. In particular, it is overly simplistic to adduce from this assessment that trials deliver justice and truth commissions establish the truth. In investigating and adjudicating upon specific cases, trials will uncover and record much of the 'truth' surrounding the commission of past abuses. Truth commissions may contribute to justice through their acknowledgement of the suffering of victims, assignation of institutional responsibility and formulation of recommendations for reform and the payment of reparations.[17] Equally, the recommendations for legal and institutional reforms frequently made by truth commissions may provide the foundation for

---

[13] Bickford, *The Encyclopaedia of Genocide and Crimes against Humanity*, 1045.

[14] See Louis Joinet, *Set of Principles for the Protection and Promotion of Human Rights through Action to Combat Impunity*, UN Doc. E/CN.4/Sub.2/1997/20/Rev.1 (1997) (Joinet Principles), updated by Dianne Orentlicher, *Updated Set of Principles for the Protection and Promotion of Human Rights through Action to Combat Impunity*, UN Doc. E/CN.4/2005/102.Add.1 (2005) (Updated Principles) and *Basic Principles and Guidelines on the Right to a Remedy and Reparation for Victims of Violations of International Human Rights and Humanitarian Law* annexed to General Assembly Res. A/C.3/60/L.24 (Bassiouni Principles).

[15] Juan E. Mendez, 'Accountability for Past Abuses' (1997) 19 *Human Rights Quarterly* 255, 259–62.

[16] *Ibid.*, 263.

[17] Priscilla B. Hayner, *Unspeakable Truths: Transitional Justice and the Challenge of Truth Commissions* (2nd edn) (New York and London: Routledge, 2010), 20.

the judicial reforms necessary for states to fulfil their obligations to take effective measures to prevent future violations. A programme of reforms cannot be compiled until the deficiencies of the old system are understood. In addition, both the findings of trials and the recommendations and conclusions of truth commissions may inform the design of reparation packages for victims. Again, before reparations are made, it must be determined who is to be compensated and for what. Thus, while it can be said that states possess four distinct duties in responding to past human rights violations, and victims four corresponding rights, the measures implemented to discharge particular duties may, in practice, contribute to the fulfilment of other transitional justice objectives.[18] Indeed, it would seem that the pursuit of trials and truth commissions, the establishment of the truth and assignation of responsibility that their operation brings, may be necessary before reparations and reforms programmes can be compiled and implemented. This book is concerned with only these two initial transitional justice mechanisms: truth commissions and trials.

3   Truth commissions, trials and the rights to truth and justice

Despite the overlapping contributions of the four primary transitional justice mechanisms, truth commissions have come to be closely aligned with the right to truth and trials with the right to, particularly criminal, justice. It is their contributions to the delivery of these rights that legitimise their place within the transitional justice framework. The right to justice has been confirmed in the jurisprudence of human rights courts, findings of supervisory bodies and UN sponsored studies. It has been argued convincingly that the right to justice does not necessarily require criminal prosecution.[19] Instead, it is proposed that a public forum in which victims can confront and challenge the perpetrators of past abuses, much in the way that some truth commissions have operated, suffices to fulfil the right of victims to justice.[20] However, international law, national practice and the demands of victims suggest that trials are a key component of the

---

[18] On the interconnectedness of the rights of victims see UN Human Rights Council, *Right to Truth, Report of the Office of the High Commissioner for Human Rights*, A/HRC/5/7, 7 June 2007, paras. 81–6.

[19] Ambos, 'The Legal Framework of Transitional Justice', 30; Angelika Schlunk, *Amnesty versus Accountability: Third Party Intervention Dealing with Gross Human Rights Violations in Internal and International Conflicts* (Berlin: Berlin Verlag Spitz, 2000), 44–5. This will be discussed further in Chapter 2.

[20] *Ibid.*, 36.

response to, certainly the most serious, human rights violations. Within the transitional justice framework, criminal trials are considered to make an important contribution to overall restoration.[21]

A number of international treaties make specific provision for the delivery of criminal justice for human rights violations through the imposition of an explicit obligation to prosecute upon states parties.[22] In other instruments, an obligation to provide justice in the form of prosecution has been developed through the jurisprudence of courts and monitoring bodies. The Inter-American Court has stated that the rights of victims to an effective remedy and judicial protection, under Articles 1(1) and 25 of the American Convention on Human Rights, impose upon states parties obligations to investigate, prosecute and sanction perpetrators of human rights violations.[23] It has also found that Article 8 of the Convention, which outlines the right to be heard, includes the right

---

[21] Anthony Duff, 'Restoration and Retribution', in Andrew Von Hirsch and Julian Roberts (eds.), *Restorative Justice and Criminal Justice: Competing or Reconcilable Paradigms* (Oxford: Hart Publishing, 2003), 43–61; Mark A. Drumbl, 'Punishment Post-genocide: From Guilt to Shame to *Civis* in Rwanda' (2000) 75 *New York University Law Review* 1221, 1263–4; Jaime Malmud-Goti, 'Transitional Governments in the Breach: Why Punish State Criminals?' (1990) 12 *Human Rights Quarterly* 1, 14–15. See also Todd Howard and William Calathes, 'The United Nations International Criminal Tribunal: Is It Justice or Jingoism for Rwanda? A Call for Transformation' (1998) 39 *Virginia Journal of International Law* 135, advocating the adoption of a restorative approach to justice for mass atrocity as a means of informing the prosecutorial policies of the International Criminal Tribunal for Rwanda (ICTR); and Maya Goldstein-Bolocan, 'Rwandan Gacaca: An Experiment in Transitional Justice', 2004 *Journal of Dispute Resolution* 355.

[22] State obligations to prosecute will be discussed in Chapter 2.

[23] *Carpio Nicolle et al.* v. *Guatemala* (Merits, Reparations and Costs), Inter-American Court of Human Rights, Series C, No. 117, 22 November 2004, para. 128; *Moiwana Community* v. *Suriname* (Preliminary Objections, Merits, Reparations and Costs), Inter-American Court of Human Rights, Series C, No. 124, 15 June 2005, para. 204; '*Mapiripan Massacre*' v. *Colombia* (Merits, Reparations and Costs), Inter-American Court of Human Rights, Series C, No. 134, 15 September 2005, para. 295; *Blanco-Romero et al.* v. *Venezuela* (Merits, Reparations and Costs), Inter-American Court of Human Rights, Series C, No. 138, 28 November 2005, para. 95; *Pueblo Bello Massacre* v. *Colombia* (Merits), Inter-American Court of Human Rights, Series C, No. 140, 31 January 2006, para. 266; *Lopez-Alvarez* v. *Honduras* (Merits, Reparations and Costs), Inter-American Court of Human Rights, Series C, No. 141, 1 February 2006, para. 207; *Ximenes-Lopes* v. *Brazil* (Merits, Reparations and Costs), Inter-American Court of Human Rights, Series C, No. 149, 4 July 2006, para. 245; *Goiburú et al.* v. *Paraguay* (Merits, Reparations and Costs), Inter-American Court of Human Rights, Series C, No. 153, 22 September 2006, para. 164; *Vargas-Areco* v. *Paraguay* (Merits, Reparations and Costs), Inter-American Court of Human Rights), Series C, No. 155, 26 September 2006, para. 153; *Almonacid Arellano et al.* v. *Chile* (Preliminary Objections, Merits, Reparations and Costs), Inter-American Court of Human Rights, Series C, No. 154, 26 September 2006, para. 1110.

of victims to have the crime investigated and to have those responsible prosecuted and, where appropriate, punished.[24] The European Court of Human Rights has stated that the duty on states to secure the rights within the European Convention for the Protection of Human Rights and Fundamental Freedoms gives rise to positive obligations on the part of the state to carry out thorough and effective investigations.[25] Similarly, the Human Rights Committee (HRC) has interpreted Article 2(3) of the International Covenant on Civil and Political Rights (ICCPR), the right to an effective remedy, as requiring states to conduct a criminal investigation that brings to justice those responsible in cases involving arbitrary detentions, forced disappearances, torture and extra-judicial executions.[26] The Joinet Principles interpret the right of victims to justice as including the trial of their oppressors. In addition, they articulate obligations for the state to investigate, prosecute and punish those responsible.[27] The Bassiouni Principles also make clear that a victim's right to access justice includes the state's duty to prosecute those responsible for human rights violations.[28] These principles, although non-binding, have been described as constituting the most comprehensive and widely accepted description of a state's human rights obligations and an individual's human rights.[29] The result of this discourse is that the victim's right to justice has become interwoven with the prosecution of those who commit serious human rights violations.

---

[24] *Paniagua Morales* v. *Guatemala* (Merits), Inter-American Court of Human Rights, Series C, No. 37, 8 March 1998.

[25] *Aksoy* v. *Turkey* (Application No. 21987/93), Judgment of 18 December 1996, (1997) 23 EHRR 553, para. 98; *M.C.* v. *Bulgaria* (Application No. 39272/98), Judgment of 4 December 2003, (2005) 40 EHRR 20, paras. 150–1; *Kurt* v. *Turkey* (Application No. 24276/94), Judgment of 25 May 1998, (1999) 27 EHRR 373, para. 140; *Hugh Jordan* v. *United Kingdom* (Application. No. 24746/94), Judgment of 4 May 2001, [2001] ECHR 327, para 105.

[26] *Vincente et al.* v. *Colombia*, UN Human Rights Committee, Communication No. 612/1995, UN Doc. CCPR/C/60/D/612/1995, 14 June 1994; *Rodríguez* v. *Uruguay*, UN Human Rights Committee, Communication No. 322/1998, UN Doc. CCPR/C/51/D/322/1988, 9 August 1994; *Tshiongo* v. *Zaire*, UN Human Rights Committee, Communication No. 366/1989, UN Doc. CCPR/C/49/D/366/1989, 8 November 1993; *Bautista de Arellana* v. *Colombia*, UN Human Rights Committee, Communication No. 563/1993, UN Doc. CCPR/C/55/D/563/1993, 27 October 1995; General Comment No. 31 on Article 2 of the Covenant: The Nature of the General Legal Obligation Imposed on States Parties to the Covenant, UN GAOR, Human Rights Committee, 80th Sess., UN Doc. CCPR/C/74/CRP.4/Rev.6, para. 18 (2004).

[27] Joinet Principles, paras. 26–7; Updated Principles, 'Summary'.

[28] Bassiouni Principles, Principles 4 and 22(f).

[29] Updated Principles, 'Summary'.

While trials are closely linked to the provision of the right to justice, truth commissions, as their name suggests, are wedded to the right to truth or the right to know. The right to truth is not explicitly stated in any human rights treaty. Its roots can be traced to Articles 32 and 33 of the 1977 First Additional Protocol to the Geneva Conventions of 1949.[30] These provide respectively for the right of families to know the fate of their relatives and oblige states parties to search for those reported missing. The closest enunciation of a right to truth is found in Article 24(2) of the draft International Convention for the Protection of All Persons from Enforced Disappearances, which states: 'each victim has the right to know the truth regarding the circumstances of the enforced disappearance, the progress and results of the investigation and the fate of the disappeared person.'[31] It has, primarily, been inferred from other rights under human rights treaties.[32] The HRC has interpreted the right to the truth as forming part of the right to be free from torture. In several cases the HRC recognised the right to know as a means to end or prevent the psychological torture of families of victims of forced disappearances[33] and clandestine executions.[34] The European Court of Human Rights has interpreted the right to be free from torture, together with the right to an effective remedy, as encompassing a right to truth through the requirement that violations be effectively investigated and those involved promptly informed of the results.[35] The Court has also found that a state's failure to conduct an effective investigation aimed at clarifying the whereabouts and fate of missing persons who disappeared in life-threatening circumstances

[30] Protocol I Additional to the Geneva Conventions on 12 August 1949 relating to the Protection of Victims of International Armed Conflict, 1125 UNTS 3.

[31] Inter-American Convention on the Forced Disappearance of Persons, Belém, Brazil, 9 June 1994, (1994) 33 *International Legal Materials* 1529.

[32] For a discussion of this see Thomas M. Antkowiak, 'Truth as Right and Remedy in International Human Rights Experience' (2002) 23 *Michigan Journal of International Law* 977.

[33] See the explanation by Bertil Wennergren, member of the Human Rights Committee, in his opinion in the cases: *R. A. V. N. et al.* v. *Argentina*, UN Human Rights Committee, Communication Nos. 343, 344 and 345/1988, UN Doc. CCPR/C/38/D/344/1988, 5 April 1990 (Appendix); *S. E.* v. *Argentina*, UN Human Rights Committee, Communication No. 275/1988, UN Doc. CCPR/C/38/D/275/1988, 4 April 1990 (Appendix). See *Sarma* v. *Sri Lanka*, UN Human Rights Committee, Communication No 950/2000, UN Doc. CCPR/C/78/D/950/2000, 31 July 2003, para. 9.5.

[34] *Lyashkevich* v. *Belarus*, UN Human Rights Committee, Communication No 887/1999, UN Doc. CCPR/C/77/D/887/1999, 24 April 2003, para. 9.2.

[35] *Kurt* v. *Turkey* (Application No. 24276/94), Judgment of 25 May 1998 (1999) 27 EHRR 373, paras. 130–4; *Tas* v. *Turkey* (Application No. 24396/94), Judgment of 14 November 2000 (2001) 33 EHRR 15, paras. 77–80; *Cyprus* v. *Turkey* (Application No. 25781/94), Judgment of 10 May 2001 (2002) 35 EHRR 30, para. 157.

constitutes a continuing violation of its obligation to protect the right to life.[36] The Inter-American Court of Human Rights has held that victims and their next of kin have a right to clarification of the facts surrounding serious human rights violations under the rights to a hearing and to an effective remedy and judicial protection in the American Convention.[37] Similarly, the African Commission on Human and Peoples' Rights has found the right to the truth to form part of the right to an effective remedy under its Principles and Guidelines on the Right to a Fair Trial and Legal Assistance in Africa.[38]

Numerous UN Resolutions have acknowledged the right to truth[39] and the importance of uncovering and delivering the truth in order to end impunity and contribute to the attainment of peace.[40] Often, the virtues of truth commissions have been espoused in this regard.[41] The Joinet and

---

[36] *Cyprus* v. *Turkey* (Application No. 25781/94), Judgment of 10 May 2001, (2002) 35 EHRR 30, para. 136.

[37] *Bamaca Velasquez* v. *Guatemala* (Merits), Inter-American Court of Human Rights, Series C, No. 70, Judgment of 25 November 2000, paras. 159–66.

[38] African Union Doc. DOC/0S(XXX)247, 2001, Principle C, which provides for the right to an effective remedy, states in para. (b)(iii) that the right to an effective remedy includes access to the factual information concerning the violations. See Yasmin Naqvi, 'The Right to Truth in International Law: Fact or Fiction?' (2006) 88 *International Review of the Red Cross* 245, 257.

[39] UN Human Rights Council Resolution 9/11, Right to Truth, 24 September 2008; UN Human Rights Council Resolution 12/12, Right to the Truth, 1 October 2009; UN Human Rights Council Resolution 14/7, Proclamation of 24 March as the International Day for the Right to the Truth Concerning Gross Human Rights Violations and for the Dignity of Victims, 17 June 2010.

[40] UN Security Council Resolution 1606 (2005), UN Doc. S/RES/1606 (2005), 20 June 2005, Preamble, paras. 2 and 7, on the peace process in Burundi; UN Security Council Resolution 1593 (2005), UN Doc. S/RES/ 1593 (2005), 31 March 2005, para. 5, on the situation in Darfur; UN General Assembly Resolution 57/105 (2003), Assistance for Humanitarian Relief, Rehabilitation and Development for Timor-Leste, UN Doc. A/RES/57/105 (2003), 13 February 2003, para. 12; UN General Assembly Resolution 57/161 (2003), United Nations Verification Mission in Guatemala, UN Doc. A/RES/57/161 (2003), 28 January 2003, para. 17; UN General Assembly Resolution 48/149 (1994), Situation of Human Rights in El Salvador, UN Doc. A/RES/48/149 (1994), 7 March 1994, para. 4; UN General Assembly Resolution 42/147 (1987), Situation of Human Rights and Fundamental Freedoms in Chile, UN Doc. A/RES/42/147 (1987), 7 December 1987, paras. 10(d) and (e); UN General Assembly Resolution 40/145 (1985), Situation of Human Rights and Fundamental Freedoms in Chile, UN Doc. A/RES/40/145 (1985), 13 December 1985, para. 6(b).

[41] UN Security Council Resolution 1468 (2003), UN Doc. S/RES/1468 (2003), 20 March 2003, para. 5 on the need to establish a truth commission in the Democratic Republic of Congo; UN Security Council Resolution 1593 (2005), para. 5, on the need to promote healing and reconciliation in Sudan through the establishment of inclusive institutions including truth commissions.

Bassiouni Principles both advocate the benefits of truth commissions in delivering the right to truth.[42] The UN Rule of Law Toolkit for Post-Conflict States considers truth commissions as a means of delivering the right to truth.[43] In 2005 the UN Commission on Human Rights affirmed the right to truth and commissioned a study to determine its scope and content.[44] The study found that the right to the truth regarding gross human rights violations, violations of international humanitarian law and international crimes is an inalienable, autonomous and non-derogable right, possessed by victims, their relatives and the wider society.[45] It implies knowing the full and complete truth as to the events that transpired, their specific circumstances and who participated in them, including knowing the circumstances in which the violations took place, as well as the reasons for them.[46] The study therefore suggests that states may have more onerous obligations in providing the right to truth than might previously have been considered. It lends support to the argument that the right to truth is a fundamental, emerging principle of international human rights law and a central means of addressing a legacy of abuse.[47]

The HRC study commends the work of trials and truth commissions in implementing the right to truth,[48] noting at the same time the limitations of both.[49] It states that trials are one means of delivering the truth, although it suggests that the primary objective of trials is to 'deal out justice', rather than to establish truth.[50] Only as a secondary consequence of the process of adjudication does the study consider that trials uncover and record the truth.[51] While it finds shared origins between the rights to truth and justice, the study elucidates a distinction between them and articulates two independent rights. This distinction, coupled with the conclusion that victims, their families and the wider society possess an autonomous right to know the complete truth about the past has significant implications. It implies that states may have to implement initiatives

---

[42] Joinet Principles, Principle 1; Updated Principles, Principle 2; Bassiouni Principles, Principle 22.

[43] Office of the UN High Commissioner for Human Rights, *Rule of Law Tools for Post-Conflict States: Truth Commissions*, 2006, New York and Geneva, 1.

[44] UN Commission on Human Rights, *Right to the Truth: Human Rights Resolution 2005/66*, E/CN.4/RES/2005/66, 20 April 2005, para. 6.

[45] UN Commission on Human Rights, *Study on the Right to the Truth, Report of the Office of the United Nations High Commissioner for Human Rights*, 8 February 2006, E/CN.4/2006/91, para. 58–60.

[46] *Ibid.*, para. 59.   [47] Naqvi, 'The Right to Truth in International Law'.

[48] UN Commission on Human Rights, *Study on the Right to the Truth*, para. 61.

[49] *Ibid.*, paras. 48 and 50.   [50] *Ibid.*, para. 48.   [51] *Ibid.*, para. 48.

that ensure the effective delivery of this right, as one distinct from the right to justice, rather than hoping that trials will deliver it as a corollary to the provision of justice, although states themselves differ on this point.[52] Overall, although the study emphasises the constraints suffered by past truth commissions, it seems to actually carve out a place for them. It affirms the current international practice of utilising both mechanisms as part of the same transitional justice programme and adds weight to previous studies, which had advocated the adoption of a multi-pronged approach to delivering the truth.[53]

4   The purpose of trials in responding to past human rights violations

Prosecution occupies something of a hallowed place within the transitional justice framework,[54] not least because empirical evidence shows that victims of human rights violations seek justice in the form of criminal trials.[55] The variety of forums in which abuses have been prosecuted illustrates the importance of trials as a response to past violations. Some, such as those committed during the Second World War,[56] and in the internal conflicts of the former Yugoslavia[57] and Rwanda,[58] have become the subject matter of international criminal tribunals. Others have been prosecuted in hybrid courts, such as the institutions established in East

---

[52] UN Human Rights Council, *Right to the Truth, Report of the Office of the High Commissioner for Human Rights*, A/HRC/5/7, 7 June 2007, 5–7.

[53] UN Commission on Human Rights, *Study on the Right to Truth*, para. 48.

[54] The strengths and weaknesses of prosecution will be considered below.

[55] Ernesto Kiza, Corene Rathgeber and C. Rohne Holger, *Victims of War: An Empirical Study on War-Victimization and Victims' Attitudes towards Addressing Atrocities* (Hamburg: Hamburger Edition Online, 2006), 97, available at www.his-online.de. In this study, 79 per cent of the victims interviewed in Afghanistan, Bosnia and Herzegovina, Cambodia, Croatia, the Democratic Republic of Congo (DRC), Israel, Kosovo, Federal Yugoslav Republic of Macedonia, Palestinian Territories, Philippines and Sudan were in favour of prosecution for past atrocities.

[56] On the operation and significance of the trials see George Ginsberg and Vladimir N. Kudriavstev (eds.), *The Nuremberg Trial and International Law* (Dordrecht: Nijhoff, 1990); Roger S. Clark, 'Nuremberg and Tokyo in Contemporary Perspective', in Timothy L. H. McCormack and Gerry J. Simpson (eds.), *The Law of War Crimes – National and International Approaches* (The Hague, London and Boston: Kluwer Law International, 1997), 171–89.

[57] The International Tribunal for the former Yugoslavia was established pursuant to Security Council Resolution 827 (1993), UN Doc S/RES/827 (1993), 25 May 1993.

[58] The International Criminal Tribunal for Rwanda was established pursuant to Security Council Resolution 955 (1994), UN Doc. S/RES/955 (1994), 8 November 1994.

Timor,[59] Sierra Leone[60] and Cambodia.[61] Others still have been dealt with through domestic proceedings, either in the state of territoriality or in the courts of sympathetic third states.[62] Most recently, the International Criminal Court has begun work on the investigation and prosecution of the most serious human rights crimes. Proceedings are underway in relation to crimes committed in Uganda,[63] Democratic Republic of Congo,[64] Central African Republic,[65] Sudan,[66] Kenya[67] and Libya.[68] However, trials are justified on a number of grounds, not only the delivery of victims' rights to justice and, to a lesser extent, truth. The multiplicity of objectives with which prosecutorial institutions have been endowed makes it difficult to discern their overriding aim. This has led to criticism that prosecution for serious human rights violations lacks a coherent theoretical

[59] United Nations Transitional Administration in East Timor (UNTAET) Regulation 2000/15, UNTAET/REG/2000/15, 6 June 2000, created the Special Panels for Serious Crimes.

[60] Special Court Agreement (Ratification) Act 2002 created the Special Court for Sierra Leone.

[61] General Assembly Resolution A/Res/57/228B on the creation of the Extraordinary Chambers for Cambodia, 13 May 2003. Hybrid institutions have also been created in Kosovo and Bosnia and Herzegovina. See United Nations Mission in Kosovo (UNMIK), Regulation 2000/64, UN Doc. UNMIK/REG/2000/64, 15 December 2000 on the creation of the 64 Panels, and Security Council Resolution 1503 (2003), S/RES/1503 (2003), 28 August 2003 on the creation of the War Crimes Chamber within the state court of Bosnia Herzegovina.

[62] Amnesty International, *Universal Jurisdiction: The Duty of States to Enact and Enforce Legislation*, AI Index IOR 53/004/2001, 1 September 2001, Chapter 2 'The Evolution of the Practice of Universal Jurisdiction'. On European attempts to prosecute see Axel Marschik, 'The Politics of Prosecution: European National Approaches to War Crimes', in Timothy L. H. McCormack and Gerry J. Simpson (eds.), *The Law of War Crimes: National and International Approaches* (The Hague: Kluwer Law International, 1997), 65–99. See also Chapter 5.

[63] *The Prosecutor v. Joseph Kony, Vincent Otti, Okot Odhiambo and Dominic Ongwen*, Case No. ICC-02/04–01/05.

[64] *The Prosecutor v. Thomas Lubanga Dyilo*, Case No. ICC-01/04–01/06; *The Prosecutor v. Germain Katanga and Mathieu Ngudjolo Chui*, Case No. ICC-01/04–01/07; *The Prosecutor v. Bosco Ntaganda*, Case No. ICC-01/04–02/06.

[65] *The Prosecutor v. Jean-Pierre Bemba Gombo*, Case No. ICC-01/05–01/08.

[66] *The Prosecutor v. Ahmad Muhammad Harun and Ali Muhammad Ali Abd-Al-Rahman*, Case No. ICC-02/05–01/07; *The Prosecutor v. Omar Hassan Ahmad Al Bashir*, Case No. ICC-02/05–01/09; *The Prosecutor v. Bahr Idriss Abu Garda*, Case No. ICC-02/05–02/09; *The Prosecutor v. Abdallah Banda Abakaer Nourain and Saleh Mohammed Jerbo Jamus*, Case No. ICC-02/05–03/09.

[67] *The Prosecutor v. William Samoei Ruto, Henry Kiprono Kosgey and Joshua Arap Sang*, Case No. ICC-01/09–01/11; *The Prosecutor v. Francis Kirimi Muthaura, Uhuru Muigai Kenyatta and Mohammed Hussein Ali*, Case No. ICC-01/09–02/11.

[68] UN Security Resolution 1970, (2011), S/Res/1970 (2011), 26 February 2011.

foundation.[69] It is not the purpose of this book to develop a theoretical framework for the operation of criminal trials within transitional states. It is, however, essential to glean a clear understanding of the purpose of criminal trials within transitional states if the possibilities for effective coexistence alongside truth commissions are to be properly assessed.

Examination of the enacting legislation of the prosecutorial institutions established to date reveals the assignation of a wealth of objectives to these bodies. Most commonly, their establishment is justified on retributive and deterrent grounds. Commentators consider this illogical, arguing that the aims of these theories are divergent and their focuses opposed.[70] Deterrence theory, as part of the utilitarian school of thought, is forward-looking and views prosecution and punishment as a means of preventing future crime through the deterrence of reoffending and of would-be offenders.[71] In contrast, the retributivist school is past-oriented and considers that the purpose of prosecution and punishment is to apportion blame and repay the offender for his wrongdoing.[72] A clear retributive function can be seen in the Nuremberg Tribunal, which was established simply to 'try and punish' those suspected of serious human rights violations.[73] Many of the prosecutorial bodies established since have been

---

[69] Immi Tallgren, 'The Sense and Sensibility of International Criminal Law' (2002) 13 *European Journal of International Law* 561; Ralph Henham, 'The Philosophical Foundations of International Sentencing' (2003) 1 *Journal of International Criminal Justice* 64; Miriam J. Aukerman, 'Extraordinary Evil, Ordinary Crime: A Framework for Understanding Transitional Justice' (2002) 15 *Harvard Human Rights Journal* 39.

[70] Mark Drumbl, 'Collective Violence and Individual Punishment: The Criminality of Mass Atrocity' (2005) 99 *Northwestern University Law Review* 539; Mark Osiel, 'Why Prosecute? Critics of Punishment for Mass Atrocity' (2000) 22 *Human Rights Quarterly* 118.

[71] Kent Greenawalt, 'Punishment' (1983) 74 *Journal of Criminal Law and Criminology* 343, 353; Ten, 'Crime and Punishment', 367. On deterrence of international human rights crimes see Payam Akhaven, 'Justice in The Hague, Peace in the Former Yugoslavia: A Commentary of the United Nations War Crimes Tribunal' (1998) 20 *Human Rights Quarterly* 739, 743–51.

[72] Hart, *Punishment and Responsibility*, 8–9; Kant, 'Justice and Punishment', 104. On retribution for serious human rights violations see Aryeh Neier, 'Rethinking Truth, Justice and Guilt after Bosnia and Rwanda', in Carla Hess and Robert Post (eds.), *Human Rights in Political Transitions: Gettysburg to Bosnia* (New York: Zone Books, 1999), 42; Julie Mertus, 'Only a War Crimes Tribunal: Triumph of the International Community, Pain of the Survivors', in Belinda Cooper (ed.), *War Crimes: The Legacy of Nuremberg* (New York: TV Books, 1999), 229; M. Cherif Bassiouni, 'Searching for Peace and Achieving Justice' (1996) 50 *Law and Contemporary Problems* 9, 26.

[73] Charter of the International Military Tribunal, 82 UNTS 279, Art. 6. See also Daniel B. Pickard, 'Proposed Sentencing Guideline for the International Criminal

endowed with multifaceted, aspirational mandates that make it difficult to ascertain their primary purpose.

For example, the International Criminal Tribunal for the former Yugoslavia (ICTY) was established to bring to justice those responsible and provide effective redress for the violations committed, halt the commission of further atrocities and contribute to the restoration and maintenance of peace in the region.[74] The International Criminal Tribunal for Rwanda (ICTR) has similar aims, but was additionally tasked with contributing to national reconciliation.[75] The founding Security Council Resolutions therefore suggest that the ad hoc tribunals are fulfilling multiple purposes and have retributive, deterrent and restorative functions, though none is prioritised over the others. Discourse on the ad hoc tribunals has clouded matters further by adding to these already ambitious mandates a 'cornucopia of objectives'.[76] After ten years of operation, their mandates had evolved to additionally include creating a historical record of the conflict, preventing historical revisionism, shaping collective memory and preventing not only the commission of further crimes in the areas within their jurisdictions, but all future wars.[77] Hybrid courts fare little better. The Special Court for Sierra Leone is tasked with ending impunity, and contributing to the process of national reconciliation and to the restoration and maintenance of peace.[78] The Cambodian Extraordinary Chambers do, however, have a 'chief goal', which is to 'provide justice to the people of Cambodia, those who died and the survivors'.[79] This aim is prioritised over its additional objectives of setting straight the historical record, educating Cambodia's youth about the past, strengthening the rule of law and setting an example to those who disobey the law in Cambodia and to cruel regimes worldwide.[80]

Court' (1997) 20 *Loyola of Los Angeles International and Comparative Law Journal* 123, 125; Stuart Beresford, 'Unshackling the Paper Tiger: The Sentencing Practices of the Ad Hoc International Criminal Tribunals for the Former Yugoslavia and Rwanda' (2001) 1 *International Criminal Law Review* 33, 41.

74 SC Resolution 827, Preamble.
75 SC Resolution 955, Preamble.
76 Developments in the Law, International Criminal Law, 'The Promises of International Prosecution' (2001) 114 *Harvard Law Review* 1957, 1961.
77 Press Release, 'Address of Antonio Cassese, President of the International Criminal Tribunal for the former Yugoslavia to the General Assembly of the United Nations', 4 November 1997; Carla Del Ponte, 'The Dividends of International Criminal Justice', Address at Goldman Sachs, London, 6 October 2005.
78 SC Resolution 1315 (2000), UN Doc. S/RES/1315 (2000), 14 August 2000, Preamble.
79 See Extraordinary Chambers in the Courts of Cambodia, 'FAQs', available at www.eccc. gov.kh.
80 *Ibid.*

The ad hoc tribunals have suffered more than other prosecutorial institutions from the assignation of lofty ideals and objectives, which is perhaps indicative of their establishment at a time when prosecution had something of a reputation as a panacea for all ills. However, the judgments of the tribunals also lack clarity on the purpose of prosecution and punishment. While retribution has been described as the ICTY's primary objective in some decisions,[81] it has been denounced, in others, as counterproductive and disruptive to the Security Council's overall purpose of restoring and maintaining peace in the region.[82] Equally, while the Trial Chamber in *Delalic* considered deterrence of future crimes the most important factor,[83] the same court in *Nikolic* stated that deterrence should not be given undue prominence.[84] The jurisprudence of the ICTR reveals similar confusion. In *Prosecutor* v. *Ruggiu* the ICTR Trial Chamber listed the principal aims of sentencing as 'retribution, deterrence, rehabilitation and justice',[85] but gave no indication as to which objective had influenced its decision.[86] The jurisprudence of the hybrid courts is confused on the purpose of the trials they have conducted. The decisions of the East Timorese Special Panels reveal no consistent reasoning, with sentences being justified on retributive, deterrent and restorative grounds.[87] The Special Court for Sierra Leone has referred heavily to the decisions of the ICTY and ICTR in its adjudication. As a result, its judgments reflect the same obfuscation on the purpose of prosecution and punishment as those of the ad hoc Tribunals.[88]

---

[81] *Prosecutor* v. *Nikolic* (Case No. IT-02-60/1-S), Judgment of the Trial Chamber, 2 December 2003, para. 59.

[82] *Prosecutor* v. *Delalic* (Case No. IT-96-21-T), Judgment of the Trial Chamber, 16 November 1998, para. 1231.

[83] *Ibid.*, para. 1234. See also *Prosecutor* v. *Aleksovski*, (Case No. IT-95-14/1-A), Judgment of the Appeals Chamber, 24 March 2000, para. 185.

[84] *Prosecutor* v. *Nikolic* (Case No. IT-02-60/1-S), Judgment of the Trial Chamber, 2 December 2003, para. 90.

[85] *Prosecutor* v. *Ruggiu* (Case No. ICTR-97-32-I), Judgment and Sentencing, 1 June 2000, para. 33.

[86] See also *Prosecutor* v. *Rutaganda* (Case No. ICTR-96-3), Judgment and Sentencing, 6 December 1999, para. 456, where retribution and deterrence were identified as justifications for punishment, but neither was identified as the overriding objective for the prosecution of serious human rights crimes.

[87] *Prosecutor* v. *Franca da Silva* (Case No. 04a/2001), Special Panels for Serious Crimes, Judgment, 5 December 2002, para. 155.

[88] See for example the sentencing judgments of *Prosecutor* v. *Brima, Kamara and Kanu* (Case No. SCSL-04-16-T), Sentencing Judgment, 19 July 2007, paras. 15–16; *Prosecutor* v. *Fofana and Kondewa* (Case No. SCSL-04-14-A), Judgment, 28 May 2008, paras. 532 and 565.

However, examination of the factors that international courts have considered as aggravating in sentencing suggests that prosecution at the international level is dominated by retributive concerns.[89] The gravity of the crimes,[90] the suffering inflicted on victims,[91] the nature of the perpetrator's involvement[92] and the youth of the victims[93] have been identified as aggravating factors. Sentences have been increased in light of the scale of offences, the fact that they were committed against innocent civilians and the impact that the offences had on the victims, their relatives and the wider community.[94] The implication that these factors increase the sentence for a particular offence supports the contention that the courts follow a retributive rationale, which demands that 'the severity of the appropriate punishment depends on the depravity of [the] act'.[95] This suggests that they are motivated more by retributive ideals and the need to punish past wrongs than by the need to deter future crimes or restore peace.

The Preamble to the ICC Statute evidences both a retributive and deterrent function,[96] although unlike other prosecutorial institutions, retribution appears to be the ICC's primary objective. The Preamble states that the Court 'aims to end impunity for the perpetrators of ... [core] crimes and thus to contribute to the prevention of such crimes'.[97] It therefore seems that the ICC will deliver retributive justice to those who

[89] On this point see Drumbl, 'Collective Violence and Individual Punishment', 561–6; Beresford, 'Unshackling the Paper Tiger'; Henham, 'The Philosophical Foundations of International Sentencing'.

[90] *Prosecutor v. Aleksovski* (Case No. IT-95–14/1-A), Judgment, 24 March 2000, para. 182; *Prosecutor v. Nahimana* (Case No. ICTR-99–52-T), Judgment and Sentencing, 3 December 2003, para. 1102; *Prosecutor v. Kayishema* (Case No. ICTR-95–1-T), Judgment and Sentencing, 21 May 1999, para. 18; *Prosecutor v. Brima, Kamara and Kanu* (Case No. SCSL-04–16-T), Sentencing Judgment, 19 July 2007, paras. 34–6; *Co-Prosecutors v. Guek Eav Kaing* (Case No:001/18–07–2007/ECCC/TC), Judgment, 26 July 2010, paras. 580, 582, 596, 600–1.

[91] *Prosecutor v. Erdemovic* (Case No. IT-96–22-T), Sentencing Judgment, 29 November 1996, para. 85.

[92] *Prosecutor v. Ntagerura* (Case No. ICTR-99–46-T), Judgment and Sentence, 25 February 2004, paras. 813–15; *Prosecutor v. Vasiljevic* (Case No. IT-98–32-A), Judgment of the Appeals Chamber, 25 February 2004, para. 182.

[93] *Prosecutor v. Kunarac* (Case No. IT-96–23/1-A), Judgment of the Appeals Chamber, 12 June 2002, para. 381.

[94] *Prosecutor v. Fofana and Kondewa* (Case No. SCSL-04–14-A), Judgment, 28 May 2008, paras. 558–65.

[95] John Rawls, 'Two Concepts of Rules' (1955) 64 *The Philosophical Review* 3, 5.

[96] Rome Statute of the International Criminal Court, A/Conf.183/9, 17 July 1998, (1998) 37 *International Legal Materials* 1002, Preamble, paras. 4–5.

[97] *Ibid.*, para. 5.

commit the most serious violations of human rights through the vehicle of prosecution and that this in turn is intended to have a deterrent effect on would-be perpetrators. The primary aim of the ICC is to prosecute and punish past conduct: a retributive goal. Linked to this primary function, is the additional utilitarian aim of deterring the future commission of human rights violations. In addition, the Court has stressed that its mandate is judicial and that issues of peace, security and restoration fall within the remit of other institutions.[98]

Overall, it is difficult to conclude with certainty as to the primary purpose of prosecution for past human rights violations. While retribution and deterrence are the objectives most commonly advanced, neither is clearly delineated, either in the enacting legislation or jurisprudence of international courts and tribunals, as the principal aim. Doubts have been expressed as to whether prosecution of international human rights crimes adheres properly to either theory.[99] International criminal law, which attaches such significance to the inherent worth and dignity of the individual, cannot easily be reconciled with utilitarian theories of deterrence, which view individuals as a means to an end. Nor does it sit easily with retributive notions. The limited and selective nature of international criminal justice means that not every perpetrator will be prosecuted and even those that are, are unlikely to suffer in proportion to their wrongdoing. Nevertheless, consideration of the reasoning of the ad hoc tribunals and hybrid courts in their sentencing decisions shows that although they acknowledge deterrence as a penal theory, they appear to be chiefly motivated by retributive concerns. Their focus is on the past conduct of the individual perpetrator and on delivering a sentence that reflects the seriousness of the crimes committed. Sentences will be more severe where the crimes committed are particularly cruel,[100] high in number[101]

---

[98] ICC, Office of the Prosecutor, *Policy Paper on the Interests of Justice*, September 2007, ICC-OTP-2007, 7–8.

[99] Aukerman, 'Extraordinary Evil, Ordinary Crime'; Drumbl, 'Collective Violence and Individual Punishment'; Carlos S. Nino, *Radical Evil on Trial* (New Haven: Yale University Press, 1996), 142; Frédéric Mégret, 'Three Dangers for the International Criminal Court: A Critical Look at a Consensual Project' (2001) XII *Finnish Year Book of International Law* 193, 213.

[100] *Prosecutor v. Nahimana* (Case No. ICTR-99–52-T), Judgment and Sentencing, 3 December 2003, para. 1102; *Prosecutor v. Kayishema* (Case No. ICTR-95-1-T), Judgment and Sentencing, 21 May 1999, para. 18.

[101] *Prosecutor v. Erdemovic* (Case No. IT-96-22-T), Sentencing Judgment, 29 November 1996, para. 85; *Prosecutor v. Fofana and Kondewa* (Case No. SCSL-04–14-A), Judgment, 28 May 2008, paras. 558–65.

or committed against vulnerable sectors of society.[102] This book therefore proceeds on the understanding that the primary aim of prosecution within the transitional justice framework is to deliver retributive justice by assigning individualised blame for the commission of these crimes and punishing those who perpetrate them.

5   The role of truth commissions in responding to past human rights violations

Truth commissions emerged in the early 1980s, as a number of states undertook the transition from authoritarian regime to democratic rule, often in the aftermath of violent internal conflicts. As these regimes fell, or voluntarily relinquished power, evidence of the systematic human rights violations committed under their rule came to light. Despite calls for criminal justice, fragile political settlements,[103] weak judicial systems[104] and the existence of national amnesty laws[105] precluded prosecutions in many states. As a concession that provided a means of investigating

[102] *Prosecutor* v. *Fofana and Kondewa* (Case No. SCSL-04-14-A), Judgment, 28 May 2008; *Prosecutor* v. *Brima, Kamara and Kanu* (Case No. SCSL-04-16-T), Sentencing Judgment, 19 July 2007, paras. 34–5.

[103] On the negotiated political settlement in South Africa see Alex Boraine, 'Truth and Reconciliation in South Africa: The Third Way', in Robert I. Rotberg and Dennis Thompson (eds.), *Truth v. Justice: The Morality of Truth Commissions* (Princeton University Press, 2000), 141–3; Marianne Guela, 'South Africa's Truth and Reconciliation Commission as an Alternate Means of Addressing Transitional Government Conflicts in a Divided Society' (2000) 18 *Boston University International Law Journal* 57. On the difficulties that faced the Chilean government following the overthrow of the Pinochet regime see Jorge S. Correa, 'Dealing with Past Human Rights Violations: The Chilean Case after Dictatorship' (1992) 67 *Notre Dame Law Review* 1455.

[104] On the impediments to justice created by the judicial systems in El Salvador and Guatemala, see Mark Vasallo, 'Truth and Reconciliation Commissions: General Considerations and a Critical Comparison of the Commissions of Chile and El Salvador' (2002) 33 *University of Miami Inter-American Law Review* 153, 159–60; Thomas Buergenthal, 'The United Nations Truth Commission for El Salvador' (1994) 27 *Vanderbilt Journal of Transnational Law* 497, 534; Terry L. Karl, 'El Salvador's Negotiated Revolution' (1992) 71 *Foreign Affairs* 147; Andrew N. Keller, 'To Name or Not to Name? The Commission for Historical Clarification in Guatemala, its Mandate and the Decision Not to Identify Individual Perpetrators' (2001) 13 *Florida Journal of International Law* 289, 294.

[105] For discussion of the South American amnesty laws see Jo Pasqualucci, 'The Whole Truth and Nothing But the Truth: Truth Commissions, Impunity and the Inter-American Human Rights System' (1994) 12 *Boston University International Law Journal* 321 and Naomi Roht-Arriaza, 'Truth Commissions and Amnesties in Latin America: The Second Generation' (1998) 92 *American Society of International Law and Proceedings* 313.

and acknowledging the past, while avoiding the controversy of pursuing individual criminal accountability, some states established truth commissions. Truth commissions were, therefore, created out of compromise, a conception that led critics to label them as weak surrogates for justice and to accusations that they fostered a culture of impunity.[106]

Truth commissions have garnered significant support since their beginnings as 'flawed compromises', aided in no small part by South Africa's world-renowned Truth and Reconciliation Commission. A more sophisticated understanding of what they can contribute to transitional states has developed[107] and since the 1990s their establishment has been considered in virtually every transitional context.[108] With the new millennium, a new breed of truth commission emerged. The transitional justice programmes implemented in East Timor and Sierra Leone saw truth commissions established alongside prosecutorial institutions as a complement to criminal justice.[109] They are now established not only where prosecution seems impossible, but as independent, transitional justice mechanisms capable of delivering unique benefits to transitional states.

There is no such thing as the typical truth commission. Each has operated differently and with varying degrees of success. As a result, truth commissions are not easily defined. In her seminal work on truth commissions, Hayner identified four features that all truth commissions share: a focus on the past; the investigation of a pattern of abuses; a temporary existence; and official authorisation from the state.[110] Some years later, Freeman developed this definition in light of the developments in truth

---

[106] Jonathan D. Tepperman, 'Truth and Consequences' (2002) 81 *Foreign Affairs* 131.

[107] This will be discussed in section 6.

[108] Freeman, *Truth Commissions and Procedural Fairness*, 11.

[109] The practice of contemporaneous establishment is also seen in the DRC and Uganda. The DRC referred the commission of serious violations in parts of the country to the ICC while simultaneously operating a truth commission. Ultimately, that commission was unable to fulfil its mandate due to political interference and ongoing instability within the country. See International Centre for Transitional Justice, Press Release, 'The DRC Elections, Reconciliation and Justice', 27 July 2006. Similarly, although the ICC has issued warrants for the arrest of those suspected of crimes in Uganda, there have been ongoing calls for the establishment of a national truth commission. International Center for Transitional Justice and the Human Rights Center, *Forgotten Voices: A Population Based Survey on Attitudes about Peace and Justice in Northern Uganda* (Berkeley: International Center for Transitional Justice and the Human Rights Center, University of California, 2005), 35; Uganda Peoples Congress, Press Release, 'Refocus the Juba Peace Talks', 19 July 2006, para. 2(a).

[110] Priscilla B. Hayner, *Unspeakable Truths. Facing the Challenge of Truth Commissions* (New York: Routledge, 2001), 14.

commission practice, listing nine additional elements.[111] He characterises truth commissions as investigatory commissions of inquiry,[112] which focus on severe acts of violence or repression[113] that have occurred during recent periods of abusive rule or armed conflict.[114] Truth commissions, he states, are concerned not only with the facts of individual cases but with providing an account of the broad causes and consequences of the violations.[115] They focus on violations committed in the sponsoring state[116] and are established within the sponsoring state.[117] In addition, he defines truth commissions as victim-centred bodies,[118] which are independent from the state,[119] yet officially authorised by it.[120]

This leads Freeman to define a truth commissions as:

> an *ad hoc* autonomous and victim-centred commission of inquiry set up in and authorised by a State for the primary purposes of (1) investigating and reporting on the principal causes and consequences of broad and relatively recent patterns of severe violence or repression that occurred in the State during determinate periods of abusive rule or conflict, and (2) making recommendations for their redress and future prevention.[121]

However, in her recent and updated work, Hayner points to the unwieldiness and rigidity of Freeman's definition.[122] Rather than adopting it, she updates her own definition, identifying five key characteristics. Thus, a truth commission: is focused on past events; investigates a pattern of events over a period of time; engages directly and broadly with the affected population; is a temporary body that aims to conclude with a final report; and is authorised by the state under review.[123] This book adopts Hayner's definition as one which captures the essential elements of past commissions and appears sufficiently flexible to accommodate the new models that are likely to emerge.

Unsurprisingly, given the different definitions, commentators differ as to how many of the investigative commissions established to date can

---

[111] Freeman, *Truth Commissions and Procedural Fairness*, 12–18.
[112] *Ibid.*, 14.   [113] *Ibid.*   [114] *Ibid.*, 15.   [115] *Ibid.*   [116] *Ibid.*, 15–16.
[117] *Ibid.*, 16.   [118] *Ibid.*, 17.   [119] *Ibid.*   [120] *Ibid.*, 18.
[121] *Ibid.* This definition is also adopted by Eric Wiebelhaus-Brahm, *Truth Commissions and Transitional Societies: The Impact on Human Rights and Democracy* (London and New York: Routledge, 2010), 3–4. For other definitions see: Updated Principles; UN Security Council, *Report of the Secretary-General on the Rule of Law and Transitional Justice in Conflict and Post-Conflict Societies*, para. 50.
[122] Hayner, *Unspeakable Truths: Transitional Justice and the Challenge of Truth Commissions*, 11.
[123] *Ibid.*, 11–12.

be considered truth commissions.[124] Generally, there is agreement that around thirty truth commissions have been created worldwide, mostly in Latin and Central America and sub-Saharan Africa. Their focus on past events, investigation of a pattern of abuses, temporary nature and independence from the state in which they operate distinguish them from other forms of investigative commission.[125] It is not the intention of this book to discuss exhaustively the details of each truth commission or to promote one truth commission model over others. Instead, it seeks to draw out common aspects of current truth commission practice in order to develop an understanding of how their operation can best be coordinated with that of prosecutorial institutions.

All truth commissions are given a mandate by the authority that creates them, whether it is by presidential decree, peace accord, legislative instrument or UN resolution.[126] The mandate sets the commission's length of operation, geographic scope and subject matter. It will also set out its primary objectives and any investigative powers with which it is to be endowed. It may additionally regulate the commission's relationship with prosecutorial institutions. Wide variation can be seen in truth commission mandates and, accordingly, their operation. Past commissions have taken from nine months to nine years to complete their work[127]

---

[124] Generally, it is agreed that truth commissions have been established in the following states: Bolivia, Argentina, Uganda, Nepal, Chile, Chad, El Salvador, Germany, Sri Lanka, Haiti, South Africa, Ecuador, Guatemala, Nigeria, Uruguay, South Korea, Peru, Panama, Serbia and Montenegro, East Timor, Sierra Leone, Ghana, Democratic Republic of Congo, Paraguay, Morocco, Liberia, Kenya. Hayner's 2001 list of truth commissions includes the commissions established in Uganda (1974), Zimbabwe (1984), Uruguay (1985), African National Congress (ANC) (1992 and 1993) and Burundi (1995). However, these are not classified by Freeman as truth commissions. Like Freeman, Wiebelhaus-Brahm excludes the 1974 Ugandan commission, those established by the ANC and that in Burundi, although, he does include the commissions established by Zimbabwe and Uruguay. Wiebelhaus-Brahm also includes in his list the 1986 Philippines commission, which is not in Freeman's list and Freeman lists the 2001 Granada commission and the 2005 Indonesian commission, while Wiebelhaus-Brahm does not. Hayner's 2010 list includes additionally, the 2000 Uruguay Peace Commission, the 2003 Chilean Valech Commission, the North Carolina Greensboro Truth and Reconciliation Commission, the Indonesian and Timor-Leste Commission for Truth and Friendship, and the Canadian Truth and Reconciliation Commission. Oddly, she admits herself that these do not fall within her definition of a truth commission, but are included for comparative purposes. She also includes more recently established truth commissions in Mauritius, Solomon Islands and Togo.

[125] Wiebelhaus-Brahm, *Truth Commissions and Transitional Societies*, 4.

[126] Freeman, *Truth Commissions and Procedural Fairness*, 27–8.

[127] *Ibid.*, Appendix 1, Table A.1: Truth Commissions and Their Key Powers.

and while most have been directed to concentrate on violations committed within their own state, the geographic scope of others has extended
beyond the territory of the country in question.[128] Specificity and subject
matter have also differed. The early commissions of Bolivia, Argentina,
Nepal and Sri Lanka were permitted only to investigate disappearances,
excluding a large number of other violations from investigation and dis-
torting the final account of the types and numbers of abuses committed.[129]
More recent commissions have been given broad mandates to investigate all types of violations, with a particular focus on those that involve
physical violence or repression and have been committed on a systematic
scale.[130] Like prosecutorial institutions, truth commissions have not been
immune to the inclusion of idealistic and, at times, somewhat unrealis-
tic aims within their mandates. Past commissions have been established
to promote national reconciliation,[131] restore the dignity of victims,[132]
reintegrate low-level perpetrators into their communities[133] and address
the experiences of vulnerable groups.[134] Some commissions have also fulfilled adjudicative functions. The South African Truth and Reconciliation
Commission (TRC) was given the authority to grant amnesty to perpetrators of human rights violations in exchange for full and truthful
testimony,[135] the East Timorese Commission for Reception, Truth and

---

[128] South Africa: Promotion of National Unity and Reconciliation Act, No. 34 of 1995, Preamble; Sierra Leone: Truth and Reconciliation Commission Act 2000, Article 6(2)(a)(i).

[129] Freeman, *Truth Commissions and Procedural Fairness*, Appendix 1, Table A.1: Truth Commissions and Their Key Powers; Peter Schey, Dinah Shelton and Naomi Roht-Arriaza, 'Addressing Human Rights Abuses: Truth Commissions and the Value of Amnesty' (1997) 19 *Whittier Law Review* 325, 332.

[130] Hayner, *Unspeakable Truths. Facing the Challenge of Truth Commissions*, 316–19.

[131] For example the Chilean TRC: Supreme Decree No. 355, Creation of the Commission on Truth and Reconciliation, 25 April 1990, Santiago, Preamble, para. 2; South African TRC: Promotion of National Unity and Reconciliation Act, No. 34 of 1995, Preamble.

[132] For example the East Timorese Commission for Reception, Truth and Reconciliation (CAVR): UN Transitional Administration in East Timor Regulation No. 2001/10 on the Establishment of a Commission for Reception, Truth and Reconciliation in East Timor, UN Doc. UNTAET/REG/2001/10, 13 July 2001, s. 3.1(f); Sierra Leonean TRC: Truth and Reconciliation Commission Act 2000, s. 6(2)(b).

[133] This was also an objective of the East Timorese CAVR. See UN Transitional Administration in East Timor Regulation No. 2001/10 on the Establishment of a Commission for Reception, Truth and Reconciliation in East Timor, UN Doc. UNTAET/REG/2001/10, 13 July 2001, s. 3.1(h).

[134] For example the Liberian TRC: An Act to Establish the Truth and Reconciliation Commission of Liberia, 2005, s. 4(e).

[135] South Africa: Promotion of National Unity and Reconciliation Act, No. 34 of 1995, Chapter 4.

Reconciliation (CAVR) drew up community service agreements between perpetrators and their communities,[136] and the Moroccan commission had the power to grant financial compensation to victims.[137]

However, all commissions share two readily discernable, interrelated primary aims: the investigation and clarification of past human rights violations and the prevention of similar violations in the future through the formulation of recommendations for reform.[138] These aims reflect the transitional justice goals of providing victims with the truth about the past and preventing human rights violations in the future. The truth-seeking function of commissions is fulfilled primarily through taking statements from victims, witnesses and, where possible, perpetrators. This enables those directly affected by the violations of the past to play a central role in the truth-seeking process and demonstrates the influence of restorative justice theory, which places victims at the centre of responses to crime, upon the work of truth commissions.[139] The mandates of many past commissions have specifically included responding to the needs of victims.[140] Truth commissions aim to contribute to the transitional justice objective of preventing human rights violations in the future through the publication of their final report, which documents their findings, outlines patterns of abuse and makes recommendations for reform. Like other aspects of truth commission operation, reporting has varied, from a focus on individuals and specific cases in Argentina, Chile[141] and El Salvador,[142] to the broad, contextual style adopted in Guatemala[143] and Sierra Leone.[144]

---

[136] UNTAET Regulation 2001/10, ss. 22–32.

[137] Freeman, *Truth Commissions and Procedural Fairness*, 35.

[138] *Ibid.*, 33.

[139] Kathleen Daly, 'Revisiting the Relationship between Retributive and Restorative Justice', in Heather Strang and John Braithwaite (eds.), *Restorative Justice: Philosophy to Practice* (Burlington: Ashgate, 2000), 36.

[140] See for example, South Africa's Promotion of National Unity and Reconciliation Act, No. 34 of 1995, Preamble; UNTAET Regulation 2001/10, ss. 3.1(f) and 21.2; An Act to Establish the Truth and Reconciliation Commission of Liberia, 2005, ss. 4(b) and (e).

[141] Schey *et al.*, 'Addressing Human Rights Abuses', 33.

[142] Margaret Popkin, 'The Salvadoran Truth Commission and the Search for Justice' (2004) 15 *Criminal Law Forum* 105, 110–11.

[143] Susan Kemp, 'The Interrelationship between the Guatemalan Commission for Historical Clarification and the Search for Justice in National Courts' (2004) 15 *Criminal Law Forum* 67, 88.

[144] William A. Schabas, 'A Synergistic Relationship: The Sierra Leone Truth and Reconciliation Commission and the Special Court for Sierra Leone' (2004) 15 *Criminal Law Forum* 3, 11.

In order to fulfil their mandates, many truth commissions have been endowed with investigative powers. This was not the case for the earliest commissions, which possessed few powers and were dependent on government and military cooperation for information and access to official documentation.[145] The South African TRC, established in 1995, gave rise to a new truth commission model, one that was endowed with powers of subpoena,[146] search and seizure[147] and witness protection,[148] as well as the capabilities to conduct questioning under oath[149] and to hold public hearings.[150] A large number of truth commissions established since the South African TRC have possessed these attributes,[151] along with the increasingly common ability to grant confidentiality to those who offer testimony.[152] These powers enable truth commissions to obtain information from sectors of society who might not otherwise offer testimony. Former perpetrators and vulnerable witnesses may not disclose their accounts of the past without either the protection of confidentiality or the impetus of compulsion. The testimony of these groups enables a truth commission to compile a more representative version of the past. Without their

---

[145] Pasqualucci, 'The Whole Truth and Nothing But the Truth', 336–9 on the limited powers possessed by the Argentinean and Chilean commissions.

[146] South Africa: Promotion of National Unity and Reconciliation Act, No. 34 of 1995, ss. 29 and 31.

[147] *Ibid.*, s. 32.

[148] *Ibid.*, s. 35. On the powers of the TRC see Boraine, 'Truth and Reconciliation in South Africa', 146–53.

[149] South Africa: Promotion of National Unity and Reconciliation Act, No. 34 of 1995, s. 29(1)(c).

[150] *Ibid.*, s. 33.

[151] For example, the commissions of Nigeria (1999), Grenada (2001), East Timor (2001), Ghana (2002), Sierra Leone (2002), DRC (2004) and Liberia (2005) were all endowed with powers of subpoena. The commissions of Nigeria (1999), East Timor (2001), Ghana (2002) and DRC (2005) were given powers of search and seizure and the commissions of Nigeria (1999), Grenada (2001), Peru (2001), East Timor (2001), Ghana (2002), Sierra Leone (2002), Morocco (2004), Paraguay (2004), DRC (2004) and Liberia (2005) possessed the power to conduct public hearings. See Freeman, *Truth Commissions and Procedural Fairness*, Appendix 1, Table A.1: Truth Commissions and Their Key Powers.

[152] In some cases the truth commission's mandate has stipulated that proceedings be conducted on a confidential basis. See Agreement on the Establishment of the Commission to clarify past human rights violations and acts of violence that have caused the Guatemalan Population to Suffer, Oslo, 23 June 1994; Supreme Decree No. 065–2001-PCM, Art. 7 on the establishment of the Peruvian TRC and Mexico Peace Agreements, Mexico City, 27 April 1991, Art. 7 on the establishment of the Commission on the Truth for El Salvador. Other commissions have had discretion to grant confidentiality. See Sierra Leone: Truth and Reconciliation Commission Act 2000, s. 7(3); East Timor, UNTAET Regulation No. 2001/10, s. 44.2.

testimony, a significant dimension of the truth may be lost. It is the possession by truth commissions of these quasi-judicial powers, and how their exercise might be coordinated with prosecutorial proceedings, which is of particular interest to this book.

6 The strengths and weaknesses of truth commissions and trials

Both trials and truth commissions are considered to deliver a range of, sometimes overlapping and complementary, benefits to transitional societies. Yet despite the academic attention that their respective strengths have received, few empirical studies testing the veracity of these claims have been carried out.[153] Although there is now a developing body of literature on the need to assess the effectiveness of transitional justice mechanisms, little is currently known about their practical impact.[154] Moreover, if both bodies can deliver the same benefits with equal efficacy there is surely no requirement for their dual operation. Only if they have unique merits can the use of both institutions be justified. Drawing on the evidence and scholarship available at present, this section seeks to explore the respective strengths and weaknesses of trials and truth commissions in responding to past violations.

Early literature evidences a belief that trials and truth commissions play important roles in truth establishment.[155] This is significant, as clarification of the truth about past events is considered essential in order for transitional societies to come to terms with their pasts, prevent recurrences of atrocities, and move forward to a reconciled future.[156] As

---

[153] Two recent exceptions are Tricia D. Olson, Leigh A. Payne and Andrew G. Reitger, *Transitional Justice in Balance: Comparing Processes, Weighing Efficacy* (Washington DC: US Institute of Peace Press, 2010); Wiebelhaus-Brahm, *Truth Commissions and Transitional Societies.*

[154] Van der Merwe *et al.*, *Assessing the Impact of Transitional Justice.*

[155] Antonio Cassese, 'Reflections on International Criminal Justice' (1998) 61 *Modern Law Review* 1, 6; Neil J. Kritz, 'Coming to Terms with Atrocities: A Review of Accountability Mechanisms for Mass Violations of Human Rights' (1996) 59 *Law and Contemporary Problems* 127, 128; Stephen Landsman, 'Alternative Responses to Serious Human Rights Abuses: Of Prosecution and Truth Commissions' (1996) 59 *Law and Contemporary Problems* 81, 83.

[156] Mark Imbleau, 'Initial Truth Establishment by Transitional Bodies and the Fight against Denial' (2004) 15 *Criminal Law Forum* 159; Rajeev Bhargava, 'Restoring Decency to Barbaric Societies', in Robert I. Rotberg and Dennis Thompson (eds.), *Truth v. Justice: The Morality of Truth Commissions* (Princeton University Press, 2000), 52–8; Richard Goldstone, 'Justice as a Tool for Peace-Making: Truth Commissions and International

understanding of these mechanisms has developed, however, their truth-finding limitations have become clear. The truth established by trials is necessarily narrow as it emerges from the prosecution of a limited range of crimes and is confined to the actions of those tried.[157] Trials have been criticised as ill-adapted to capturing the multiple sources of mass violence due to their focus on guilt and innocence.[158] The restrictive rules of evidence and procedure may lead to useful information being excluded.[159] Moreover, the inaccessibility of the operations and findings of prosecutorial institutions by affected populations means that criminal trials may not provide the most effective forum for establishing a historical record of past violations that is accepted by the general populace.[160] Although the ICTY has taken seriously the need for a historical record in affected communities and has included detailed records of past events in its decisions, this is rare among prosecutorial institutions.[161]

At first glance, truth commissions fare better. They are, after all, established with the objective of documenting and disseminating the history of the political, social and economic structure of the system that permitted the commission of abuses and leaving the country with an official record of past events.[162] However, truth commissions too have inherent truth-finding deficiencies. Typically, they suffer from underfunding and this, coupled with time constraints, limits their abilities to conduct investigations, take statements and transcribe collected data.[163] Concerns have

---

Criminal Tribunals' (1996) 28 *NYU Journal of International Law and Politics* 485; Luc Huyse, 'Dealing with the Past and Imagining the Future', in Luc Reychler and Thania Paffenholz (eds.), *Peacebuilding: A Field Guide* (Boulder: Lynne Rienner Publishers, 2002), 327; Sabine Kurtenbach, 'Dealing with the Past in Latin America', in Luc Reychler and Thania Paffenholz (eds.), *Peacebuilding: A Field Guide* (Boulder: Lynne Rienner Publishers, 2002), 356; Tristan Anne Borer, 'Truth Telling as a Peace Building Activity', in Tristan Anne Borer (ed.), *Telling the Truths: Truth Telling and Peace Building in Post-Conflict Societies* (University of Notre Dame Press, 2006), 1, 17–18.

[157] Imbleau, 'Initial Truth Establishment by Transitional Bodies', 165–6.

[158] Martha Minow, 'The Hope for Healing: What Can Truth Commissions Do?', in Robert I. Rotberg and Dennis Thompson (eds.), *Truth v. Justice: The Morality of Truth Commissions* (Princeton University Press, 2000), 235–61, 238.

[159] Laura Olson, 'Mechanisms Complementing Prosecution' (2002) 84 *International Review of the Red Cross* 173, 175.

[160] *Ibid.* See also Jose E. Alvarez, 'Crimes of States/Crimes of Hate: Lessons from Rwanda' (1999) 24 *Yale Journal of International Law* 365, 397–8.

[161] Richard A. Wilson, 'Judging History: The Historical Record of the International Criminal Tribunal for the Former Yugoslavia' (2005) 27 *Human Rights Quarterly* 908.

[162] Olson, 'Mechanisms Complementing Prosecution', 175.

[163] Joanna Quinn and Mark Freeman, 'Lessons Learned: Practical Lessons Gleaned from inside the Truth Commissions of Guatemala and South Africa' (2003) 25 *Human Rights Quarterly* 1117.

been raised that those who appear before truth commissions seldom tell the full truth[164] and that testimony based on memory is subjective and vulnerable to change over time.[165] Ultimately, the truth presented may be one-dimensional as a result of an inability to obtain testimony from all parties to a conflict.[166] The truth which emerges will be shaped by the investigative methodologies employed by the commission, the commissioners' interpretation of the mandate, and the abilities of the commission to gain cooperation from officials and access to relevant documentation.[167]

What is also increasingly clear is that the idea of a single, objective truth is a false construct. In its final report, the South African TRC referred to four notions of truth: factual or forensic; personal or narrative; social; and healing or restorative. Wilson argues that this can be reduced to two models: forensic and narrative. For him, forensic truth is the only real truth. It is compiled of facts and corroborating evidence and leads to the establishment of patterns of violence, the nature, scope and methods of repression and the responsibility for it. Narrative truth relates to the experiences of individuals, and therefore involves an element of subjectivity.[168] Mendez makes a similar distinction, between 'structural' and 'individualized' truth.[169] There are, in reality, different types and levels of truth.

Understanding the truth-finding merits of trials and truth commissions may lie within Chapman's distinction between macro and micro truth.[170] She argues that due to their reliance on personal testimony as a primary source of data, truth commissions are best suited to establishing macro truth. Macro truth encompasses the structural causes of violence,

---

[164] Tim Kelsall, 'Truth, Lies, Ritual: Preliminary Reflections on the Truth and Reconciliation Commission in Sierra Leone' (2005) 27 *Human Rights Quarterly* 361.

[165] Nora Strejilevich, 'Testimony: Beyond the Language of Truth' (2006) 28 *Human Rights Quarterly* 701.

[166] Jennifer Schirmer, 'Whose Testimony? Whose Truth? Where Are the Armed Actors in the Stoll-Menchu Controversy?' (2003) 25 *Human Rights Quarterly* 60.

[167] Audrey R. Chapman and Patrick Ball, 'The Truth of Truth Commissions: Comparative Lessons from Haiti, South Africa, and Guatemala' (2001) 23 *Human Rights Quarterly* 1; Audrey R. Chapman 'Truth Finding in the Transitional Justice Process', in Hugo Van der Merwe, Victoria Baxter and Audrey R. Chapman (eds.), *Assessing the Impact of Transitional Justice: Challenges for Empirical Research* (Washington DC: United States Institute of Peace Press, 2009), 91–115.

[168] Richard A. Wilson, *The Politics of Truth and Reconciliation in South Africa* (New York: Cambridge University Press, 2001), 36–7.

[169] Juan E. Mendez, 'The Human Right to Truth: Lessons Learned from Latin American Experiences with Truth Telling', in Tristan Anne Borer (ed.), *Telling the Truths: Truth Telling and Peace Building in Post-Conflict Societies* (University of Notre Dame Press, 2006), 115–51.

[170] Chapman, 'Truth Finding in the Transitional Justice Process', 104–5.

the identification of the broader causes and the intellectual authors of it.[171] The subjectivity and discrepancies inherent in personal testimony are unlikely to impact on the determination of macro truth.[172] These deficiencies make truth commissions unsuitable to determining micro truth, which identifies the circumstances of particular crimes and the individuals and groups responsible for their commission.[173] The establishment of micro truth would seem to lie more appropriately with prosecutorial institutions, which engage in close scrutiny of specific cases and whose focus is to establish the culpability of individuals.[174] As indicated in the UN Study on the Right to the Truth, there is an individual and societal dimension to the right to truth. While individual victims and their relatives are likely to desire clarification of the details pertaining to particular cases, society as a whole is likely to focus upon the broader picture of the nature of the violations committed and the institutional responsibility for them. This is not to suggest that individuals have no interest in macro truths or society no interest in the micro truth of individual cases.[175] However, there are different dimensions to the right to truth and different types of truth that can be established. There is a need for both micro and macro truth if the rights of victims and society are to be fulfilled, and consequently a role for both truth commissions and trials. Any transitional truth is likely to be imperfect and contested by some and it must be acknowledged that both institutions have shortcomings in establishing it. However, trials and truth commissions contribute to the clarification of different truths. They have different but complementary contributions to make to truth establishment.

Truth commissions and trials are also understood to contribute to the healing of victims. As discussed above, empirical studies suggest that the majority of victims of serious violations of human rights seek criminal justice.[176] As non-judicial bodies, truth commissions cannot assign criminal responsibility for the crimes they investigate or impose any form of punishment on the perpetrators. They will always fall short of delivering

---

[171] *Ibid.*, 105.   [172] *Ibid.*   [173] *Ibid.*

[174] Janet Cherry, 'Truth and Transitional Justice in South Africa', in Hugo Van der Merwe, Victoria Baxter and Audrey R. Chapman (eds.), *Assessing the Impact of Transitional Justice: Challenges for Empirical Research* (Washington DC: United States Institute of Peace Press, 2009), 249–65, 251.

[175] Paul Gready, *The Era of Transitional Justice: The Aftermath of the Truth and Reconciliation Commission in South Africa and Beyond* (Oxford and New York: Routledge, 2011), 24–5.

[176] Kiza *et al.*, *Victims of War*, 97.

full and formal accountability and cannot meet the demands of victims for retributive, criminal justice.

Despite the symbolic significance of prosecution, the trial process itself has traditionally only offered victims a peripheral role. Commentators have noted that victim testimony is only of relevance to the court if it can be used as evidence to prove elements of the crime charged and, at that, only the testimony of a relatively small number of victims will be required as evidence.[177] Further criticism has been made of the exclusion of victims' accounts of their suffering under evidentiary rules and the rigorous defence challenges to their testimony through cross-examination.[178] These factors, it is argued, have lead to a sense of marginalisation among the victim community.[179] The ICC has made significant steps forward in recognising the rights and role of victims within prosecutorial proceedings, providing a statutory right for victims' participation where their personal interests are affected.[180] However, there will necessarily be limits to the participation of victims. Article 68(3) of the ICC Statute states that victims' participation in proceedings will be permitted where 'it is determined to be appropriate by the Court' and where it would not be 'prejudicial to or inconsistent with the rights of the accused and a fair and impartial trial'. The Office of the Prosecutor (OTP) has stated that this must be assessed on a case-by-case basis.[181] Already, the Court has held that there is no room for those granted victim status to present additional evidence at the pre-trial stage.[182] While the ICC's creation of a right of victim participation is innovative in international criminal justice, it must operate within parameters that protect the integrity of the Court's proceedings.[183]

Truth commissions do not operate under the same procedural constraints as criminal trials and can offer victims a central role. Victim testimony is of primary importance for truth commissions as they build an

---

[177] For discussion of the experiences of some witnesses who testified at the ICTY see Eric Stover, 'Witnesses and the Promise of Justice in the Hague', in Eric Stover and Harvey M. Weinstein (eds.), *My Neighbor, My Enemy: Justice and Community in the Aftermath of Mass Atrocity* (Cambridge University Press, 2004), 104–20.

[178] Minow, 'The Hope for Healing', 238.

[179] *Ibid.*

[180] Rome Statute, Art. 68(3). ICC Rules of Procedure and Evidence (RPE) rr. 85, 89 and 91.

[181] ICC, Office of the Prosecutor, *Policy Paper on Victims' Participation*, April 2010, 16.

[182] *Prosecutor v. Germain Katanga and Mathieu Ngudjolo Chui*, Decision on the Set of Procedural Rights Attached to Procedural Status of Victim at the Pre-Trial Stage of the Case, ICC-01/04–01/07–474, 13 May 2008, para. 113.

[183] ICC, *Policy Paper on Victims' Participation*, 18.

overall picture of the abuses of the past.[184] It is argued that commissions provide victims with a platform on which they can bring their experiences to the awareness of the public and, as formally established institutions, provide official acknowledgement of their suffering.[185] It is this aspect of truth commission operation that has given rise to a belief that they play a central role in the healing of victims. However, the assertion that offering testimony publicly to a truth commission affords opportunities for victims to heal[186] is largely untested and is therefore being increasingly challenged.[187] The limited studies that have been carried out show that the opportunity to recount experiences may be empowering or cathartic for some victims, but for others, it may reignite anger and prove highly traumatic; the experience is variable.[188] The prosecution of perpetrators may also prove to be an important aspect of healing for some victims.[189] Ultimately, however, the healing process is complex, slow and subjective,[190] and while truth commissions and prosecutions may contribute, in different ways, to the healing of some victims, it seems likely that they can only act as one small component of that overall process.

---

[184] Hayner, *Unspeakable Truths: Facing the Challenge of Truth Commissions*, 28.

[185] Martha Minow, *From Vengeance to Forgiveness: Facing History after Genocide and Mass Violence* (Boston: Beacon Press, 1998), 58.

[186] *Ibid.*, 61.

[187] Jonathan Allen, 'Balancing Justice and Social Unity: Political Theory and the Idea of a Truth and Reconciliation Commission' (1999) 49 *University of Toronto Law Journal* 315, 316–17; Brandon Hamber, ' "Nunca Más" and the Politics of Person', in Tristan Anne Borer (ed.), *Telling the Truths: Truth Telling and Peace Building in Post-Conflict Societies* (University of Notre Dame Press, 2006), 207–31, 215; Richard Goldstone 'Exposing Human Rights Abuses: A Help or a Hindrance to Reconciliation?' (1995) *Hastings Constitutional Law Quarterly* 22; Audrey R. Chapman, 'Truth Commissions as Instruments of Forgiveness and Reconciliation', in Raymond G. Helmick and Rodney L. Peterson (eds.), *Forgiveness and Reconciliation: Religion, Public Policy and Conflict Transformation* (Radnor: Templeton Foundation Press, 2002), 257–79. Wiebelhaus-Brahm, *Truth Commissions and Transitional Societies*, 11.

[188] Ruth Picker, *Victims' Perspectives about the Human Rights Violations Hearings* (Johannesburg: Centre for the Study of Violence and Reconciliation, 2005).

[189] Debra Kaminer *et al.*, 'The Truth and Reconciliation Commission in South Africa: Relation to Psychiatric Status and Forgiveness among Survivors of Human Rights Abuses' (2001) 178 *British Journal of Psychiatry* 373; Hugo Van der Merwe, 'What Survivors Say about Justice: An Analysis of the TRC Victim Hearings', in Audrey R. Chapman and Hugo Van der Merwe (eds.), *Truth and Reconciliation: Has the TRC Delivered?* (Philadelphia: University of Pennsylvania Press, 2008), 23–45. On the inadequacies of prosecution in bringing about healing see Laurel E. Fletcher and Harvey M. Weinstein, 'Violence and Social Repair: Rethinking the Contribution of Justice to Reconciliation' (2002) 24 *Human Rights Quarterly* 573.

[190] Hamber, ' "Nunca Más" ', 216.

Transitional states are also thought to benefit from the assignation of responsibility that arises from the work of trials and truth commissions. The individualisation of guilt brought about through prosecution is considered essential at individual and societal levels. For victims, the prosecution and punishment of individuals can 'meet the desire for revenge'.[191] At a societal level, the individualisation of responsibility is thought to help alleviate inter-ethnic and religious tensions. Thus, 'the emphasis on individual responsibility offers an avenue away from the cycles of blame that lead to revenge, recrimination and ethnic and national conflicts'.[192] Linked to this is the notion that collective guilt is also eased through the individualisation of responsibility. Research indicates that members of groups, whether national, religious or ethnic, have a strong desire to be free from collective moral guilt.[193] However, like the healing of victims, early studies suggest that the alleviation of collective blame and the easing of guilt are likely to be lengthy, complex processes.[194] The prosecution of individuals may make a contribution to this process, although how significant that contribution might be remains uncertain.

Truth commissions are not generally concerned with individualising guilt, although some have made findings in specific cases.[195] They focus instead on assigning institutional responsibility.[196] As a result, their recommendations frequently centre on reform of the military, security forces and judiciary.[197] By reforming corrupt institutions it is hoped, although

---

[191] Cassese, 'Reflections on International Criminal Justice', 6.

[192] Minow, *From Vengeance to Forgiveness*, 40.

[193] Karl Jaspers, *The Question of German Guilt*, trans. E. B. Ashton (New York: Dial Press, 1947), 39–41, Dinka Corkalo *et al.*, 'Neighbours Again? Intercommunity Relations after Ethnic Cleansing', in Eric Stover and Harvey M. Weinstein (eds.), *My Neighbor, My Enemy: Justice and Community in the Aftermath of Mass Atrocity* (Cambridge University Press, 2004), 143–8.

[194] *Ibid.*

[195] Popkin, 'The Salvadoran Truth Commission', 110–11; Buergenthal, 'The United Nations Truth Commission for El Salvador', 528. On the difficulties associated with publishing findings of individual responsibility see Freeman, *Truth Commissions and Procedural Fairness*, Chapter 7. See also Quinn and Freeman, 'Lessons Learned', 1144–6.

[196] See for example, the reports of the El Salvadoran and Guatemalan commissions: *From Madness to Hope: The 12 Year War in El Salvador: Report of the Commission on the Truth for El Salvador*, UN Doc. S/25500, Annex, 1993 Part VI, A; *Guatemala: Memoria del Silencio: Informe de la Comisión para el Esclarecimiento Histórico* (Guatemala City: Commission for Historical Clarification: distributed by F&G Editores, 1999), Conclusions, Part II, paras. 82, 94–6.

[197] *From Madness to Hope: The 12-Year War in El Salvador*, Part V, Recommendations; *Guatemala: Memoria del Silencio*, Recommendations. To date the record for implementation of truth commission recommendations has been poor. Recently, however, clauses

by no means proven,[198] that the likelihood of violations being committed in the future is diminished. Interestingly, a recent study demonstrates that truth commissions promote more significant improvements in long-term human rights standards when they operate alongside trials and amnesties.[199] It is contended that where these three mechanisms operate together a 'justice balance' is struck.[200] Trials deter human rights violations, amnesties stabilise the political system and truth commissions enhance accountability by exposing the systemic, institutional nature of abuses. Truth commissions do not undermine amnesty or prosecutions, and they provide a blueprint for reform.[201] The study again points to the complementary and mutually reinforcing roles played by trials and truth commissions within the transitional justice framework.

The role of truth commissions in determining institutional responsibility as a basis for formulating proposals for reform is closely linked to strengthening the rule of law. The findings of a truth commission may stimulate social dialogue about the past and inspire broader participation in the political process.[202] The recommendations for reform, if put into practice, may create more democratic, accountable state institutions which respect, protect and promote human rights and this, in turn, may foster civic trust.[203] Of course, the very establishment of truth commissions and pursuit of criminal justice go some way to strengthening the rule of law. The operation of these processes is indicative of a break with the past, an acknowledgement by the state that the abuses of the past were wrong and an attempt to re-establish the orderly function of the state and hold wrongdoers to account.[204] Trials and truth commissions again,

---

have been included in truth commission legislation making implementation mandatory. See for example Sierra Leone: Truth and Reconciliation Commission Act 2000, Art. 14, which imposes an obligation on the Sierra Leonean government to implement the recommendations of the TRC directed at state bodies and facilitate the implementation of those directed at others.

[198] Hamber, '"Nunca Más"', 214–21.

[199] Tricia D. Olsen, Leigh A. Payne, Andrew G. Reitger and Eric Wiebelhaus-Brahm, 'When Truth Commissions Improve Human Rights' (2010) 4 *International Journal of Transitional Justice* 457.

[200] *Ibid.*, 469–70.

[201] *Ibid.*, 475.

[202] Pablo De Greiff, 'Truth Telling and the Rule of Law', in Tristan Anne Borer (ed.), *Telling the Truths: Truth Telling and Peace Building in Post-Conflict Societies* (University of Notre Dame Press, 2006), 181, 188.

[203] *Ibid.*, 188–90.

[204] Ruti Teitel, *Transitional Justice* (Oxford University Press, 2000), 28–30; Malmud-Goti, 'Transitional Governments in the Breach, 11–12; Fletcher and Weinstein, 'Violence and

however, operate at the very beginning of this long process. They may lay important foundations on which to build a society based on the rule of law but the achievement of that goal will ultimately depend on a host of variables, outside the operational period of trials and truth commissions.[205]

The final and oft-cited benefit of trials and truth commissions to be considered here is their power to bring about national reconciliation. Truth commissions, in particular, have become inextricably linked to the concept of reconciliation, both in their names and mandates. Exactly what is meant by reconciliation remains unclear. Transitional justice scholars are divided on the definition of reconciliation, whether it is a process or a goal and the level(s) on which it occurs.[206] There seems to be some consensus that national reconciliation is both long term and multidimensional.[207] Defining national reconciliation on these criteria has therefore led to conclusions that transitional justice mechanisms such as trials and truth commissions are generally unsuited to promoting national reconciliation, due to their temporary nature and their operation at a time when memories of the past are most painful.[208]

Past commissions have not underestimated the complexity of national reconciliation. Both the TRC for South Africa and that for Sierra Leone undertook a range of initiatives to promote national reconciliation but acknowledged that they could not reconcile their respective nations, particularly in their short life spans.[209] However, both documented their

Social Repair', 596; Juan E. Mendez, 'In Defence of Transitional Justice', in A. James McAdams (ed.), *Transitional Justice and the Rule of Law in New Democracies* (London: University of Notre Dame Press, 1997) 1–27, 4.

[205] On the failure of truth commissions established to date to bring any meaningful reform in the areas of human rights and democracy see Wiebelhaus-Brahm, *Truth Commissions and Transitional Societies*, Parts II and III.

[206] Joanna R. Quinn (ed.), *Reconciliation(s): Transitional Justice in Post-Conflict Societies* (Montreal and Kingston, London, Ithaca: McGill Queen's University Press, 2009), 5.

[207] Brandon Hamber and Grainne Kelly, *A Place for Reconciliation? Conflict and Locality in Northern Ireland* (Belfast: Democratic Dialogue, 2005), 38–40; Audrey R. Chapman, 'Approaches to Studying Reconciliation', in Hugo Van der Merwe, Victoria Baxter and Audrey R. Chapman (eds.), *Assessing the Impact of Transitional Justice: Challenges for Empirical Research* (Washington DC: United States Institute of Peace Press, 2009), 143–73, 151; David Bloomfield, Teresa Barnes and Luc Huyse, *Reconciliation After Violent Conflict: A Handbook* (Stockholm: International Institute for Democracy and Electoral Assistance, 2003), 214.

[208] Chapman, 'Approaches to Studying Reconciliation', 158–9.

[209] *Truth and Reconciliation Commission of South Africa Report* (Cape Town: Truth and Reconciliation Commission, distributed by Juta and Co., 2002), vol. 5, Chapter 9, 350–91; SLTRC, *Witness to Truth: Report of the Sierra Leone Truth and Reconciliation Commission* (Accra: Graphic Packaging Ltd, 2004), vol. 3b, Chapter 7.

sense that they had begun a process that other stakeholders could take forward. Chapman acknowledges the useful role that can be played by truth commissions, and indeed trials, in the early stages of reconciliation. She considers that truth commissions can be a source of public education and socialisation and can offer former adversaries a cooperative experience. In addition, both truth commissions and trials can act as an early shared experience in a divided country.[210] Much work remains to be done on developing both a conceptual understanding of reconciliation and empirical tools to assess the contribution made by transitional justice mechanisms to reconciliation. At this early stage, it seems likely that, as with the healing of victims and the strengthening of the rule of law, truth commissions and trials have a small contribution to make to the lengthy and complex process of national reconciliation.

7   Conclusion

This chapter has explained the place of truth commissions and criminal prosecution within the transitional justice framework and has explored the various aims and objectives assigned to these mechanisms. It has shown that the primary objective of trials is to deliver retributive criminal justice, while truth commissions aim to clarify and document the truth about the past.

The chapter has also demonstrated that trials and truth commissions can make positive contributions to transitional states. Their contributions are overlapping, and indeed complementary, in that both appear, on some level, to respond to the needs of victims, assign responsibility for past violations, uncover the truth, and contribute to peace and the prevention of further atrocities. The methods they employ in delivering these benefits are of course different, as is their effectiveness in fulfilling them. The nature of prosecution means that criminal trials will necessarily focus on specific cases, proving particular facts and assigning criminal responsibility to a limited number of individuals. Trials may strengthen the national and international rule of law, provide acknowledgement of the suffering of victims and deliver a sense of justice. In so doing, they may lay favourable conditions for national reconciliation and contribute to the overall healing process of victims. Broadly, the strength of prosecution lies in its retributive function and its ability to deliver criminal justice to those in transitional states.

---

[210] Chapman, 'Approaches to Studying Reconciliation', 159.

Truth commissions, as non-judicial mechanisms, cannot fulfil the desire of victims for criminal justice. However, commissions possess unique abilities to engage in broad, historical inquiry, to provide affected populations with an accessible account of the past and to conduct an inclusive and interactive truth-seeking process. In the process of truth seeking and telling, truth commissions too may contribute to the healing of victims and the strengthening of the rule and law and lay some of the groundwork for long-term reconciliation. Together, trials and truth commissions have the potential to deliver a range of benefits to transitional states. The remaining chapters of this book seek to determine whether and how their modes of operation can be coordinated in order to secure the delivery of these benefits to transitional societies.

2

Truth commissions and international jurisdiction to prosecute

1 Introduction

The way in which states respond to serious human rights violations is, or at least ought to be, in large part determined by their international legal obligations. The commission of certain human rights crimes gives rise to duties to prosecute under international treaty law. Other violations, while not the subject of specific treaties or customary duties, may give rise to international condemnation, pressure to prosecute those responsible at the national level and, failing that, international efforts to do so. It is in light of these obligations and influences that the operation of truth commissions and trials must be coordinated. Legal frameworks impact the role played by truth commissions within transitional states, their subject matter mandates, the powers they can be endowed with and their personal jurisdiction.

The establishment of the International Criminal Court (ICC) creates additional complexities in the efforts to coordinate truth commissions with prosecutorial proceedings. The significance of the ICC Statute lies not simply in the creation of the Court or its prioritisation of prosecution at the national level through the principle of complementarity, although this latter innovation may of itself affect the ways in which truth commissions are used in future. The Statute imposes a range of obligations on states parties to cooperate with and provide assistance to the Court.[1] How those obligations will be reconciled with the investigations of national truth commissions, the powers they exercise and the protection of the information they uncover raises difficult questions.

Before an evaluation can be carried out of how the operations of these bodies can be coordinated in practice, it is necessary to understand the nature and extent of the prosecutorial obligations possessed by states and how these shape the choices made in responding to past violations. It is

---

[1] This will be considered in Chapter 4.

also vital to develop an appreciation of the likely impact of the ICC regime upon the future operation of truth commissions. This chapter will therefore consider treaty and customary sources requiring the prosecution of serious human rights violations, their overlap with the subject matter mandates of truth commissions and the implications of these obligations for the establishment and operation of commissions. The potential for overlap between truth commission mandates and the jurisdiction of the ICC will also be demonstrated and the implications for truth commissions considered. The chapter will show that where there are obligations to prosecute past violations, these will influence the role that can be played by truth commissions within transitional states. It will argue that where crimes within the jurisdiction of the ICC have been committed, truth commissions will fulfil a subsidiary role to that of prosecution.

2   International law obligations to prosecute and the overlap with truth commission mandates

2.1   Truth commissions and treaty obligations to prosecute

A number of international and regional treaties impose upon their states parties an explicit obligation to prosecute should the crimes enumerated within those treaties occur. The Genocide Convention,[2] the Geneva Conventions,[3] the Apartheid Convention,[4] the Convention against Torture,[5] the International Convention on Enforced Disappearance[6] and the Inter-American Convention on the Forced Disappearance of Persons[7]

---

[2] UN Convention on the Prevention and Punishment of the Crime of Genocide, 9 December 1948, 78 UNTS 227, Art. 6.

[3] Geneva Convention I for the Amelioration of the Condition of the Wounded and Sick in Armed Forces in the Field, 12 August 1949, 75 UNTS 31, Art. 49; Geneva Convention II for the Amelioration of the Condition of Wounded, Sick and Shipwrecked Members of Armed Forces at Sea, 12 August 1949, 75 UNTS 85, Art. 50; Geneva Convention III Relative to the Treatment of Prisoners of War, 12 August 1949, 75 UNTS 135, Art. 129; Geneva Convention IV Relative to the Protection of Civilian Persons in Time of War, 12 August 1949, 75 UNTS 287, Art. 146.

[4] International Convention on the Suppression and Punishment of the Crime of Apartheid, 30 November 1973, 1015 UNTS 243, Art. 4(b).

[5] UN Convention against Torture and Other Cruel, Inhuman or Degrading Treatment or Punishment, 10 December 1984, 1465 UNTS 85, Arts. 4(2) and 7.

[6] International Convention for the Protection of All Persons from Enforced Disappearance, New York, 20 December 2006, General Assembly Resolution 61/177.

[7] Inter-American Convention on the Forced Disappearance of Persons, Belém, Brazil, 9 June 1994, (1994) 33 *International Legal Materials* 1529.

are all examples. In other instruments an obligation to prosecute human rights violations is arguably, although by no means definitively, implicit.[8] It has been developed through the jurisprudence of human rights courts and supervisory bodies on state obligations to respect and ensure the rights within the Conventions and to provide victims with an effective remedy.[9]

States parties have not always strictly adhered to their treaty obligations to prosecute specific human rights violations or to provide victims of violations with effective remedies.[10] Indeed, many states established truth commissions instead of carrying out criminal trials. Recent practice evidences a move away from impunity towards accountability and demonstrates the beginnings of a commitment at national levels to pursuing criminal responsibility. Although they do not result from treaty obligations, national efforts at accountability can be seen in the Rwandan *gacaca* trials,[11] the Sierra Leonean request for the establishment of the Special Court,[12] prosecutions for violations committed under the military regimes of Latin and Central America[13] and the trials at the Iraqi High Tribunal.[14] The role of the truth commission is also evolving. Those created in East Timor, Sierra Leone and, to some extent, Kenya, have operated as complements to trials rather than alternatives to them. These initiatives suggest the emergence of a more proactive and nuanced approach to accountability, particularly for the most serious violations of human rights. As part of this, greater rigour in adherence to treaty obligations also seems likely.

---

[8] Kai Ambos, 'The Legal Framework of Transitional Justice: A Systematic Study with a Special Focus on the ICC', in Kai Ambos *et al.* (eds.), *Building a Future on Peace and Justice: Studies on Transitional Justice, Peace and Development* (Heidelberg and Berlin: Springer-Verlag, 2009), 30.

[9] See Chapter 1.

[10] Louise Mallinder, *Amnesty, Human Rights and Political Transitions: Bridging the Peace and Justice Divide* (Oxford: Hart Publishing, 2008), 119–37, 266–83.

[11] For an extensive analysis see Phil Clark, *The Gacaca Courts and Post-Genocide Justice and Reconciliation in Rwanda: Justice without Lawyers* (Cambridge University Press, 2010).

[12] *Fifth Report of the Secretary-General in the United Nations Mission in Sierra Leone*, S/2000/751, 31 July 2000, 2.

[13] Pablo F. Parenti, 'The Prosecution of International Crimes in Argentina' (2010) 10 *International Criminal Law Review* 491; Girão Monteconrado *et al.*, 'International Criminal Law and Transitional Justice in Brazil' (2010) 10 *International Criminal Law Review* 509; Guzmán Dalbora and José Luis, 'The Treatment of International Crimes in Chilean Jurisprudence: A Janus Face' (2010) 10 *International Criminal Law Review* 535.

[14] M. Cherif Bassiouni, 'Post-Conflict Justice in Iraq: An Appraisal of the Iraq Special Tribunal' (2005) 38 *Cornell International Law Journal* 327.

It is against this backdrop of increasing national accountability that future truth commissions will be designed and, ultimately, will carry out their operations. If they are established in conjunction with trials and are endowed with mandates similar to those of the past, there will be overlap between their investigations and the treaty obligations of states to prosecute human rights violations. A large number of past commissions have, for example, had authority to investigate the crime of torture. Sometimes a specific reference to the crime has been included within the mandate,[15] or authority has been given implicitly by way of a general mandate to investigate 'human rights violations', which includes those committed by public institutions.[16] Some commissions have interpreted and defined their subject matter mandates in accordance with international treaty definitions[17] and many have documented instances of torture by state officials within their final reports.[18] The prohibition of torture is a customary international law norm and has been described as a *jus cogens* rule.[19] For states parties to the Convention against Torture (CAT), torture by, or with the acquiescence of, public officials is prohibited,[20] regardless of war, the threat of it, political instability or national emergency.[21] The CAT also imposes obligations upon its states parties in order to regulate their responses to the occurrence of torture. States parties are under a duty to criminalise torture under domestic law[22] and to ensure their capability of exercising jurisdiction over acts of torture committed on their territory or

---

[15] Chilean Supreme Decree 355 on the Creation of the Commission on Truth and Reconciliation, Santiago, 25 April 1990, Art. 1; Peruvian Supreme Decree 065–2001-PCM, Lima, 2 June 2001, Art. 3(c).

[16] An Act to Establish the Truth and Reconciliation Commission of Liberia 2005, s. 4(a), South African Promotion of National Unity and Reconciliation Act, No. 34 of 1995, s. 4; Ghanaian National Reconciliation Commission Act 2002, ss. 3 and 4.

[17] See for example, *Truth and Reconciliation Commission of South Africa Report* (Cape Town: Truth and Reconciliation Commission, distributed by Juta and Co., 2002), vol. 1, Chapter 4, 78.

[18] See for example: *Report of the Chilean National Commission on Truth and Reconciliation* (University of Notre Dame Press, 1993), 159–61; *From Madness to Hope: The Twelve Year War in El Salvador, Report of the Commission on the Truth for El Salvador*, UN Security Council, S/25500, 1993, Annex, Part IV A.

[19] *Al-Adsani v. United Kingdom* (Application No. 35763/97), Judgment of 21 November 2001, (2002) 34 EHRR 273, para. 61; *Caesar v. Trinidad and Tobago* (Merits, Reparations and Costs), Inter-American Court of Human Rights, Series C, No. 123, 11 March 2005; UN Human Rights Committee General Comment 29, HRI/GEN/1/Rev.9 (vol. I) 234, para. 3; UN Committee against Torture, General Comment 2, HRI/GEN/1/Rev.9 (vol. I) 376, para. 1; *Prosecutor v. Furundzija* (Case No. 17–95–17/1-T), Trial Judgment, 10 December 1998, paras. 153–7.

[20] CAT, Arts. 1 and 4.   [21] CAT, Art. 2(2).   [22] CAT, Art. 4.

by their nationals.[23] The commission of the offence additionally carries, for states parties, an obligation to prosecute or extradite those suspected of it.[24] With 147 states parties, the CAT is widely ratified and a large number of states therefore possess obligations to prosecute or extradite in relation to the crime of torture. Given the regularity with which torture has formed a component of the crimes committed in past transitional contexts, it seems likely to feature again in the future. It is therefore foreseeable that in future transitional states where past violations have included torture, that crime may form part of the subject matter of both prosecutorial proceedings, in line with international treaty obligations, and national truth commission investigations.

Enforced disappearance has also commonly been included in truth commission mandates.[25] Truth commissions were born in large part from the legacy of state involvement in forced disappearances in Central and Latin America in the 1970s and early 1980s and the very earliest commissions were established purely to investigate this crime.[26] State policies relating to enforced disappearance have been widely documented in final truth commission reports.[27] Enforced disappearance is also the subject of two international treaties,[28] which, like the CAT, impose upon states parties obligations to criminalise the offence under domestic law and to prosecute or extradite offenders.[29] The Inter-American Convention on the Forced Disappearance of Persons came into force in 1996 and, currently, the International Convention on Enforced Disappearance requires one additional ratification to enter into force, making it likely that it too will soon form part of international law. Forced disappearance is not the mainstay of truth commission investigation that it once was, reflecting the fact that many of the most recent commissions have operated following

---

[23] CAT, Art. 5(1) and (2).   [24] CAT, Art. 7.

[25] Argentinean Decree No 187/83, Comisión Nacional sobre la Desaparición de Personas, Argentina, 15 December 1983, Art. 2(b); Chilean Supreme Decree 355, Art. 1; Peruvian, Supreme Decree 065–2001-PCM, Art. 3(b).

[26] See Chapter 1.

[27] *Report of the Chilean National Commission on Truth and Reconciliation*, 161–6; UN Security Council, *From Madness to Hope*, Part IV B 3; *Guatemala: Memoria del Silencio: Informe de la Comisión para el Esclarecimiento Histórico* (Guatemala City: Commission for Historical Clarification, distributed by F&G Editores, 1999), Conclusions, para. 89; *Chega!*, Final Report of the Commission for Reception, Truth and Reconciliation for East Timor, January 2006, Part 7.2.

[28] Inter-American Convention on the Forced Disappearance of Persons and International Convention for the Protection of All Persons from Enforced Disappearance.

[29] Inter-American Convention on the Forced Disappearance of Persons, Arts. III and VI; International Convention for the Protection of All Persons from Enforced Disappearance, Arts. 4 and 9.

internal conflict rather than dissolution of authoritarian regimes. The issue of forced disappearance has, however, been brought back to attention by the ongoing attempts to confront the past in Brazil. A bill creating a truth commission, which seems likely to have disappearances included within its mandate, is making its way through parliament. While the government, heavily influenced by the military, is currently resistant to the idea of prosecutions,[30] past experience in Latin America demonstrates that truth commissions pave the way for trials. Brazil ratified the International Convention on Enforced Disappearance in November 2010 and is a signatory to the Inter-American Convention on the Forced Disappearance of Persons, although it has not ratified that Convention. The crimes in question took place prior to ratification and would not therefore be the subject of obligations to prosecute even if the Convention was in force. However, there is the beginning of a newfound commitment to accountability in Brazil, making it a possibility that disappearances may become the subject matter of both a truth commission and trials within the country. Again, the potential for overlap between truth commission and prosecutorial mandates can be seen in this experience.

Some commissions have been instructed to investigate violations of international humanitarian law, including the crimes within the Geneva Conventions of 1949 and their Additional Protocols.[31] Where 'grave breaches' of the Conventions have been committed, states parties are under an obligation to prosecute those responsible or extradite them to a requesting state.[32] However, the 'grave breaches' regime pertains only to international armed conflicts. There is a body of literature calling for a uniform law applicable to all armed conflict,[33] some of which

---

[30] Eduardo González, 'Brazil's Hour of Truth and Justice', International Centre for Transitional Justice, 2011.

[31] An Act to Establish the Truth and Reconciliation Commission of Liberia 2005, s. 4(a); Sierra Leone: Truth and Reconciliation Commission Act 2000, s. 6(1). Note too that the East Timorese CAVR interpreted its mandate of investigating 'human rights violations' to include investigations into violations of international humanitarian law, including the Geneva Conventions, 1949. See *Chega!*, Part 2, 5.

[32] Geneva Convention I, Arts. 49, 50; Geneva Convention II, Arts. 50, 51, Geneva Convention III, Arts. 129, 130, Geneva Convention IV, Arts. 146, 147; Protocol I Additional to the Geneva Conventions of 12 August 1949 and Relating to the Protection of Victims in International Armed Conflict, 1125 UNTS 3, Arts. 11, 85, 86, 88.

[33] James G. Stewart, 'Towards a Single Definition of Armed Conflict in International Humanitarian Law: A Critique of Internationalized Armed Conflict' (2003) 85 *International Review of the Red Cross* 313; Michael Reisman and James Silk, 'Which Law Applies to the Afghan Conflict?' (1988) 82 *American Journal of International Law* 465; Ingrid Detter, *The Law of War* (Cambridge University Press, 2002), 49.

claims that customary law demonstrates a narrowing gap between the two regimes.[34] Nevertheless, for the time being the distinction remains and has been adopted in the ICC Statute.[35] Truth commissions generally investigate violations committed under repressive national regimes or during civil conflict, thus violations committed in non-international armed conflict. Although many serious violations are committed during civil war, the internal nature of the conflict means that the *aut dedere, aut judicare* principle does not apply to them. Future transitional states may choose to exercise criminal jurisdiction over violations of international humanitarian law and, indeed, it would seem proper to do so. Prosecutorial proceedings might then overlap the subject matter jurisdiction of any truth commission that is also established, but the overlap will not result from a prosecutorial obligation imposed by the Geneva Conventions.

No past commission has been endowed with a subject matter mandate specifically including the crime of apartheid. This may seem surprising given that the most famous truth commission, that established in South Africa, was created to address the legacy of apartheid era violations. However, the South African TRC was instructed to investigate the causes, nature and extent of gross human rights violations, including their antecedents and context.[36] Although the South African TRC interpreted this aspect of its mandate to require examination of the system of apartheid,[37] the crime was not included explicitly within the enacting legislation. Neither has genocide been included, although the Peruvian commission was directed to investigate collective violations of the Andean and native communities' rights,[38] and the Guatemalan Commission concluded that

---

[34] Sonja Boelaert-Suominen, 'Grave Breaches, Universal Jurisdiction and Internal Armed Conflict: Is Customary Law Moving towards a Uniform Enforcement Mechanism for All Armed Conflicts?' (2000) 5 *Journal of Conflict and Security Law*, 63; Allison Danner, 'When Courts Make Law: How the International Criminal Tribunals Recast the Laws of War' (2006) 59 *Vanderbilt Law Review* 1. See also *Prosecutor* v. *Tadic* (Case No. IT-94-1-AR72), Decision on the Defence Motion for Interlocutory Appeal on Jurisdiction, 2 October 1995, para. 127.

[35] Art. 8(2)(b). See Heike Spieker, 'The International Criminal Court and Non-International Armed Conflicts' (2000) 13 *Leiden Journal of International Law* 417. On the reduction of the distinction following the Kampala Review Conference see Amal Alamuddin and Philippa Webb, 'Expanding Jurisdiction over War Crimes under Article 8 of the ICC Statute' (2010) 8 *Journal of International Criminal Justice* 1219.

[36] South African Promotion of National Unity and Reconciliation Act, No. 34 of 1995, s. 3(a).

[37] *Truth and Reconciliation Commission of South Africa Report*, vol. 1, Chapter 4, 95.

[38] Peruvian Supreme Decree 065–2001-PCM, Art. 3(d).

the state had committed genocide against the indigenous Mayan people between 1981 and 1983.[39] It is conceivable that should either apartheid or genocide occur again, the state of territoriality may prosecute the perpetrators in compliance with international obligations under the Genocide and Apartheid Conventions and establish truth commissions to investigate and record the same events.

If states parties have duties to prosecute serious violations as a result of their obligations to respect and ensure treaty rights and provide a remedy for their violation, as suggested by the Inter-American Court of Human Rights and, to a lesser extent, the European Court of Human Rights,[40] the potential for overlap will be much wider. In addition to torture and forced disappearance, prosecution of other serious violations frequently committed during conflict or authoritarian regime, such as extra-judicial killings and assassinations, ill-treatment of individuals by security forces, unlawful detention and violations of due process, might also be required as a result of treaty obligations. Given that truth commissions are now most commonly mandated to investigate 'the human rights violations of the past',[41] the investigations of commissions and prosecutorial bodies would overlap considerably. However, many commentators doubt whether the jurisprudence on positive duties under human rights treaties can be taken to create an absolute duty to prosecute all serious violations in all circumstances.[42] Indeed, readily assuming the existence of an obligation to prosecute and punish all human rights violations has been cautioned against.[43]

Even absent a prosecutorial obligation in respect of all human rights violations, the potential for overlap between the mandates of truth commissions and treaty obligations of states to prosecute certain crimes is apparent. Any overlap is likely to be partial. Truth commissions typically investigate a much broader range of violations than those whose prosecution is mandated by treaty and past commissions have documented a wide range of economic, social and cultural rights violations, as well as

---

[39] *Guatemala: Memoria del Silencio*, 34–5.

[40] Anja Seibert-Fohr, *Prosecuting Serious Human Rights Violations* (Oxford University Press, 2009), Chapters 3 and 4.

[41] South African Promotion of National Unity and Reconciliation Act, No. 34 of 1995, s. 3(1)(a); UNTAET Regulation No. 2001/10 on the Establishment of a Commission for Reception, Truth and Reconciliation in East Timor, UNTAET/REG/2001/10, 13 July 2001, s. 3.1; An Act to Establish the Truth and Reconciliation Commission of Liberia 2005, s. 4(a); Sierra Leone: Truth and Reconciliation Commission Act 2000, s. 6(1).

[42] Ambos, 'The Legal Framework of Transitional Justice', 30.

[43] Seibert-Fohr, *Prosecuting Serious Human Rights Violations*, 9–10.

civil and political rights abuses.[44] This does not mean that the overlap will always be inconsiderable. Depending on the nature of the crimes and how significant a dimension of the overall picture of past abuses they form, their investigation may be a central focus for both truth commissions and prosecutorial institutions.

For example, where crimes such as torture and forced disappearance have operated as part of a state's policy of repression, as in Argentina and Chile,[45] victims of those particular crimes may form a high proportion of the overall victim community and, therefore of the testimony received by the commission. The investigation, documentation and assignation of responsibility for those crimes may then become a substantial component of a truth commission's work, as it receives victims' accounts and seeks to explain the violations within a broader context. Investigation of the institutional apparatus that permitted or authorised the commission of those crimes will also be of key relevance to prosecutorial institutions as they seek to identify the individuals responsible and carry out prosecutions in line with treaty obligations. The result will be overlap between the work of the truth commission and the prosecutorial institutions. A similar situation may arise in the event of apartheid. Apartheid as a legal policy and social practice may, as in South Africa, give rise to many different human rights violations which will become the subject of truth commission investigations. The truth commission is unlikely to simply catalogue the different types of violations committed. As the South African TRC did,[46] it will seek to situate them within the historical, legal and cultural environments that gave rise to their commission and develop an understanding of responsibility for them. At the same time, for states parties to the Apartheid Convention, obligations arise to investigate and prosecute those responsible for the architecture and implementation of those overarching policies of racial segregation and the violations they gave rise to.[47] The system of apartheid itself will be the focus of both truth commission and prosecutorial investigation. Likewise, investigation of the crime of genocide may create an overlap between prosecutorial and truth commission proceedings. The Rwandan experience demonstrates that prosecuting genocide

---

[44] Priscilla B. Hayner, *Unspeakable Truths: Transitional Justice and the Challenge of Truth Commissions* (2nd edn) (London and New York: Routledge, 2010), Appendix 2, Chart 3.

[45] *Nunca Más: The Report of the Argentine National Commission on the Disappeared* (New York: Farrar Straus Giroux, 1986); *Report of the Chilean National Commission on Truth and Reconciliation.*

[46] See Chapter 3.   [47] Apartheid Convention, Art. 4(b).

requires investigation into the creation of a climate that enabled such crimes to occur and the role played by individuals in fostering it.[48] Any truth commission established post-genocide is equally likely to explore the milieu that gave rise to genocide, creating an overlap between its operations and those of prosecutorial institutions. Although the ultimate objectives of truth-seeking and prosecutorial investigations are different, they are reliant upon the same broad categories of information and personnel in order to fulfil their respective purposes. Moreover, both typically possess powers to access the information they require.

In short, if states in which these crimes are committed in future are party to the relevant international treaties, there may be overlap between the operations of prosecutorial bodies and any truth commission established to investigate past violations. For states parties, prosecution must take priority as it forms part of a state's international treaty obligations. Truth commissions, however worthwhile an enterprise they are perceived to be, are a national level option. Nevertheless, the establishment of truth commissions now forms a staple of transitional justice practice. How states will coordinate their international obligations to prosecute certain human rights crimes with the operation of national truth commissions and manage their potentially overlapping mandates raises a range of questions. The potential relevance of the information collected by one mechanism to the mandate of the other, coupled with the exercise of investigatory powers by both, seems bound to create an array of dilemmas.

2.2   Customary duties to prosecute

Overall, human rights violations whose prosecution is unequivocally demanded by treaty are few in number. Many of the most serious crimes, those for which prosecution is arguably most important, are not the subject of treaties that impose duties to prosecute on states parties. Any obligation to prosecute human rights violations that are not the subject of international treaties must therefore stem from customary law.[49] The extent to which there is any customary duty to prosecute international

---

[48] See particularly *Prosecutor* v. *Karemera* (Case No. ICTR 98–44-T), Decision on Appeals Chamber Remand of Judicial Notice, P 17, Judgment of 11 December 2006, taking judicial notice of the fact that between 6 April 1994 and 17 July 1994 there was a genocide in Rwanda against the Tutsi ethnic group, based on the previous findings of the Tribunal.

[49] Statute of the International Court of Justice, reprinted in (1945) 39 *American Journal of International Law* (Supp.) 215, Art. 38(1).

human rights violations is contentious.[50] The majority of states and authoritative commentators view genocide, crimes against humanity, war crimes and aggression as international crimes[51] and acknowledge the right of all states to exercise criminal jurisdiction over them.[52] Jurisdiction can be exercised on the grounds of territoriality or nationality, as the traditionally accepted principles of jurisdiction, or, more controversially, on the basis of the passive personality or protective principles.[53] More controversial still is the exercise of jurisdiction on the grounds of universality, particularly its assertion *in absentia*.[54] Historically, despite the academic

---

[50] Some commentators have argued strongly in favour of a customary duty to prosecute serious human rights violations. See Miles M. Jackson, 'The Customary International Law Duty to Prosecute Crimes against Humanity: A New Framework' (2007) 16 *Tulane Journal of International and Comparative Law* 117; Dianne Orentlicher, 'Settling Accounts: The Duty to Prosecute Human Rights Violations of a Prior Regime' (1991) 100 *Yale Law Journal* 2537; Dianne Orentlicher, 'Swapping Amnesty for Peace: The Duty to Prosecute Human Rights Crimes' (1997) 3 *ILSA Journal of International and Comparative Law* 713; M. Cherif Bassiouni, *Introduction to International Criminal Law* (New York: Transnational Publishers, 2003), 167–8. Others, however, are dubious of the existence of such an obligation and point to the lack of uniformity in state practice as regards prosecution. See Michael P. Scharf, 'The Letter of the Law: The Scope of the International Legal Obligation to Prosecute Human Rights Crimes' (1996) 59 *Law and Contemporary Problems* 41; Roman Boed, 'The Effect of a Domestic Amnesty on the Ability of Foreign States to Prosecute Alleged Perpetrators of Serious Human Rights Violations' (2000) 33 *Cornell International Law Journal* 297; Emily W. Schabacker, 'Reconciliation or Justice and Ashes: Amnesty Commissions and the Duty to Punish Human Rights Offences' (1999) 12 *New York International Law Review* 1, 39; Angelika Schlunk, *Amnesty versus Accountability: Third Party Intervention Dealing with Gross Human Rights Violations in Internal and International Conflicts* (Berlin: Berlin Verlag Spitz, 2000), 49; Ben Chigara, *Amnesty in International Law: The Legality under International Law of National Amnesty Laws* (Harlow: Pearson Education Ltd, 2002).
[51] Gerhard Werle, *Principles of International Criminal Law* (2nd edn) (The Hague: T. M. C. Asser Press, 2009), 29; Ian Brownlie, *Principles of Public International Law* (7th edn) (Oxford University Press, 2008), 589; Antonio Cassese, *International Criminal Law* (2nd edn) (Oxford University Press, 2008), 12.
[52] Werle, *Principles of International Criminal Law*, 69–70; Brownlie, *Principles of Public International Law*, 593; Cassese, *International Criminal Law*, 12. Some also include torture within this definition, as a crime distinct from one of the categories of crimes against humanity or war crimes. See Cassese, *International Criminal Law*, 12; Brownlie, *Principles of Public International Law*, 592.
[53] A full discussion of the exercise of jurisdiction in relation to international crimes does not fall within the scope of this text. See Robert Cryer, *Prosecuting International Crimes* (Cambridge University Press, 2005), 75–101.
[54] Case Concerning Arrest Warrant of 11 April 2000 *(Democratic Republic of Congo v. Belgium)*, International Court of Justice, General List, Judgment of 14 February 2002, Separate Opinion of President Guillaume, para. 12 and Joint Separate Opinion of Judges Higgins, Kooijmans and Buergenthal; Neil Boister, 'The ICJ in the Belgian Arrest Warrant

attention received by the universality principle, there have been only a small number of cases based upon this ground.[55] It may take on a previously unseen relevance in future. In response to ratification of the ICC Statute, many states parties have passed implementing legislation containing provisions that enable them to exert universal jurisdiction over international crimes.[56] It is therefore possible that in future, states may more frequently exercise jurisdiction on the principle of universality in an attempt to plug the impunity gap, in accordance with ICC objectives.[57]

There is no general consensus as to the existence or scope of a customary duty to prosecute international crimes. It has been suggested that a customary obligation to prosecute international crimes flows from their categorisation as *jus cogens*[58] norms of international

---

Case: Arresting the Development of International Criminal Law' (2002) 7 *Journal of Conflict and Security Law* 293; Claus Kress, 'Universal Jurisdiction over International Crimes and the *Institut de Droit International*' (2006) 4 *Journal of International Criminal Justice* 561.

[55] Cedric Ryngaert, 'Applying the Rome Statute's Complementarity Principle: Drawing Lessons from the Prosecution of Core Crimes by States Acting under the Universality Principle' (2008) 19 *Criminal Law Forum* 153.

[56] For discussion of some implementing legislation see: Goran Sluiter, 'Implementation of the ICC Statute in the Dutch Legal Order' (2004) 2 *Journal of International Criminal Justice* 158; Juliet Hay, 'Implementing the Rome Statute in New Zealand' (2004) 2 *Journal of International Criminal Justice* 533; Max du Plessis, 'South Africa's Implementation of the ICC Statute: An African Example' (2007) 5 *Journal of International Criminal Justice* 460; Fannie Lafontaine, 'Canada's Crimes against Humanity and War Crimes Act on Trial: An Analysis of the Munyareza Case' (2010) 8 *Journal of International Criminal Justice* 269. See also David Turns, 'Aspects of National Implementation of the Rome Statute: The United Kingdom and Selected Other States', in Dominic McGoldrick, Peter Rowe and Eric Donnelly (eds.), *The Permanent International Criminal Court: Legal and Policy Issues* (Portland, OR: Hart Publishing, 2004), 337–89. This will be discussed further in Chapter 5.

[57] Rome Statute, Preamble, para. 5. The coordination of truth commissions with prosecutions in third states will be considered in Chapter 5.

[58] *Jus cogens* are a set of norms with a superior status to all other rules of the international community. They may not be derogated from either by treaty or through the ordinary customary process and any derogating rules may be declared null and void. See Vienna Convention on the Law of Treaties 1969, 1155 UNTS 331, Art. 53. It should be noted, however, that academic writers disagree as to what constitutes a peremptory *jus cogens* norm, how norms rise to that level and how to determine their existence. See M. Cherif Bassiouni, 'International Crimes: *Jus Cogens* and *Obligatio Erga Omnes*' (1996) 59 *Law and Contemporary Problems* 63, 67. In addition, some scholars treat *jus cogens* and customary law as the same, others distinguish between them and others still question whether the term *jus cogens* is not merely another way of describing general principles. See Anthony D'Amato, *The Concept of Custom in International Law* (New York: Cornell University Press, 1971), 132; Gordon A. Christenson, 'Jus Cogens: Guarding Interests Fundamental to International Society' (1988) 28 *Virginia Journal of International Law* 585.

law.[59] It is argued that this *jus cogens* status gives rise to *erga omnes*[60] obligations not to grant impunity to those who commit them and a duty to prosecute or extradite.[61] However, the precise nature and scope of obligations *erga omnes* remain ambiguous. Although some commentators have questioned whether the *jus cogens* quality of international crimes might have the consequence of states having a duty to prosecute, they stop short of stating categorically that this is the case.[62] Support for the existence of a customary duty can be found in the 1996 International Law Commission Draft Code of Crimes against the Peace and Security of Mankind, which argued for a duty to prosecute or extradite individuals accused of genocide, crimes against humanity and war crimes and to prohibit such crimes regardless of where or by whom they were committed.[63] The ICTY Appeals Chamber has also held that there is a customary obligation to prosecute or extradite those who have allegedly committed grave breaches of international humanitarian law.[64] The reference to the 'duty' to prosecute within the ICC Statute Preamble has been held out as evidence of a customary duty to prosecute international crimes,[65] albeit only in relation to crimes committed within a state's own territory.[66] Indeed, the crimes within the ICC Statute are increasingly framed in terms of a duty to prosecute, at

---

[59] Some scholars assert that genocide, crimes against humanity and war crimes all have *jus cogens* status. See Bassiouni, *Introduction to International Criminal Law*, 139–42; Antonio Cassese, *International Law* (Oxford University Press, 2005), 202–3. However, others include only genocide and crimes against humanity within this category. See Brownlie, *Principles of Public International Law*, 511 and Theodor Meron, 'On a Hierarchy of International Human Rights' (1986) 80 *American Journal of International Law* 1, 15.

[60] In the *Barcelona Traction* case the ICJ stated: 'An essential distinction should be drawn between the obligations of a State towards the international community as a whole and those arising vis-a-vis another State in the field of diplomatic protection. By their very nature the former are the concern of all States. In view of the importance of the rights involved all States can be held to have a legal interest in their protection; they are obligations *erga omnes*.' Barcelona Traction Case *(Belgium* v. *Spain)*, Judgment of 5 February 1970, ICJ Rep. 4, 32.

[61] Bassiouni, 'International Crimes: *Jus Cogens* and *Obligatio Erga Omnes*', 65–6.

[62] Brownlie, *Principles of Public International Law*, 597.

[63] *Yearbook of the International Law Commission*, 1996, vol. II, Arts. 8–9.

[64] *Prosecutor* v. *Blaskic* (Case No. IT-95-14), Judgment on the Request of the Republic of Croatia for Review of the Decision of Trial Chamber II of 18 July 1997, 29 October 1997, para. 29.

[65] Ambos, 'The Legal Framework of Transitional Justice' 19, 29–31.

[66] Morten Bergsmo and Otto Triffterer, 'Preamble', in Otto Triffterer (ed.), *Commentary on the Rome Statute of the International Criminal Court* (2nd edn) (Oxford: Hart Publishing, 2008), 1.

least for states parties,[67] although the jurisdictional scope of this 'duty' has been questioned.[68] Some argue that customary law now recognises a duty to prosecute on the part of the state in which an international crime is committed.[69] The more convincing argument is that there is an emerging customary duty to prosecute international crimes based on territoriality and, to some extent, nationality jurisdiction, as a result of recent rejections of amnesties, declarations affirming the duty to prosecute, jurisprudence of human rights courts and monitoring bodies and the subject matter jurisdiction of the ICC.[70]

State practice remains the major impediment to the crystallisation of a customary duty to prosecute international crimes.[71] Rather than supporting the existence of a duty to prosecute, it has tended to veer in the opposite direction. States have traditionally been reluctant to prosecute even crimes which occurred on their own territory and have frequently enacted amnesty laws absolving those responsible for the most serious violations from criminal accountability.[72] National prosecutions of international crimes have been both rare and sporadic. State practice cannot therefore be said to support the position, at present, that states have a duty under customary law to prosecute international crimes.[73] Nevertheless,

---

[67] John Dugard, 'Possible Conflicts of Jurisdiction with Truth Commissions', in Antonio Cassese, Paulo Gaeta and John Jones (eds.), *The Rome Statute of the International Criminal Court: A Commentary*, 2 vols. (Oxford University Press, 2002), vol. 2, 693–704, 696–9; Mohammed M. El Zeidy, 'The Principle of Complementarity: A New Machinery to Implement International Criminal Law' (2002) 32 *Michigan Journal of International Law* 869, 947–8.

[68] Robert Cryer *et al.*, *An Introduction to International Criminal Law and Procedure* (Cambridge University Press, 2010), 72.

[69] Werle, *Principles of International Criminal Law*, 69; Claus Kress, 'War Crimes Committed in Non-International Armed Conflict and the Emerging System of International Criminal Justice' (2001) 30 *Israel Yearbook on Human Rights* 103, 163; Naomi Roht-Arriaza, 'Amnesty and the International Criminal Court', in Dinah Shelton (ed.), *International Crimes, Peace and Human Rights: The Role of the International Criminal Court* (New York: Transnational Publishers, 2000), Chapter 8, 78; Christian Tomuschat, 'The Duty to Prosecute International Crimes Committed by Individuals', in Hans-Joachim Cremer *et al.* (eds.), *Tradition und Weltoffenheit des Rechts: Festschrift fur Helmut Steinberge* (Berlin: Springer, 2002) 315–51, 342.

[70] Seibert-Fohr, *Prosecuting Serious Human Rights Violations*, chapter 7; Darryl Robinson, 'Serving the Interests of Justice: Amnesties, Truth Commissions and the International Criminal Court' (2003) 14 *European Journal of International Law* 481.

[71] Cryer, *Prosecuting International Crimes*, 110–17.

[72] For a comprehensive account of the practice of states in enacting amnesties see Mallinder, *Amnesty, Human Rights and Political Transitions*.

[73] Seibert-Fohr, *Prosecuting Serious Human Rights Violations*, chapter 7; Cryer, *Prosecuting International Crimes*, 60, 102–3.

notwithstanding the absence of treaty and customary obligations, the commission of the most serious human rights violations is likely to result in international pressure to prosecute, either at the national level or through the medium of an international tribunal. The next section of this book explores the potential overlap between truth commission mandates and efforts to prosecute the most serious human rights crimes: those within the jurisdiction of the International Criminal Court.

3   The jurisdiction of the ICC and its overlap with truth commission mandates

3.1   Subject matter overlap

The jurisdiction of the ICC is 'limited to the most serious crimes of concern to the international community as a whole'.[74] Specifically, the Court has jurisdiction over genocide, crimes against humanity, war crimes and aggression.[75] Jurisdiction is prospective and applies to crimes committed since July 2002,[76] by individuals over the age of eighteen at the time of the alleged commission of the crime.[77] Jurisdiction can be triggered by reference by a state party,[78] reference by the UN Security Council[79] or by the initiation of an investigation by the prosecutor.[80] Importantly, despite its status as a treaty institution, the ICC's jurisdiction has the potential to extend beyond the territory and nationals of its states parties. The Statute makes provision for non-party states to accept the jurisdiction of the Court.[81] Moreover, the Security Council's power to refer situations to the ICC, when acting pursuant to Chapter VII of the UN Charter, can be exercised even where the crimes were not committed on the territory of or

---

[74] Rome Statute, Art. 5.

[75] Rome Statute, Art. 5. Under Article 15(3) *ter* the ICC will exercise jurisdiction over the crime of aggression, subject to a decision by the states parties after 1 January 2017. ICC, Assembly of States Parties, Resolution RC/Res.6, The Crime of Aggression, adopted at the 13th plenary meeting on 11 June 2010. See Claus Kress and Leonie von Holtzendorff, 'The Kampala Compromise on the Crime of Aggression' (2010) 8 *Journal of International Criminal Justice* 1179.

[76] Rome Statute, Arts. 11 and 24(1).

[77] Rome Statute, Art. 26. For a brief discussion of the age of responsibility in the Rome Statute see John T. Holmes, 'The Protection of Children's Rights in the Statute of the International Criminal Court', in Mauro Politi and Guiseppe Nesi (eds.), *The Rome Statute of the International Criminal Court: A Challenge to Impunity* (Aldershot: Ashgate, 2001), 119–22.

[78] Rome Statute, Art. 13(a).   [79] Rome Statute, Art. 13(b).

[80] Rome Statute, Art. 13(c).   [81] Rome Statute, Art. 12(3).

by the citizens of a state party.[82] This enables the Court to proceed even if the state concerned has not ratified the ICC Statute or accepted the jurisdiction of the ICC.[83]

The Rome Statute's definition of genocide is found in Article 6 and derives directly from the Genocide Convention. It therefore involves one of the following acts when committed 'with intent to destroy, in whole or in part, a national, ethnical, racial or religious group as such': killing members of the group, causing bodily or mental harm, inflicting conditions of life likely to bring about the physical destruction of the group, imposing measures to prevent birth or transferring children of the group.[84]

Article 7 defines crimes against humanity, building upon the definitions in the Nuremberg Charter and the statutes of the ICTY and ICTR and the jurisprudence of the ad hoc tribunals. It lists, as crimes against humanity, murder, extermination, enslavement, deportation or forcible transfer, imprisonment or severe deprivation of liberty, torture, rape and other sexual offences, persecution against an identifiable group on political, racial, national, ethnic, cultural, religious or gender grounds, enforced disappearance and the crime of apartheid.[85] In order for these crimes to constitute crimes against humanity they must be committed as part of a widespread or systematic attack against a civilian population.[86] The attack must be carried out 'pursuant to or in furtherance of a State or organizational policy to commit such attack',[87] indicating that crimes against humanity can be committed by non-state actors.[88] The perpetrator must additionally possess 'knowledge of the attack'.[89] Notably, the absence within Article 7 of any link between crimes against humanity and the existence of an armed conflict confirms that crimes against humanity can be committed in peacetime and provides protection for civilians living under abusive regimes.[90]

---

[82] Rome Statute, Art. 12(2).
[83] On the role of the Security Council under the Rome Statute see Luigi Condorelli and Santiago Villalpando, 'Referral and Deferral by the Security Council', in Antonio Cassese, Paulo Gaeta and John R. W. D. Jones (eds.), *The Rome Statute of the International Criminal Court: A Commentary*, 2 vols. (Oxford University Press, 2002), 627–55.
[84] Genocide Convention, Art. 2; Rome Statute, Art. 6.
[85] Rome Statute, Art. 7(1).   [86] *Ibid.*   [87] Rome Statute, Art. 7(2)(a).
[88] For discussion of this point see William A. Schabas, *An Introduction to the International Criminal Court* (Cambridge University Press, 2007), 102–4.
[89] Rome Statute, Art. 7(1).
[90] For a full discussion of the evolutionary nature of crimes against humanity see Meg McAuliffe deGuzman, 'The Road from Rome: The Developing Law of Crimes against Humanity' (2000) 22 *Human Rights Quarterly* 335.

War crimes are defined in Article 8, which states that, in particular, the Court will have jurisdiction over the most serious instances of war crimes.[91] Article 8 consists of four categories of war crimes, two relating to international armed conflict and two directed at non-international armed conflict. 'Grave breaches' of the Geneva Conventions makes up the first category of war crimes,[92] with the second consisting of other serious violations of the laws and customs applicable in international armed conflict.[93] The other categories include violations of common Article 3 to the Geneva Conventions[94] and other serious violations of the laws and customs applicable in non-international armed conflicts.[95]

The Court's jurisdiction will, therefore, only come into play where the most serious human rights crimes are committed. Truth commissions may also form an important component of national transitional justice programmes implemented to respond to serious violations. Many of the states in which the most serious crimes have been committed of recent times have established truth commissions, or have at least considered doing so. In East Timor, Sierra Leone and Liberia, states that saw the commission of crimes against humanity and war crimes, truth commissions were established. As the Democratic Republic of Congo referred the commission of the most serious crimes on its territory to the ICC, it also established a national truth commission.[96] In Uganda, where those responsible for war crimes and crimes against humanity have been indicted by the ICC, there has been prolonged national dialogue concerning the establishment of a truth commission.[97] A truth commission is in operation in Kenya, another state where the ICC is undertaking investigations. In Cote d'Ivoire where, at the time of writing, the Court seems poised to open investigations into alleged war crimes and crimes against humanity,[98] there are efforts being made towards the establishment of a national truth

---

[91] Rome Statute, Art. 8(1).   [92] Rome Statute, Art. 8(2)(a).   [93] Art. 8(2)(b).

[94] Rome Statute, Art. 8(2)(c) and (d).   [95] Rome Statute, Art. 8(2)(e).

[96] On the establishment of the TRC see Frederico Borello, 'A First Few Steps: The Long Road to a Just Peace in the Democratic Republic of Congo', International Center for Transitional Justice, October 2004, Part IV. Unfortunately, a restrictive mandate and political interference has prevented the truth commission from undertaking any meaningful investigations.

[97] 'Uganda: Country Needs National Reconciliation', *The Monitor* (Kampala), 18 September 2007; Kintu Nyago, 'We Need a Truth Commission', *New Vision* (Uganda), 23 September 2006.

[98] ICC, Office of the Prosecutor Statement, 'Cote d'Ivoire: ICC Prosecutor Ready to Request Judges for Authorization to Open an Investigation', 22 June 2011.

commission.[99] Although they have never come to fruition, there have also been numerous attempts to establish commissions in the former Yugoslav states and Rwanda.[100]

Not only are truth commissions operational within states where the worst human rights crimes have been committed, they have been tasked with investigating and reporting upon them. The East Timorese CAVR was established to investigate, among other abuses, violations of international humanitarian law, including violations of the Geneva Conventions and the Additional Protocols,[101] crimes that now fall within the ICC's jurisdiction under Article 8 of the Rome Statute. Both war crimes and crimes against humanity were included in the mandate of the Liberian TRC.[102] The TRC for Sierra Leone had a less precise mandate, but was also instructed to investigate violations of international humanitarian law and human rights abuses, with a particular focus on their nature and extent and whether they were the result of deliberate planning, policy or authorisation by any government, group or individual.[103] Serious violations of international humanitarian law are included as war crimes within Article 8 of the ICC Statute and the concepts of nature, extent and official planning are key in establishing whether the commission of certain violations amounts to crimes against humanity under Article 7. If this trend continues, there is likely to be real similarity and overlap in the investigations carried out by some future commissions and those of the ICC.

---

[99] Eric Agnero, 'Ivory Coast Announces Commission to Investigate Post-Election Crimes', CNN, 16 June 2011.

[100] US Institute of Peace, Special Report 13, *Rwanda: Accountability for War Crimes and Genocide*, January 1995. See also Jeremy Sarkin, 'The Necessity and Challenges of Establishing a Truth and Reconciliation Commission in Rwanda' (1999) 21 *Human Rights Quarterly* 767; Erin Daly, 'Transformative Justice: Charting a Path to Reconciliation' (2001/2002) 12 *International Legal Perspectives* 73; Neil J. Kritz and Jakob Finci, 'A Truth and Reconciliation Commission in Bosnia and Herzegovina: An Idea Whose Time Has Come' (2001) 3 *International Law Forum* 50, 53. For a discussion of some of the problems that faced the TRC for Serbia and Montenegro see Tatjana Peric, 'Facing the Past: Religious Communities, Truth and Reconciliation in Post-Milosevic Serbia', Harvard University Kokkalis Progamme, 2004; Jelena Pejic, 'The Yugoslav Truth and Reconciliation Commission: A Shaky Start' (2001–2002) 25 *Fordham International Law Journal* 1.

[101] UNTAET Regulation 2001/10, ss. 3.1, 1(c) and (d).

[102] An Act to Establish the Truth and Reconciliation Commission of Liberia, 2005, ss. 2 and 4(a).

[103] Sierra Leone: Truth and Reconciliation Commission Act 2000, ss. 6(1) and (2)(a).

As with treaty obligations to prosecute, the overlap between the subject matter mandate of the ICC and those of national truth commissions will be partial. Truth commissions investigate a broader range of violations than those that fall within the ICC's jurisdiction, focusing not only on the most serious violations but also on lower level crimes that have an impact on society. The Liberian TRC had economic crimes included within its mandate,[104] the Kenyan commission has been instructed to investigate the exploitation of land and public resources and their illegal acquisition[105] and the East Timorese CAVR operated a community reconciliation process in relation to minor criminal and civil offences.[106] However, the typical objective of investigating and documenting the causes of abuses and broad responsibility for them means that truth commissions frequently interview and comment upon the roles played by senior military and political figures, those who might ultimately become the subjects of ICC prosecutions. The testimony of victims may be equally relevant to a truth commission, as it seeks to ascertain the nature, causes and patterns of abuses, as it will be to the ICC as it investigates the extent of the violations committed, determines whether the thresholds for its exercise of jurisdiction are met and establishes individual responsibility for the most serious crimes. Official documentation of government, security forces and the military may also prove relevant to the investigations of both bodies. While the overlap in subject matter mandate might be partial and the objectives of truth commissions and the ICC different, the requirements to access the same evidence, information and witnesses in order to fulfil those mandates is likely to give rise to questions of how best to coordinate these operations in future.

3.2   Truth commissions and the complementarity principle

The potential for overlap with ICC proceedings is only one aspect of the Rome Statute model that is likely to affect future truth commissions. The complementarity regime along with the obligations imposed upon states parties will also impact the shape of future truth commissions[107] and the options open to states where the most serious crimes are committed. The complementarity principle underpins the prosecutorial regime envisaged by the ICC and ensures that primary responsibility for the prosecution of

---

[104] An Act to Establish the Truth and Reconciliation Commission of Liberia, 2005, s. 4(a).
[105] Kenyan Truth, Justice and Reconciliation Act 2008, ss. 6(n) and (o).
[106] UNTAET Regulation 2001/10, s. 22.   [107] See Chapter 4.

the crimes set out in the Statute remains with national courts. Under the Statute, domestic courts are given presumptive jurisdiction.[108] The ICC is obliged to declare a case inadmissible where it is being or has been investigated or prosecuted by a state that has jurisdiction over it and a decision has been taken not to prosecute.[109] Only in circumstances where states are 'unable or unwilling genuinely to carry out the investigation or prosecution'[110] does jurisdiction fall to the ICC. This respects the sovereign right of states to prosecute their own nationals and crimes that occur on their territory.

The Court itself has responsibility for ascertaining admissibility. In order to determine inability, the Court must consider whether, due to a total or substantial collapse or unavailability of its national judicial system, the state is unable to obtain the accused or the necessary evidence and testimony or otherwise unable to carry out its proceedings. Unwillingness must also be determined by reference to a number of factors. The Court must consider whether national proceedings have or had the purpose of shielding those concerned from criminal responsibility,[111] whether there has been unjustified delay in those proceedings[112] and whether they were conducted with the necessary impartiality and independence, consistent with an intent to bring those concerned to justice.[113] The 'unwilling' state may not simply be one that chooses outright not to exercise its jurisdiction. States that depart significantly from normal legal procedures, indulge in sham trials in an attempt to prevent retrial by virtue of the double jeopardy rule, or appear to be 'going through the motions' without real resolve to see justice done, may all find the legitimacy of their proceedings and their genuine willingness to prosecute questioned by the ICC.[114] Pre-Trial Chamber 1 has suggested that a further component for consideration in admissibility determinations is the inactivity of the national judicial system.[115]

Past practice demonstrates that transitional states that find themselves 'unable' to prosecute, due to weakened legal and administrative systems, often establish truth commissions as a means of reckoning with past

---

[108] See Gerry Simpson, 'Politics, Sovereignty and Remembrance', in Dominic McGoldrick, Peter Rowe and Eric Donnelly (eds.), *The Permanent International Criminal Court: Legal and Policy Issues* (Portland, OR: Hart Publishing, 2004), 47–65, 55.

[109] Rome Statute, Art. 17(1)(a) and (b).   [110] Rome Statute, Art. 17.

[111] Rome Statute, Art. 17(2)(a).   [112] Rome Statute, Art. 17(2)(b).

[113] Rome Statute, Art. 17(2)(c).

[114] Schabas, *An Introduction to the International Criminal Court*, 184.

[115] *Prosecutor* v. *Lubanga*, Case No: ICC-01/04–01/06–08, Decision on the Prosecutor's Application for a Warrant of Arrest, 10 February 2006, para. 38–9.

abuses. This can be seen in the experiences of El Salvador and Guatemala, both of which established truth commissions after prolonged civil wars that left judicial institutions incapable of carrying out impartial and effective trials.[116] States parties in this situation now seem likely to become the targets of ICC investigations and prosecutions. Indeed, the creation of a permanent international institution with the ability to pursue prosecution for the most serious crimes where national authorities cannot is the very purpose of the ICC regime. Thus, in future, truth commissions established due to national inability to prosecute will almost certainly find themselves operating alongside ICC proceedings.

However, the 'unwilling' state may also be one that establishes a truth commission, either as an alternative to trials or as a forerunner to them. Certainly, truth commissions established in conjunction with sweeping national amnesty laws[117] that foreclose the possibility of prosecution for even the most serious crimes, seem likely to give rise to findings of unwillingness. Far-reaching amnesties are fundamentally at odds with the ICC's *raison d'être* of ending impunity.[118] Such laws may be perceived as a means of shielding those responsible from criminal accountability, rendering the case admissible before the Court on the ground that the state is unwilling to prosecute. While commonplace at one time, the use of truth commissions and amnesties as alternatives to trials is declining as a transitional justice model in favour of limited amnesty programmes alongside trials for the most serious crimes.[119] However, the issue of granting amnesty for such crimes has not disappeared. In 1999 the Lomé Peace Accord between the Sierra Leonean government and the Revolutionary United Front (RUF) purported to establish a truth commission and grant amnesty to combatants and collaborators in respect of all violations

---

[116] Andrew N. Keller, 'To Name or Not to Name? The Commission for Historical Clarification in Guatemala, Its Mandate and the Decision Not to Identify Individual Perpetrators' (2001) 13 *Florida Journal of International Law* 289, 294; Thomas Buergenthal, 'The United Nations Truth Commission for El Salvador' (1994) 27 *Vanderbilt Journal of Transnational Law* 497, 534.

[117] See for example the commissions established in Chile and Ghana: Chilean Decree Law No. 2191, April 18, 1978, published in *Diario Oficial*, No. 30,042, 19 April 1978 and Ken A. Attafuah, 'An Overview of Ghana's National Reconciliation Commission and Its Relationship with the Courts' (2004) 15 *Criminal Law Forum* 125.

[118] Rome Statute, Preamble, para. 5.

[119] See the use of limited amnesty programmes excluding amnesty for the most serious crimes in East Timor, UNTAET Regulation No. 2000/11 on the Organisation of Courts in East Timor, UNTAET/REG/2000/11, 6 March 2000, s. 10.1; Liberia: An Act to Establish the Truth and Reconciliation Commission of Liberia, 2005, s. 26(g); Kenya: Truth, Justice and Reconciliation Act 2008, s. 34(3).

committed, including war crimes and crimes against humanity.[120] In 2005 Algeria approved a decree implementing the Charter for Peace and National Reconciliation, which granted amnesty to members of armed groups responsible for gross human rights violations in the interests of national harmony.[121] In addition, in 2006 Uganda considered offering amnesty to the leaders of the Lord's Resistance Army, now indicted by the ICC for crimes against humanity and war crimes,[122] in an attempt to bring the conflict to an end.[123] It therefore remains possible that some states may, in future, decide to pass national amnesty laws for human rights crimes and establish truth commissions as an alternative to pursuing prosecution. If, as is likely, the ICC assumes jurisdiction in such a situation, any national truth commission will operate in tandem with ICC proceedings.

The establishment of truth commissions in conjunction with broad amnesty laws provides a clear example of a situation in which the ICC might legitimately assume jurisdiction due to national unwillingness to prosecute. A more complex situation arises where a state establishes a commission, which is intended as a forerunner to trials. The Argentinean commission was established as a precursor to prosecutions and its records were passed to prosecutors for use in building cases against those responsible for past violations.[124] In Liberia the TRC was established on the understanding that prosecutions might follow when the judicial

---

[120] Peace Agreement between the Government of Sierra Leone and the Revolutionary United Front of Sierra Leone, Lomé, 3 June 1999, Arts. IX and XXVI. This idea was later abandoned when renewed fighting caused the Government to rethink its position. It should also be noted that the UN refused to support the amnesty provision. See *Seventh Report of the Secretary-General on the United Nations Observer Mission in Sierra Leone*, Security Council, UN Doc. S/1999/836.

[121] Laura Scully, 'Neither Justice Nor Oasis: Algeria's Amnesty' (2008) 33 *Brooklyn Journal of International Law* 975.

[122] *The Prosecutor* v. *Joseph Kony, Vincent Otti, Okot Odhiambo and Dominic Ongwen*, International Criminal Court, Case No. ICC-02/04–01/05, 8 June 2010.

[123] 'War Crimes Amnesty for Rebels Is Necessary, Uganda Tells UN General Assembly', UN News Service, 20 September 2006. See also; Kathleen E. MacMillan, 'The Practicability of Amnesty as a Non-Prosecutory Alternative in Post-Conflict Uganda' (2007) 6 *Cardozo Public Law, Policy and Ethics Journal* 199; Alexander K. A. Greenawalt, 'Complementarity in Crisis: Uganda, Alternative Justice and the ICC' (2009) 50 *Virginia Journal of International Law* 107; Alex K. Kriksciun, 'Uganda's Response to ICC Arrest Warrants: A Misguided Approach?' (2007) 16 *Tulane Journal of International and Comparative Law* 213.

[124] Jo Pasqualucci, 'The Whole Truth and Nothing But the Truth: Truth Commissions, Impunity and the Inter-American Human Rights System' (1994) 12 *Boston University International Law Journal* 321, 338.

system was stronger.[125] The Kenyan truth commission was designed with the power to make recommendations for prosecution, suggesting that its work might have been intended to contribute to subsequent national trials.[126] Although the ICC has assumed jurisdiction in the Kenyan situation, the Court has not developed any general policy on how to respond to such situations. It is possible that a clearly stated intention to pursue prosecutions, following the operation of a truth commission might be sufficient to stay proceedings by the Court. Equally, however, this could be perceived as a stalling device and interpreted as an 'unjustified delay' in commencing prosecutions, thereby giving rise to a determination of unwillingness to prosecute and rendering a case admissible before the Court. The Pre-Trial Chamber's recent decision on the Kenyan situation points in the latter direction. There, despite efforts to try those responsible for low-level violations and to establish a special tribunal, Kenya's failure to actively pursue prosecution of those who bear responsibility for the most serious crimes has rendered the case admissible before the Court.[127] The operation of the Kenyan truth commission received no consideration in this decision. This may indicate that the establishment and operation of national truth commissions is not a relevant consideration in determining the admissibility of cases before the Court and will not prevent the exercise of jurisdiction by the ICC.

This decision may go some way to settling a long-debated issue. Since the creation of the ICC Statute, commentators have questioned whether the operation of a national truth commission might prevent the exercise of jurisdiction by the ICC under Article 17 and enable the Court to defer permanently to national truth commission proceedings. Most of this discussion has focused on Article 17(1)(b) and the notion that a case might be inadmissible if the state can show: that the crime has been 'investigated' by a truth commission; that it has 'decided' not to prosecute; and that the decision not to prosecute did not result from the unwillingness or inability genuinely to do so.[128] Arguments have been advanced that the 'investigation' referred to in Article 17 is not required by the Statute

---

[125] Priscilla B. Hayner, 'Negotiating Peace in Liberia: Preserving the Possibility for Justice', Report for the Center for Humanitarian Dialogue and the International Center for Transitional Justice, November 2007, 25.

[126] Kenya: Truth, Justice and Reconciliation Act 2008, s. 5(d)

[127] Decision Pursuant to Article 15 of the Rome Statute on the Authorization of an Investigation into the Situation in the Republic of Kenya, Pre-Trial Chamber II, Case No. ICC-01/09–19, 31 March 2010, paras. 181–7.

[128] Robinson, 'Serving the Interests of Justice', 499.

to be criminal in nature.[129] It is also contended that the unwillingness criterion under Article 17(2) that proceedings be consistent with an intent to bring those concerned to justice does not necessarily refer to criminal justice.[130] However, if, as in the Kenyan situation, the ongoing operations of a truth commission do not even constitute 'the case being investigated' under Article 17(1)(a) to prevent the assumption of jurisdiction, it seems most unlikely that the operation of a truth commission alone, without any criminal trials, will act as a permanent barrier to the exercise of ICC jurisdiction under Article 17 (1)(b). Indeed, it would seem from the Trial Chamber's recent decision that the national proceedings referred to in the Statute must be of a criminal nature in order to render a case inadmissible before the ICC.

The complementarity regime therefore holds some significant consequences for truth commission establishment. On a practical level, the use of truth commissions as an alternative to trials for the most serious crimes seems likely to end. Where a state party is unable or unwilling to pursue prosecutions, the ICC will assume jurisdiction and undertake investigations and prosecutorial proceedings. This is a positive development in the battle against impunity and reinforces the trend already underway, where the most serious crimes are not dealt with solely through the mechanism of a national truth commission. Notwithstanding the recent decision in the Kenyan situation, exactly how the Court will interpret the admissibility criteria of unwillingness and inability in respect of truth commissions remains to be seen in large part. The Court has not been forthcoming on whether the initial establishment of a truth commission will be taken as a prima facie indication of unwillingness or inability to prosecute. The lack of certainty in this area means that states will have to consider carefully before establishing a truth commission as an initial response to past violations rather than instituting a policy of prosecution if they wish to exclude the possibility of the Court assuming jurisdiction. The recent Trial Chamber decision on the Kenyan situation is a stark warning in this regard.

[129] Carsten Stahn, 'Complementarity, Amnesties and Alternative Forms of Justice: Some Interpretative Guidelines for the International Criminal Court' (2005) 3 *Journal of International Criminal Justice* 695, 711–12; Anja Seibert-Fohr, 'The Relevance of the Rome Statute of the International Criminal Court for Amnesties and Truth Commissions' (2003) 7 *Max Planck Yearbook of United Nations Law* 553, 569; Hector Olásolo, 'The Triggering Procedure of the International Criminal Court: Procedural Treatment of the Principle of Complementarity and the Role of the Office of the Prosecutor' (2004) 5 *International Criminal Law Review* 121, 139.

[130] Robinson, 'Serving the Interests of Justice', 501–2.

The creation of a truth commission rather than the immediate pursuit of trials should not automatically be assumed as an indication of unwillingness to prosecute. The establishment of a strong truth commission may be indicative of a state's determination to address the past and, as part of that longer term process, to pursue prosecutions. For affected populations there are distinct advantages of trials being carried out in an accessible, national forum rather than through an international tribunal operating at a distance. In light of this, the ICC should not rush to assume jurisdiction until it is clear that prosecution within the state of territoriality is not a possibility. In states such as Argentina and Liberia, the prosecutions that were intended to follow national truth commissions did not, at least in the short term, come to fruition. These experiences should not tarnish perceptions of all national truth-seeking initiatives and the Court should make every effort to support national attempts at accountability. A flexible and lateral approach to complementarity should be adopted and the premature assumption of jurisdiction, without providing adequate opportunity for domestic institutions to address their own legacy of abuse, resisted. As part of this lateral approach, it is suggested that the Court should not assume that the initial establishment of a national truth commission before the pursuit of criminal accountability is indicative of unwillingness or inability to prosecute in the longer term. This is not to suggest that the Court should delay initiation of its own proceedings until a national truth-seeking process has ended. This can take several years, during which time relevant evidence may be lost or contaminated. However, the Court should be open to dialogue with national authorities and should accept that it may be easier to initiate truth commission proceedings before putting in place a prosecutorial system to address past crimes.[131]

The significance of the complementarity principle lies not only in its practical impact upon future truth commission use, but also in its alteration of their place within the transitional justice framework. The complementarity regime's prioritisation of prosecution through its demands that trials be carried out, whether at the national level or by the Court itself, implies a subordination of truth commissions to criminal trials. Complementarity alters and, to a large extent, dictates

---

[131] Neil J. Kritz, 'War Crimes and Truth Commissions: Some Thoughts on Accountability Mechanisms for Mass Violations of Human Rights', presented at a USAID Conference, *Promoting Democracy, Human Rights, and Reintegration in Post-conflict Societies*, 30–1 October 1997.

national priorities, as if states parties wish to avoid intervention by the ICC, they will have to ensure that, should the crimes within the statute be committed, they undertake proceedings aimed at bringing those responsible to criminal justice. Moreover, the ability of the UN Security Council to refer situations to the ICC means that the Court's reach extends beyond its states parties, and may give rise to a greater focus on prosecutorial policies even in non-states parties. Criminal trials will therefore take on a place of elevated importance among transitional justice mechanisms in future. Prosecution will become the primary objective of at least states parties in addressing past atrocities and the creation and operation of other transitional justice initiatives, including truth commissions, will, necessarily, become secondary considerations. At both ideological and practical levels, prosecution will occupy a place of unparalleled significance as a consequence of the complementarity regime. Truth commissions will become, at best, a complement to trials and their operation will have to accommodate prioritised prosecutorial objectives.

4 Possibilities for coordination: sequencing work, dividing labour?

Notwithstanding the altered nature of the transitional justice framework following the creation of the ICC, at operational levels a practical dilemma persists: where the subject matter mandates of truth commissions and prosecutorial institutions overlap, how should their operations be coordinated? Without careful consideration of how these institutions ought to interact, their need to access the same evidence, information and witnesses may give rise to conflict. Two key proposals have emerged in this regard: sequencing the operation of truth commissions and trials and dividing work between them, with trials targeted at those most responsible and truth commissions dealing with those left over.[132] As Hayner explains, neither of these proposals presents a logical or workable solution.[133]

It has been suggested that the potential for conflict may be minimised by carrying out trials before the commencement of truth commission

---

[132] Hayner, *Unspeakable Truths: Transitional Justice and the Challenge of Truth Commissions*, 110–11.
[133] *Ibid.*

proceedings.[134] This proposal would have the advantage of diminishing the prospects for tension around access to witnesses and information that may occur where operation is concurrent. However, on balance it presents more problems than it solves. The length of time alone that prosecutorial proceedings take to complete makes this an unfeasible option. Initiating truth commission proceedings perhaps a decade or more after the point of transition will likely have weakened the public appetite for participation in truth seeking that exists at the time of transition. The benefits that truth commission proceedings can bring would be denied to transitional societies at a time when they can be most useful. Legislative and institutional reforms will likely have been implemented without the benefit of truth commission proposals based on a thorough examination of the past. In addition, given the time that it can take to mobilise criminal trials, there may be a transitional justice lull if truth commissions are to follow trials. Sequencing the other way around does not provide a solution either. While truth commissions generally complete their work more quickly than prosecutorial institutions, they remain likely to operate for a number of years. In that time, prosecutorial investigations too would lose the momentum present at the point of transition. As time passes evidence becomes more difficult to obtain and personal accounts are altered and influenced by subsequent events. Delaying trials until the end of a truth commission may also detract from the truth-seeking process. As a truth commission brings to light the nature and extent of past violations, it is likely that demands for criminal justice will increase. Where that demand is not being met, dissatisfaction with truth seeking as the primary response may develop.

Dividing labour is equally unworkable, despite some evidence of role division with contemporary transitional justice practice. Prosecutorial initiatives tend to focus on those who bear the greatest responsibility for the most serious crimes. This accords with the mandate of the ICC and was the approach adopted in East Timor and Sierra Leone.[135] As a result, lower level perpetrators may be granted amnesty in the interests of national reconciliation as suggested in the enacting legislation of the Liberian[136] and Kenyan[137] truth commissions or reintegrated to society

---

[134] William W. Burke-White, 'Proactive Complementarity: The International Criminal Court and National Courts in the Rome System of Justice' (2008) 49 *Harvard International Law Journal* 53, 104.

[135] See Chapter 3.

[136] An Act to Establish the Truth and Reconciliation Commission of Liberia, 2005, s. 26(g).

[137] Kenya: Truth, Justice and Reconciliation Act 2008, ss. 34–9.

through a traditional justice mechanism as in East Timor.[138] However, to divide labour so as to require truth commissions to investigate only lower level violations negates one of their central purposes. One of the key strengths of truth commissions is their documentation of patterns of abuses and their ability to situate their commission within institutional frameworks. That objective requires consideration of the roles played by senior figures within political, military and security institutions, who may also become subjects of criminal prosecutions. To document a history of past violations without explaining why and how they occurred or who was responsible for them removes a significant and important dimension of the work of truth commissions.

The solution to how to coordinate truth commissions and trials must therefore lie elsewhere. Sequencing operations and drawing divisions within their work seems likely to undermine the valuable contribution that these mechanisms can make to transitional states. Delaying the commencement of either of these mechanisms may weaken their potential impact. This leads to the necessary conclusion that in order to maximise the benefits of their operation, they should be established as close to the point of transition as possible and, as a result, operate simultaneously, or at least with some overlap. Trials have not always been possible in the past as many states found that their political settlements or judicial systems were simply too fragile to pursue prosecutions at the time of transition.[139] Truth commissions were often established instead. However, where the most serious crimes are concerned, the creation of the ICC narrows the possibilities for problems of this nature, as the Court will be able to initiate proceedings where national authorities are unable or unwilling to do so. It therefore enhances the likelihood of contemporaneous operation by creating a means of pursuing prosecution where states, which may nevertheless establish national level truth commissions, are unable to do so.

5 Conclusion

This chapter has shown that many of the crimes that commonly form part of the subject matter mandate of truth commissions are also those that require prosecution. At national levels, trials may be required as a result of international treaty obligations or in accordance with the ICC Statute regime. Internationally, prosecution of the most serious violations may

---

[138] See Chapter 3.   [139] See Chapter 1.

occur as a result of their status as ICC crimes. Where states have treaty obligations to prosecute or are parties to the ICC, criminal trials for the relevant crimes must be prioritised in order to fulfil international obligations or avoid the assumption of jurisdiction by the ICC. How states will coordinate such trials with the operation of any truth commission that is also established remains to be seen.

Violations that require prosecution will form only a portion of those investigated by truth commissions. However, questions remain as to how proceedings will be coordinated where trials and truth commissions do overlap. States will have to consider whether truth commissions ought to investigate crimes that will also be the subject of prosecutorial proceedings and whether demarcation is possible if the truth commission is to compile a complete account of the past. If there is to be subject matter overlap between trials and truth commissions, decisions will be required upon the possibility of information exchange and the powers to be exercised by the commission. Consideration of how to manage the perceptions of the affected populace and ensure their engagement with both processes will be necessary. A delicate balance will need to be struck in order to ensure the successful fulfilment of prosecutorial obligations with effective national truth seeking.

While the coordination of these bodies will undoubtedly be difficult at the national level, the issue will become significantly more complex if prosecutorial proceedings are carried out by the ICC.[140] In this situation, trials and truth commissions will not be operating as part of a coordinated domestic programme and, as things stand, there will be no joined-up policy governing the relationship between them or how they ought to interact. The truth commission will be a national body acting in accordance with domestic legislation and criminal investigations and prosecutions will be pursued by an independent, international treaty institution with its own judicial objectives. Additional challenges are posed by the possibility of prosecutions in bystander states, under the universality principle.[141] Nevertheless, access to some of the same information, evidence and witnesses will be required by both truth commissions and prosecutorial institutions if they are to fulfil their mandates. Decisions will be needed on whether to endow truth commissions with the quasi-judicial powers they typically exercise in light of the difficulties this might create in contemporaneous operations alongside the ICC

---

[140] See Chapter 4.   [141] See Chapter 5.

and third state trials. At the same time, the need to minimise the potential for conflict will need to be balanced against creating truth commissions with relevant mandates and sufficient capability to fulfil those mandates. These issues form the topics of analysis in the remaining chapters of this book.

3

Coordinating truth commissions and criminal courts at the national level

1 The absence of a common approach

Despite the extensive and ever-increasing use of trials and truth commissions within transitional states, past practice provides little direction on how their operations should be coordinated. In large part, this may be explained by the fact that these bodies have rarely been established together as part of a planned national response to past violations. Early truth commissions were often created as an alternative to trials[1] or on the understanding that their findings would have no judicial effect.[2] Although in some states the violations investigated by these commissions have subsequently become the subject of prosecutions, trials have been conducted long after the dissolution of the commissions.[3] In other states, truth commissions and prosecutorial institutions built cooperative relationships, with the commission forwarding information relating to human rights crimes.[4] This has, however, generally been at the behest of the commission

---

[1] This was the situation in Chile. See Jose Zalaquett, 'Balancing Ethical Imperatives with Political Constraints: The Dilemma of New Democracies Confronting Past Human Rights Violations' (1992) 43 *Hastings Law Journal* 1425. On similar difficulties in Ghana see Ken A. Attafuah, 'An Overview of Ghana's National Reconciliation Commission and Its Relationship with the Courts' (2004) 15 *Criminal Law Forum* 125.

[2] See for example, the Agreement on the Establishment of the Commission to Clarify Past Human Rights Violations and Acts of Violence that have caused the Guatemalan Population to Suffer, Oslo, 17 June 1994, (1997) 36 *International Legal Materials* 283 on the protection of the Guatemalan Commission's information and Ghana's National Reconciliation Commission Act 2002.

[3] See Kathryn Sikkink and Carrie Booth Walling, 'Argentina's Contribution to Global Trends in Transitional Justice', in Naomi Roht-Arriaza and Javier Mariezcurrena (eds.), *Transitional Justice in the Twenty-First Century: Beyond Truth versus Justice* (Cambridge University Press, 2006), 301–25.

[4] See Argentina: Trial of the Members of the Former Military Junta, Federal Criminal and Correctional Court of Appeals, Federal District of Buenos Aires, reprinted in Neil J. Kritz, *Transitional Justice: How Emerging Democracies Reckon with Former Regimes*, 3 vols. (Washington DC: United States Institute of Peace Press, 1995), vol. III, Laws, Rulings and Reports, 483–4. On the Haitian Commission's passing of information to the Ministry of Justice see République d'Haiti, *Rapport de la Commission Nationale*

rather than the result of any national attempt to coordinate operations. Overall, early transitional justice practice evidences a distinct absence of successful trials and convictions for past crimes and a conspicuous use of truth commissions as substitutes for criminal justice. It therefore sheds minimal light on how trials and truth commissions can best be used effectively together.

Even in contemporary practice, trials and truth commissions have been used as part of a multifaceted and tailored response to past abuses in only three states. The relationship models implemented between them varied widely. In South Africa, prosecution and truth seeking were inextricably linked. The threat of prosecution before the courts provided the impetus for former perpetrators to participate in the truth for amnesty process operated by the Truth and Reconciliation Commission. Consideration of a case by the Commission's Amnesty Committee suspended court proceedings and a grant of amnesty from the Committee brought a permanent end to civil and criminal proceedings for the crime concerned.[5] The Commission for East Timor had a close working relationship with the prosecutorial institutions of the country and was under a duty to share information and refer serious cases to the Office of the General Prosecutor.[6] In contrast, the Sierra Leonean Truth and Reconciliation Commission and the Special Court operated as two entirely separate entities.[7] Each of these models gave rise to a unique set of issues and challenges as overlapping mandates, interlinked operations, reliance on the same evidence and requirements to access the same witnesses brought them into contact, and sometimes conflict.

The objective of this chapter is to identify means by which to coordinate the respective operations of trials and truth commissions at the national

---

de Vérité et de Justice, 2001, Chapter 2, Art. 9. On the cooperative arrangements between the Peruvian TRC and the Attorney General's office see Eduardo G. Cueva, 'The Peruvian Truth and Reconciliation Commission and the Challenge of Impunity', in Naomi Roht-Arriaza and Javier Mariezcurrena (eds.), Transitional Justice in the Twenty-First Century: Beyond Truth versus Justice (Cambridge University Press, 2006), 70–94, 81–3; Institutional Cooperation Agreement between the Prosecutor's Office and the Truth and Reconciliation Commission, Lima, 15 August 2002. Eduardo G. Cueva, 'The Contribution of the Peruvian Truth and Reconciliation Commission to Prosecutions' (2004) 15 Criminal Law Forum 55–66, 60.

[5] South Africa: Promotion of National Unity and Reconciliation Act, No. 34 of 1995, ss. 19(6) and 20(7)(a).

[6] UNTAET Regulation No. 2001/10 on the Establishment of a Commission for Reception, Truth and Reconciliation in East Timor, UNTAET/REG/2001/10, 13 July 2001, s. 3.1(e).

[7] William A. Schabas, 'The Relationship between Truth Commissions and International Courts: The Case of Sierra Leone' (2003) 25 Human Rights Quarterly 1035.

level in order to facilitate their effective coexistence and minimise the potential for friction. This is essential if the transitional justice theory that trials and truth commissions deliver different but complementary benefits to transitional states is to be realised in practice. The chapter will examine the relationships between past commissions and prosecutorial institutions and identify areas of potential operational difficulty that may compromise their abilities to function effectively together. It will focus on the experiences of South Africa, East Timor and Sierra Leone. Through analysis of the models implemented in these states, it will ascertain whether there are optimal working conditions, which enable truth commissions and prosecutorial institutions to function effectively together at the national level without one undermining the work of the other.

2   South Africa's truth for amnesty model

South Africa was the first state to design a transitional justice programme in which a truth commission and criminal trials were to play interconnected and complementary roles. The Truth and Reconciliation Commission (TRC) was created to establish the nature, causes and extent of gross human rights violations committed during the apartheid era, facilitate the granting of amnesty, restore the dignity of victims by granting them an opportunity to relate their accounts and recommend reparation measures.[8] The TRC was mandated to operate through three committees: the Committee on Human Rights Violations; the Committee on Amnesty; and the Committee on Reparation and Rehabilitation.[9] It was endowed with a wealth of truth-seeking powers, including search and seizure, the ability to conduct inspections and the authority to call upon any person to produce material or appear before the Commission to give evidence.[10]

The unique feature of the South African model was its truth for amnesty process. It is through this aspect of its operation that truth seeking and prosecution were utilised as an integrated and multifaceted approach to past violations. The Amnesty Committee was tasked with granting amnesty to individuals who submitted timely applications making full disclosure of politically motivated acts involving a gross violation of human rights.[11] The benefits of a grant of amnesty were significant.

---

[8] South Africa: Promotion of National Unity and Reconciliation Act, No. 34 of 1995, s. 3(1).
[9] *Ibid.*, s. 3(3).   [10] *Ibid.*, ss. 29–32.   [11] *Ibid.*, s. 20(1).

All criminal and civil liability relating to the act for which amnesty was granted was extinguished, both for the applicant and anybody that might have been vicariously liable for the applicant's act. Any criminal conviction based upon the act was expunged from all official records.[12] Amnesty therefore acted as a 'carrot' to encourage former perpetrators to offer testimony to the Commission so that it could fulfil its mandate of establishing the truth about the past and creating a shared understanding from which to move forward. The possibility of prosecution was intended as the 'stick' in the truth for amnesty model. Although incriminating information obtained by the Commission was not admissible in any subsequent court proceedings,[13] those who did not apply for amnesty, or were not granted it, remained liable to criminal and civil trial through ordinary legal proceedings. The South African model is therefore one in which truth seeking was prioritised over the pursuit of criminal justice. The primary role of prosecution, or the threat of it, was to enhance truth seeking and create a more robust truth commission by incentivising appearance and disclosure before the TRC.

2.1   Truth seeking and prosecution in practice

The integral place of prosecution within the South African model meant that prosecutorial proceedings would necessarily impact the operation of the TRC. The overall focus was on uncovering the truth and promoting national reconciliation. However, using the threat of prosecution as the impetus for perpetrators to offer testimony tied the success of the Commission to the credibility of that threat. The possibility of trial and conviction had to be perceived as real to provide the incentive for perpetrators to offer testimony and for the TRC to fulfil its mandate by obtaining information from all sectors. The TRC's findings demonstrate that where investigations and prosecutions were pursued and convictions secured, applications for amnesty and participation in the truth-seeking process increased. The conviction of Eugene de Kock, former commander of Vlakplaas, in conjunction with his extensive disclosures before the TRC and during sentencing mitigation hearings, is considered to have led to applications for amnesty from large numbers of security police officials.[14]

---

[12] Ibid., s. 20(7).   [13] Ibid., s. 31(3).

[14] Truth and Reconciliation Commission of South Africa Report (TRC Report) (Cape Town: Truth and Reconciliation Commission, distributed by Juta and Co., 2002), vol. 5, Chapter 6, 202.

The TRC also identified links between local criminal investigations and amnesty applications from those regions.[15]

Conversely, it is argued that the inadequacies of the prosecutorial programme impacted negatively on the truth-seeking process.[16] The prioritisation of truth seeking and the concentration of resources within the TRC resulted in a failure to ensure the capacity of the justice system to fulfil its role within the transitional justice model. No dedicated body was established to undertake the prosecution of apartheid era crimes. As TRC operations began, only two small inquiries were involved in fulfilling the prosecutorial component of the transitional model.[17] While one inquiry ultimately led to the conviction of de Kock, and a small number of others,[18] the other lacked support from regional prosecuting authorities. The Natal Attorney General refused to prosecute in a number of key cases. The one significant case that he did pursue resulted in the acquittal of senior politicians and military and security force members, including former Minister of Defence, Magnus Malan.[19] This outcome is argued to have reduced the incentive for many perpetrators from the military, who had awaited the outcome of the Malan trial, to apply for amnesty.[20] With the threat of effective prosecution diminished, so did the need to offer the truth in exchange for amnesty.[21] While it is overly simplistic to suggest that amnesty applications were made purely due to the likelihood or

---

[15] *TRC Report*, vol. 6, s. 3, chapter 6.

[16] Howard Varney, 'Case study: The Malan Trial (South Africa)', Presentation to International Center for Transitional Justice, *Domestic Prosecutions and Transitional Justice Conference*, 16–19 May 2005, Magaliesburg, South Africa; Janine Rauch, *Police Transformation and the South African TRC*, Race and Citizenship in Transition Series, Centre for the Study of Violence and Reconciliation, 2004.

[17] Jonathan Klaaren and Howard Varney, 'A Second Bite at the Amnesty Cherry? Constitutional and Policy Issues around Legislation for a Second Amnesty' (2000) 117 *South African Law Journal* 572, 575.

[18] Louise Mallinder, 'Indemnity, Amnesty, Pardon and Prosecution Guidelines in South Africa', *Working Paper No. 2 from Beyond Legalism: Amnesties, Transition and Conflict Transformation*, Institute of Criminology and Criminal Justice, Queen's University Belfast, February 2009, 105–7.

[19] For an analysis of the case see Howard Varney and Jeremy Sarkin, 'Failing to Pierce the Hit Squad Veil: An Analysis of the Malan Trial' (1997) 10 *South African Journal of Criminal Justice* 141.

[20] *Ibid.*, 141.

[21] Ken Oh and Theresa Edlmann, 'Reconciliatory Justice: Amnesties, Indemnities and Prosecutions in South Africa's Transition', in Centre for the Study of Violence and Reconciliation (ed.), *After the Transition: Justice, The Judiciary and Respect for the Law in South Africa: A Collection of Papers from a Project on Justice and Transition* (Johannesburg: CSVR, 2007), 9–10.

otherwise of prosecution, it was certainly an influential factor. Pedain's analysis of TRC data demonstrates that amnesty applications were low among political groups and elements of state security forces that had not seen effective prosecutions of their members. In contrast, groups that were under investigation and/or had experienced the trial and conviction of members, submitted applications in more significant numbers.[22] Where prosecution seemed a credible possibility, it motivated former perpetrators to apply for amnesty, with the result that the TRC gained access to information in accordance with its truth-seeking mandate.

In reality, the limited capacity, and in some cases lack of inclination, of the prosecutorial institutions meant that only a few high-profile trials were carried out during the TRC's lifespan.[23] Prosecutorial institutions were not sufficiently resourced to fulfil their role of incentivising truth telling by providing a realistic threat of trial and conviction for those who did not seek amnesty. The TRC nevertheless concluded that the appeal to self-interest through the truth for amnesty process was well conceived and that it enabled the Commission to uncover information that it would not otherwise have accessed.[24] It cannot be denied that the Amnesty Committee received a significant response from those who had been involved in past crimes.[25] How much greater that response might have been had prosecution been perceived as a more significant threat and how much more information the Commission might then have received cannot be known. It seems logical that truth seeking would have been enhanced by a more proactive and effective prosecutorial policy.

While the lack of a complementary criminal prosecution process has been criticised for undermining the amnesty process,[26] it is also argued that the amnesty system hampered prosecutions.[27] No framework to regulate the practical operation and interaction of trials and the TRC was developed prior to the commencement of the Commission's operations.

---

[22] Antje Pedain, 'Was Amnesty a Lottery? An Empirical Study of the Decisions of the Truth and Reconciliation Commission's Committee on Amnesty' (2004) 121 *South African Law Journal* 785, 813–14.

[23] Mallinder, 'Indemnity, Amnesty, Pardon and Prosecution Guidelines in South Africa', 106.

[24] *TRC Report*, vol. 1, Chapter 5, 64; vol. 6, s. 3, Chapter 1, 263.

[25] Pedain, 'Was Amnesty a Lottery?', 804–6.

[26] Jeremy Sarkin, *Carrots and Sticks: The TRC and the South African Amnesty Process* (Antwerp: Intersentia, 2004), 127–34.

[27] Paul Gready, *The Era of Transitional Justice: The Aftermath of the Truth and Reconciliation Commission in South Africa and Beyond* (Oxford and New York: Routledge, 2011), 102–3.

In its final report the TRC discussed the tension that arose between it and prosecutorial institutions in relation to overlapping investigations, a lack of cooperation in information flows and slow progress in investigations.[28] Gready notes the frustration experienced by prosecutorial bodies as a result of the TRC's ability to take over investigations in the short term and the inability to utilise the Commission's materials in prosecutorial proceedings even where amnesty was denied.[29] Had the prosecutorial component of the transitional model been more proactive, these issues might have become contentious, rather than occupying only a few sentences in the TRC's report. Nevertheless, this latent tension suggests a failure to fully comprehend the role to be played by prosecution within the transitional justice model and an inadequate consideration of how the TRC and prosecutorial institutions were to play mutually supporting roles in practice.

Overall, the prioritisation of truth seeking obfuscated the vital role that prosecution occupied within the transitional justice model. Truth seeking might have been the priority but the efficacy of the TRC was linked to and dependent upon the effective functioning of the prosecutorial institutions. This required the adequate and equal resourcing of the truth commission and the prosecutorial bodies. The failure to create robust, well-resourced, prosecutorial institutions meant that the threat of prosecution could not be realised. Its absence undermined the TRC's work, as it seems probable that some perpetrators failed to apply for amnesty, and therefore share their accounts, because they did not consider prosecution likely. This was a significant shortcoming as the truth for amnesty process provided the only real means of holding perpetrators to account. The distinct lack of criminal accountability for apartheid era crimes is a source of much dissatisfaction among some South Africans who had always understood that those who did not apply for amnesty, or were not granted it, would be prosecuted.[30] In short, the combined use of truth seeking and prosecution within the South African model was not as successful as it might have been. This stemmed from a failure within the design of the transitional model to recognise how crucial effective prosecution would be and to equip prosecutorial bodies accordingly. As a result, prosecution could not provide the TRC with the support that it ought to have had.

---

[28] *TRC Report*, vol. 1. Chapter 11, 343.

[29] Gready, *The Era of Transitional Justice*, 102.

[30] David Backer, 'Watching a Bargain Unravel: A Panel Study of Victims' Attitudes about Transitional Justice in Cape Town, South Africa' (2010) 4 *International Journal of Transitional Justice* 443.

2.2 Linking truth seeking and prosecution: judicialising the truth-seeking process

Generally, the truth for amnesty model has serious weaknesses in its willingness to forego criminal prosecution of those most responsible for human rights crimes and its creation of a judicialised truth commission. The decision to link amnesty and truth seeking, and endow the TRC with the power to grant individualised amnesty, created a quasi-judicial truth commission from the outset. The principle that those denied amnesty and those who failed to apply for it should face criminal prosecution further tied the TRC's operations to the formal judicial system. It also meant that every aspect of the transitional justice model – truth, amnesty and accountability – was rooted within the TRC. As a result, both victims and perpetrators had deeply vested interests in its operations. For victims and their families, the TRC processes provided the only means of calling to account those responsible for past violations.[31] For perpetrators, the power wielded by the TRC through the 1995 Act made it the subject of resentment and apprehension.[32] Not only was the TRC vested with quasi-judicial, truth-seeking abilities, it had the competence to grant amnesty to those whom it considered met the relevant criteria under a mandate which it was itself authorised to interpret. As TRC decisions impacted these groups, they sought legal scrutiny of the Commission's procedures and findings.[33] Some of the courts' rulings on these issues had a significant effect on truth seeking through their necessitation of the adoption of a more legalistic process by the TRC. While this is the result of interaction with the judicial system as a whole, rather than the direct impact of prosecutions upon truth seeking, it stems from the creation of a transitional

---

[31] Before the Amnesty Committee began work, victims called upon the courts to examine the constitutionality of the truth for amnesty process claiming that it was incompatible with section 22 of the interim Constitution, which guaranteed the right to have justiciable disputes settled by a court of law or other impartial and independent forum. The Constitutional Court rejected their claim on the grounds that the epilogue to the interim Constitution, which committed South Africa to a transitional policy of reconciliation and reconstruction, and included the granting of amnesty for past violations, trumped section 22. The judgment stressed the importance of amnesty within the 1993 political settlement and emphasised its significance in providing an incentive for truth telling. *Azanian Peoples Organisation (AZAPO) and Others* v. *President of the Republic of South Africa* 1996 (4) SALR 671. For an analysis of the case see John Dugard, 'Reconciliation and Justice: The South African Experience' (1998) 8 *Transnational Law and Contemporary Problems* 277.

[32] *TRC Report*, vol. 5, Chapter 6, 196–7.   [33] *TRC Report*, vol. 6, s. 1, Chapter 4, 80–2.

model, which links truth seeking with prosecutions. For perpetrators, in particular, TRC decisions had potentially serious, legal consequences and could either open or close the door to criminal prosecution. It is therefore unsurprising that the TRC's operations became the subject of legal challenge.

Those implicated to their detriment in TRC proceedings brought a number of cases challenging various aspects of the Commission's work. In practice, the courts acted as a system of checks and balances on the TRC's operations. They were called upon to interpret the provisions of the 1995 Act, assess the fairness and impartiality of TRC proceedings, carry out judicial review of amnesty decisions[34] and provide legal sanction for those who refused to comply with the TRC's orders.[35] One of the most significant rulings related to section 30 of the 1995 Act, and the requirement to enable those implicated in past violations during TRC hearings to address the allegations.[36] After a series of low-level decisions, the Appellate Division held that section 30 required the Commission to provide those implicated with reasonable and timeous notice of public hearings so as to allow them or their legal representatives to be present to hear the evidence, have the opportunity to rebut it and to see the demeanour of the witness. It was also held that the Commission might be under a duty to permit immediate cross-examination.[37]

Prima facie, it seems extraordinary for a court to impose such cumbersome and legalistic procedural requirements upon a truth commission. The introduction of adversarial trial features into the truth-seeking process appears at odds with the traditionally non-judicial status of truth commissions and inconsistent with their victim-centred approach. The TRC itself concluded that this ruling had the effect of imposing not only administrative burdens on the Commission as it sought to identify implicated persons and ensure that they were supplied with necessary information, it had a traumatising effect on victims who did testify.[38]

---

[34] *TRC Report*, vol. 1, chapter 7; vol. 6, s. 1, chapter 4.

[35] On the action taken against P. W. Botha following his failure to comply with the Commission's subpoena see Alex Boraine, *A Country Unmasked: Inside South Africa's Truth and Reconciliation Commission* (Oxford University Press, 2001), Chapter 6.

[36] *Nieuwoudt v. Chairman, South African Truth and Reconciliation Commission* (1996) 2 All SA 660 (SE); *Du Preez and Van Rensburg v. Chairman, South African Truth and Reconciliation Commission*, Case No. 4443/96 (unreported decision of Cape of Good Hope Provisional Division, 30 April 1996); *Du Preez and Van Rensburg v. Chairman, South African Truth and Reconciliation Commission*, 1996 (3) SA 997 (C).

[37] *Du Preez and Van Rensburg v. Chairman, South African Truth and Reconciliation Commission*, 1997 (3) SA 204 (SCA).

[38] *TRC Report*, vol. 1, 185.

Thus, it is argued that this ruling was anathema to the supportive environment that the TRC sought to create during human rights violations hearings.[39] It seems likely that the prospect of giving testimony in the presence of those allegedly responsible for past violations, and the possibility of facing cross examination by them, may have inhibited a number of victims from offering their account altogether, restricting the breadth of information available to the Commission. The section 30 ruling also obliged the TRC to give alleged perpetrators a prior view of the findings it intended to publish. Many of those implicated could not be traced and this resulted in the TRC having to delete from its final report the names of many alleged perpetrators. The incidents in which they were allegedly involved were therefore omitted or not fully described.[40] Thus, the final report does not provide as full and thorough an account of the past as it could have.

Yet it is not difficult to see why the courts felt it necessary to impose such requirements upon the TRC. In reality, the TRC was not a truly non-judicial body. It was involved in legalistic proceedings that gave it a judicial aura. The sole purpose of the high-profile Amnesty Committee was to adjudicate on individual involvement in politically motivated crimes and delicts. Its proceedings followed an adversarial process. Committee members had legal training and panels were chaired by active or retired judges.[41] Its decisions determined whether individuals qualified for amnesty and therefore whether they were indemnified against future legal proceedings. Moreover, consideration of a case by the Amnesty Committee suspended action relating to the same incident in the courts. These proceedings bore many of the hallmarks of a formal judicial process. The Human Rights Violations Committee and that on Reparation and Rehabilitation were not engaged in such legalistic tasks. However, together the three would issue one final report, which would draw together their conclusions and include findings on the involvement of individuals in past crimes. Given how much was at stake for individuals as a result of the TRC process, it is understandable that the courts sought to secure individual rights within it. It is the direct consequence of implementing a transitional justice model that created a truth commission with a judicial role, which in turn opened it to legal challenge and the imposition of due process protections in its proceedings.

---

[39] Antje du Bois-Pedain, *Transitional Amnesty in South Africa* (Cambridge University Press, 2007), 185.

[40] *TRC Report*, vol. 5, Chapter 6, 260.

[41] Pedain, 'Was Amnesty a Lottery?', 789–90.

Ironically, the amnesty process was justified in large part by its ability to assist the truth-seeking process by encouraging perpetrators to admit their crimes. However, it is widely argued that the legalistic procedure followed by the Amnesty Committee limited truth discovery in some respects.[42] The requirement to make 'full disclosure of the relevant facts'[43] was interpreted by the Amnesty Committee as requiring disclosure of only the facts that pertained directly to the act for which amnesty was sought.[44] This has been criticised for inhibiting the richness of the truth that could be uncovered by narrowing the focus of the Committee's work and excluding the wider context from its investigations.[45] Moreover, many amnesty applicants sought legal advice and representation, with the result that legal representatives heavily influenced the nature and scope of perpetrator testimony.[46] It must be concluded that endowing the TRC with responsibility for granting individualised amnesty caused it problems. It is this aspect of its operation that made it a judicialised body in design. Without that quasi-judicial status it is unlikely that it would have faced the legal challenges that led to the imposition of cumbersome procedural requirements, which inhibited victims and hampered the fulfilment of the truth and reconciliation mandate.

Overall, the TRC concluded that the amnesty initiative allowed for more truth to be uncovered than would have been the case if prosecutions had been carried out.[47] However, a transitional policy, which in design has the potential to forego prosecution of international crimes entirely, is unlikely to be an option in future.[48] Criminal accountability for the most

---

[42] Mallinder, 'Indemnity, Amnesty, Pardon and Prosecution Guidelines in South Africa', 93.

[43] South Africa: Promotion of National Unity and Reconciliation Act, No. 34 of 1995, s. 201(1).

[44] *TRC Report*, vol. 6, Chapter 1, para. 25.

[45] Jeremy Sarkin, 'An Evaluation of the South African Amnesty Process', in Audrey R. Chapman and Hugo van der Merwe (eds.), *Truth and Reconciliation in South Africa: Did the TRC Deliver?* (Philadelphia: Pennsylvania Studies in Human Rights, University of Pennsylvania Press, 2008), 95–6; Madeleine Fullard and Nicky Rousseau, 'Truth, Evidence and History: A Critical Review of Aspects of the Amnesty Process', in Erik Doxtader and Charles Villa-Vicencio (eds.), *The Provocations of Amnesty: Memory, Justice, and Impunity* (Claremont, South Africa: David Philip Publishers, 2003), 202–6; Audrey R. Chapman and Patrick Ball, 'The Truth of Truth Commissions: Comparative Lessons from Haiti, South Africa, and Guatemala' (2001) 23 *Human Rights Quarterly* 1, 26.

[46] Piers Pigou, 'False Promises and Wasted Opportunities? Inside South Africa's Truth and Reconciliation Commission', in Deborah Posel and Graeme Simpson (eds.), *Commissioning the Past: Understanding South Africa's Truth and Reconciliation Commission* (Johannesburg: Witwatersrand University Press, 2002), 48.

[47] *TRC Report*, vol. 1, Chapter 5, para. 66.

[48] Paul Gready, *The Era of Transitional Justice*, 98.

serious crimes is at the centre of international transitional justice policy in the ICC era and many states possess treaty obligations to prosecute serious human rights crimes.[49] While not all states are party to the ICC Statute and its prosecutorial regime, none lie beyond the reach of its powers due to the Security Council's power to refer cases to the Court. Even 'accountable' amnesty seems at odds with the international commitment to combat impunity through prosecution and is unlikely to prevent proceedings by the ICC. The South African model may have enabled an enhanced level of truth discovery, but it fell short of delivering the individual accountability that many desired.[50] If current practice becomes future practice, there will be prosecution of those most responsible for international crimes. The accountability component will be delivered in the form of criminal justice and there will be no requirement to vest all transitional elements within one institution. This will avoid the problems of the South African model, enable truth commissions to fulfil a non-judicial, victim-centred, truth-seeking role and leave the pursuit of individual accountability to prosecutorial institutions.

3   Prioritising prosecution in East Timor

Unlike in South Africa, prosecution was the central focus of the East Timorese transitional justice programme. The UN Transitional Administration in East Timor (UNTAET)[51] created a hybrid prosecutorial model[52] to respond to the human rights violations committed during the period of Indonesian military withdrawal.[53] Special Panels for Serious Crimes were created within the existing court structure[54] and were given exclusive jurisdiction over human rights crimes, murder and sexual violence committed between 1 January and 25 October 1999.[55] A department

---

[49] See Chapter 2.

[50] On the ongoing issues caused by the lack of accountability in South Africa see Backer, 'Watching a Bargain Unravel'.

[51] UNTAET was established under Security Council Resolution 1272 (1999), S/RES/1272 (1999), 25 October 1999.

[52] For a discussion of the hybrid court established in East Timor see Susannah Linton, 'New Approaches to International Justice in Cambodia and East Timor' (2002) 84 *International Review of the Red Cross* 93.

[53] For an extensive discussion of the history of East Timor see James Dunn, *Timor: A People Betrayed* (Sydney: ABC Books, 1983).

[54] UNTAET Regulation No. 2000/15 on the Establishment of Panels with Exclusive Jurisdiction over Serious Criminal Offences, UNTAET/REG/2000/15, 6 June 2000, s. 1.1.

[55] *Ibid.*, s. 1.3. Under s. 22.2 Appeals Panels were created within the District Court of Dili.

for the investigation of serious crimes was established within the Office of the General Prosecutor (OGP)[56] and provision was made for a prosecution support unit,[57] which became known as the Serious Crimes Unit (SCU).[58] One year later, UNTAET established a Commission for Reception, Truth and Reconciliation (CAVR) to operate alongside the prosecutorial institutions as part of a multilateral response to the human rights violations of the past.[59] The CAVR's mandate overlapped that of the Special Panels. It was tasked with investigating the nature, causes and extent of past human rights violations and establishing personal and institutional responsibility for their commission.[60]

The relationship between the CAVR and the OGP was laid down in the truth commission's enacting legislation.[61] It was unique in two ways that distinguish the CAVR from truth commissions established prior to and since its creation. First, a provision was included within the Commission's mandate, which imposed an obligation on it to refer human rights violations to the OGP, with recommendations for the prosecution of offences where appropriate.[62] This was consistent with the exclusivity of the jurisdiction of the Special Panels in relation to serious human rights violations as laid down in their enacting legislation.[63] The obligation to refer impacted the powers given to the Commission and, therefore, its operational capabilities. As information given to the Commission could be passed to the OGP and used in subsequent prosecutions, unlike in South Africa, witnesses could not be compelled to give self-incriminating evidence or evidence that would incriminate a close relative.[64] Witnesses could be ordered to appear before the Commission and to answer questions under oath.[65] However, the Commission was then rendered relatively weak, because it did not possess the necessary powers to obtain all relevant information. This obligatory information-sharing relationship also meant that the CAVR could not incentivise truth telling by guaranteeing

---

[56] UNTAET Regulation No. 2000/16 on the Organisation of the Public Prosecution Service in East Timor, UNTAET/REG/2000/16, 6 June 2000, s. 5.1.

[57] *Ibid.*, s. 14.6.

[58] On the lack of a corresponding defence unit see Caitlin Reiger and Marieka Weirda, *The Serious Crimes Process in Timor-Leste: In Retrospect*, International Center for Transitional Justice, 2006, 26–8.

[59] UNTAET Regulation No. 2001/10.

[60] *Ibid.*, s. 13.1(a).   [61] *Ibid.*, s. 3.1(e).   [62] *Ibid.*

[63] UNTAET Regulation No. 2000/15, s. 1.3. See also UNTAET Regulation No. 2001/10, s. 22.2.

[64] UNTAET Regulation No. 2001/10, ss. 17.1 and .17.2.   [65] *Ibid.*, s. 14.

the confidentiality and non-disclosure of witness testimony, a tool that many past commissions have used to obtain information.[66]

The East Timorese model was therefore one in which prosecution was prioritised over truth seeking from the outset. The Commission's final report makes clear that the CAVR understood itself as fulfilling a secondary and complementary role to the Serious Crimes Process and makes little of the resultant constraints on truth-seeking powers. It acknowledges that the duty to refer and inability to guarantee the confidentiality of witness testimony may have prevented it from gaining important information that would have assisted its truth-seeking function.[67] However, it accepted this as a natural consequence of its complementary role to criminal prosecutions and the policy decision that the work of the prosecution service should not be compromised by the truth-seeking function of the Commission.[68]

The second distinguishing feature of the CAVR–prosecution relationship was the CAVR's operation of the Community Reconciliation Process (CRP). The CRP allowed perpetrators of minor offences to obtain immunity from prosecution[69] by submitting a statement to the Commission, admitting responsibility for past crimes in a community hearing and undertaking an act of reconciliation.[70] Again, the superiority of the prosecutorial institutions was evident in this scheme as initial statements had to be forwarded to the OGP where it was decided whether the Prosecutor's jurisdiction would be exercised or whether the case could be dealt with through a CRP.[71] By the end of the Community Reconciliation Process, the CAVR had received 1,541 requests to participate,[72] involved 30,000 to 40,000 community members in a CRP procedure[73] and facilitated

---

[66] On the use of confidentiality powers to obtain sensitive information see Mark Freeman, *Truth Commissions and Procedural Fairness* (Cambridge University Press, 2006), 181–6.

[67] *Chega!*, Final Report of the Commission for Reception, Truth and Reconciliation for East Timor, January 2006, Part 2: The Mandate of the Commission, paras. 23–4.

[68] *Ibid.*   [69] *Chega!* Part 9: Community Reconciliation, paras. 3–4.

[70] *Chega!* Part 9.2, Community Reconciliation Process, para. 10. For a full discussion of the Community Reconciliation Process see Padraig McAuliffe, 'East Timor's Community Reconciliation Process as a Model for Legal Pluralism in Criminal Justice', 2008, *Law, Social Justice and Global Development Journal*, section 4.

[71] *Chega!*, Part 9.2, Community Reconciliation Process, para. 10.

[72] *Ibid.*, para.102.

[73] Patrick Burgess, 'Justice and Reconciliation in East Timor: The Relationship Between the Commission for Reception, Truth and Reconciliation and the Courts' (2004) 15 *Criminal Law Forum* 153.

the successful completion of the process by 1,371 applicants.[74] The OGP retained eighty-five cases and thirty-two were adjourned mid-hearing as credible evidence of involvement in a serious crime came to light.[75] In practice, limited resources meant that the SCU was not able to investigate these cases.[76] The Commission was critical of this failure. It concluded that this had resulted in a 'justice deficit' and a situation of 'unequal accountability', where many low-level perpetrators had participated in CRP hearings, while those guilty of more serious crimes seemed unlikely ever to be held to account.[77]

The under-resourcing of the prosecutorial institutions in East Timor undermined the achievement of criminal justice for past crimes and has cast a shadow over the transitional justice programme. Nevertheless, the East Timorese model provides useful insights into one basis for the relationship between truth commissions and prosecutorial institutions. It demonstrates acutely that the relationship between a truth commission and the prosecutorial institutions it is established alongside will dictate the powers that the commission can exercise and influence the effectiveness of its operations. Where a decision is taken to prioritise prosecution and make all information available to prosecutorial institutions, including that gathered by a truth commission, the powers of the commission must be curtailed to reflect this. Thus, in the East Timorese case, the commission could not guarantee confidentiality and was not endowed with the power to compel the disclosure of self-incriminating information due to its duty to pass evidence of involvement in serious crimes to the OGP. Limiting truth-seeking powers in this way is necessary if the integrity of the commission and the prosecutorial institutions is to be maintained.[78] The credibility of a truth commission will be undermined if it exercises a power to compel the provision of self-incriminating information, supposedly in order to optimise truth seeking, but later passes that information to a prosecutorial body for use in criminal trials. Equally, the integrity of prosecutorial proceedings, their adherence to fair trial and human rights standards may be questioned, and indeed jeopardised, if

---

[74] *Chega!*, Part 9: Community Reconciliation Process, para. 6.
[75] *Ibid.*, para. 102.   [76] *Ibid.*, para. 169.
[77] *Ibid.*, para. 170. Security Council Resolution 1704 (2006), S/RES/1704 (2006), 25 August 2006, para. 4(i), provided for the creation of a team of experienced investigative personnel to resume the investigative function of the former SCU. See *Report of the Secretary General on the United Nations Integrated Mission in Timor-Leste* (for the period from 9 July 2008 to 20 January 2009), UN Doc. S/2009/72, 4 February 2009.
[78] The question of whether it is necessary will be addressed below.

they make use of incriminating evidence obtained under the powers of compulsion of another body in later trials.

It has been suggested that 'investigative authorities should be permitted to use [compelled truth commission testimony] ... to further investigations, provided that they can ultimately prove that the evidence offered at a future trial could reasonably have been discovered in the absence of the compelled testimony'.[79] However, the legality of such an action is dubious. National and regional courts have held that where self-incriminating evidence is obtained under the powers of compulsion of a body established by law, a category into which truth commissions fall, that evidence will not be admissible in subsequent criminal proceedings against the accused.[80] As in the East Timorese model, it would seem prudent to avoid such an eventuality and the potential damage to public perceptions of truth seeking and prosecutorial processes by coordinating the operations and capabilities of the two mechanisms in accordance with the priorities of the transitional justice model. However, Burgess questions whether even the system in place between the OGP and the CAVR may fall foul of due process principles.[81] He notes that the CRP process resulted in a situation where the OGP had access to all deponent statements on their involvement in past events, which they had made without legal advice. Although deponents were advised that statements could be used in prosecutions, they provided information in the belief that they would not be prosecuted, but reintegrated through CRP. Burgess believes that this system provides inadequate protection for participants and should be remedied in any similar future programmes.[82] Indeed, a sense of injustice arises where individuals are encouraged to confess their involvement in past crimes in order to participate in one process only to discover that they are not eligible for inclusion in that process and are to be prosecuted in relation to the crimes they have disclosed. As in the South African model, this points to the dangers of interlinking the operations of trials and truth commissions and suggests that these mechanisms should operate separately, without interconnected functions.

---

[79] Freeman, *Truth Commissions and Procedural Fairness*, 253.
[80] *Ferreira v. Levin and Others*, [1995] ZACC 13, Judgment of 6 December 1995; *Saunders v. UK* (Application No. 19187/91), Judgment of 17 December 1996, (1996) 23 EHRR 313.
[81] Patrick Burgess, 'East Timor's Community Reconciliation Process', in Naomi Roht-Arriaza and Javier Mariezcurrena (eds.), *Transitional Justice in the Twenty-First Century: Beyond Truth versus Justice* (Cambridge University Press, 2006), 176–205, 195–6.
[82] *Ibid.*, 196.

The East Timorese experience also highlights a fundamental tension between the operations of truth commissions and those of prosecutorial institutions. For a truth commission to operate at its optimum efficiency and to access all relevant information, it must be endowed with powers to grant confidentiality and compel the disclosure of incriminating evidence. However, if the integrity of the truth commission is to be maintained and fair trial standards safeguarded, this would necessitate the withholding of information from prosecutorial institutions. In this situation the prosecutorial institution would not have access to all available information and the pursuit of criminal justice could be compromised in favour of truth seeking. In contrast, as was the case in East Timor, if prosecutorial institutions are to be able to access all relevant testimony and information, truth commissions will be unable to grant confidentiality to witnesses and subpoena others to provide information. Thus, the optimal operation of one mechanism is at the expense of the other. At a time when prosecution has assumed a role of unrivalled importance within transitional justice practice and discourse, such a finding is significant. For states parties to the ICC Statute, and those party to some treaty regimes, prosecution for the most serious human rights crimes ought to be a national priority. If prioritisation is interpreted as requiring the availability of all information to prosecuting bodies, then the powers of any truth commission that is also established will have to be restricted accordingly. The East Timorese experience demonstrates that this will not necessarily result in the failure of the truth commission to fulfil its mandate. It does suggest, however, that there is potential in this era of accountability for the prioritisation and pursuit of criminal justice to undermine truth seeking by limiting the powers that truth commissions can be endowed with and thereby hampering their ability to obtain information.

4   Sierra Leone: an uncoordinated approach

The Sierra Leonean Truth and Reconciliation Commission (SLTRC) and the Special Court for Sierra Leone were not the result of one overarching plan to address the human rights violations committed during the civil war. The Commission emerged from the Lomé Peace Agreement of 1999.[83] The Special Court was not suggested until renewed fighting caused the government of Sierra Leone to reassess its position regarding the

---

[83] Peace Agreement between the Government of Sierra Leone and the Revolutionary United Front of Sierra Leone, Lomé, Togo, 7 July 1999.

amnesty granted at Lomé, a year later.[84] As a result of their independent establishment, the relationship between the SLTRC and the Special Court was not defined, either in the legislation creating the Commission[85] or in the agreement on the establishment of the Special Court.[86] UN bodies and NGOs formulated proposals on how the SLTRC and Special Court ought to interact [87] but no coordination agreement was ever drawn up. Neither the Commission nor the Special Court made any attempt to establish a working relationship. Despite their overlapping mandates,[88] both appeared to consider that it was important to maintain clear boundaries.[89]

Notwithstanding the attempts of the Special Court and Commission to emphasise a division between their roles, a general perception arose early in operations that information was shared between them. Their simultaneous operation and overlapping investigations meant that there was public confusion surrounding the distinction between the two.[90] Although

---

[84] *Fifth Report of the Secretary-General on the United Nations Mission in Sierra Leone*, S/2000/751, 31 July 2000, 2. For discussion of the background to the establishment of the TRC and Special Court and their bases of jurisdiction see Abdul Tejan-Cole, 'Complementary and Conflicting Relationship between the Special Court for Sierra Leone and the Truth and Reconciliation Commission' (2003) 6 *Yale Human Rights and Development Law Journal* 139.

[85] Sierra Leone: Truth and Reconciliation Commission Act 2000.

[86] Letter dated 6 March 2002 from the Secretary General addressed to the President of the Security Council, S/2002/246, 8 March 2002, Appendix II, Agreement between the United Nations and the Government of Sierra Leone on the Establishment of a Special Court for Sierra Leone.

[87] *Report of the Secretary-General on the Establishment of a Special Court for Sierra Leone*, UN Doc. S/2000/915, 4 October 2000, para. 8. See also Letter dated 12 January 2001 from the Secretary-General to the President of the Security Council, UN Doc. S/2001/40, at para. 9; UN Commission on Human Rights, *Report of the High Commissioner for Human Rights Pursuant to Commission on Human Rights Resolution 2001/20, Situation of Human Rights in Sierra Leone*, E/CN.4/2002/37, 18 February 2002, para. 70; Marieka Wierda, Priscilla B. Hayner, and Paul van Zyl, *Exploring the Relationship between the Special Court and the Truth and Reconciliation Commission of Sierra Leone*, International Center for Transitional Justice, New York, 24 June 2002, 4, 12–13; Human Rights Watch, *Policy Paper on the Interrelationship between the Sierra Leone Special Court and Truth and Reconciliation Commission*, 18 April 2002.

[88] Statute of the Special Court for Sierra Leone, Arts. 2–5; Truth and Reconciliation Commission Act 2000, s. 6.

[89] SLTRC, *Witness to Truth: Report of the Sierra Leone Truth and Reconciliation Commission* (Accra: Graphic Packaging Ltd, 2004), chapter 6 'The TRC and the Special Court for Sierra Leone', paras. 47–8. See also the interview with the Chief Investigator of the Special Court: 'Sierra Leone's Special Court: Will It Hinder or Help?', *All Africa News Service*, 21 November 2002; Schabas, 'The Relationship between Truth Commissions and International Courts', 1051.

[90] SLTRC, *Witness to Truth*, Chapter 6, paras. 52–8, and Weirda *et al.*, *Exploring the Relationship between the Special Court and the Truth and Reconciliation Commission of*

there was no information-sharing relationship, studies show that former perpetrators were inhibited from offering testimony to the Commission for fear that it would be passed to the Special Court.[91] They were fearful not only of their own prosecution but of being called to testify against commanders.[92] As a result, only a small percentage of the testimony received by the SLTRC came from former perpetrators.[93] Thus, contemporaneous operation in the Sierra Leonean context impeded the Commission's compilation of the broadest and most balanced account possible by excluding from its report the accounts of an important stakeholder group within the conflict.[94]

In practice, the most problematic aspect of the Sierra Leonean model stemmed from the failure to regulate the relationship between the Court and the Commission and coordinate their operations. Separate conception resulted in the creation of a truth commission and court with potentially conflicting powers. Unlike in East Timor, the powers of the truth commission were not designed to take account of its contemporaneous operation alongside a prosecutorial institution. The SLTRC was given powers to issue summonses and subpoenas,[95] interview any individual,[96] offer guarantees of confidentiality to witnesses and prevent the disclosure of information received confidentially.[97] The Court was given powers to issue binding orders to any natural person, corporation or other body, notwithstanding any other law.[98] These powers gave each institution the potential to encroach upon the work of the other. The SLTRC had, in theory, the ability to subpoena those subject to proceedings by the Court, compel them to answer questions under oath, in

Sierra Leone, 40–1. See also Tejan-Cole, 'Complementary and Conflicting Relationship between the Special Court for Sierra Leone and the Truth and Reconciliation Commission', 150–5, and Gearoid Millar, 'Assessing Local Experiences of Truth-Telling in Sierra Leone: Getting to "Why" through a Qualitative Case Study Analysis' (2010) 4 *International Journal of Transitional Justice* 477, 491.

[91] SLTRC, *Witness to Truth*, Chapter 6, para. 59; PRIDE, *Ex-Combatant Views of the Truth and Reconciliation Commission and the Special Court for Sierra Leone*, A Study in Partnership with the International Center for Transitional Justice, Freetown, 12 September 2002, 19.

[92] SLTRC, *Witness to Truth*; PRIDE, *Ex-Combatant Views of the Truth and Reconciliation Commission and the Special Court for Sierra Leone*.

[93] SLTRC, *Witness to Truth*, Appendix 1, Statistical Report at 3, Figure 4.A1.1b, Percent of Statement Givers by Source, Type and Sex.

[94] *Ibid.*, Chapter 6, para. 59.

[95] Sierra Leone: Truth and Reconciliation Commission Act 2000, s. 8.1(g).

[96] *Ibid.*, s. 8(1)(c).   [97] *Ibid.*, s. 7(3).

[98] Special Court Agreement (Ratification) Act 2002, s. 21(2).

private interviews, and maintain the confidentiality of any information provided. At the same time, the Court was empowered to issue orders to the Commission and to instruct it to disclose any information that it considered relevant to prosecutorial proceedings. The Court understood its status as superior, due to its power to issue orders regardless of the content of any other law.[99] The Commission never accepted that interpretation and considered itself an institution of equal standing.[100] The failure to regulate their relationship when operations began meant that they commenced proceedings without any operational coordination, in full possession of their respective powers and with the potential for conflict a live issue.

It seems naive to have assumed that institutions with extensive investigatory powers, overlapping mandates and requirements to access the same information and personnel could have operated simultaneously without one impacting the other. Predictably, conflict did arise when the SLTRC sought to exercise its powers to interview indictees awaiting trial by the Court. In response to a request from detainees to give testimony to the SLTRC, the Commission sought to hold confidential, private interviews, as provided by the TRC Act, with a small number of those indicted by the Court.[101] The Court, in accordance with its prosecutorial mandate, sought a means to access any information that might be relevant to investigations and future trials and to guard the fairness of proceedings. It adopted a Practice Direction stipulating that interviews were to be observed by legal officers,[102] recorded and transcribed[103] and made available to any party to the criminal proceedings upon order of the Presiding judge.[104] The SLTRC condemned this as 'dismissive of the spirit and purpose behind the [TRC]' and considered it at variance with its powers to

---

[99] *Prosecutor v. Samuel Hinga Norman* (Case No. SCSL-03-08-PT-122-I and II), Decision on Appeal by the Truth and Reconciliation Commission for Sierra Leone and Chief Samuel Hinga Norman JP against the Decision of his Lordship, Mr Justice Bankole Thompson to Deny the TRC's Request to Hold a Public Hearing with Chief Samuel Hinga Norman JP, Delivered on 30 October 2003, 28 November 2003, para. 4.

[100] SLTRC, *Witness to Truth*, chapter 6, para. 66. See also on this point, William A. Schabas, 'A Synergistic Relationship: The Sierra Leone Truth and Reconciliation Commission and the Special Court for Sierra Leone' (2004) 15 *Criminal Law Forum* 3, 36–9.

[101] Letter of 9 September 2003 from the Truth and Reconciliation Commission to the Registrar of the Special Court, Robin Vincent, cited in SLTRC, *Witness to Truth*, chapter 6, para. 87.

[102] Practice Direction on the procedure following a request by a State, the Truth and Reconciliation Commission, or other legitimate authority to take a statement from a person in the custody of the Special Court for Sierra Leone, adopted 9 September 2002.

[103] *Ibid.*, para. 8(b).   [104] *Ibid.*, para. 4(c).

conduct confidential interviews.[105] It changed tack and sought instead to hold public hearings, primarily with Sam Hinga Norman, former leader of the Civil Defence Forces.[106] The attempt to do so led to proceedings before the Special Court.[107]

The *Norman* case provides the only example to date of litigation on the competing interests of truth commissions and criminal trials.[108] Significantly, the refusal of both the trial and appeal chamber judges to allow a public hearing provides a precedent for the limitation of truth commission operations where they are perceived to threaten prosecutorial proceedings. The initial judgment of Justice Bankole Thompson held that the request to hold a public hearing with an indictee indicated the perceived centrality of his role in the conflict.[109] As only three categories of people could testify before the SLTRC – victims, perpetrators and other interested parties – it was clear that he was being invited to testify as a perpetrator. This, Bankole Thompson concluded, was inconsistent with the presumption of innocence.[110] He stated that where there are competing public interests, such as between the entitlement of accused persons to a fair and public trial and the establishment of a historical record of the conflict, the accused's right to a fair trial must always prevail.[111] The decision was upheld by Justice Robertson on appeal, but with the understanding that indictees could submit testimony in writing to the Commission.[112] The Appeal Court considered that public hearings would

---

[105] Letter of 9 September 2003 from the Truth and Reconciliation Commission to the Registrar of the Special Court, Robin Vincent.

[106] *Prosecutor* v. *Samuel Hinga Norman* (Case No. SCSL-03-08-PT-101), Decision on the Request by the Truth and Reconciliation Commission of Sierra Leone to Conduct a Public Hearing with Samuel Hinga Norman, 29 October 2003.

[107] On the Prosecutor's objections to public hearings see Inter-Office Memorandum of 21 October 2003 from Desmond de Silva QC, Deputy Prosecutor (on behalf of the Prosecutor) to Judge Bankole Thompson, Presiding Judge of the Trial Chamber, entitled: Samuel Hinga Norman and the TRC.

[108] For an analysis of the case see Neil Boister, 'Failing to Get to the Heart of the Matter in Sierra Leone? The Truth Commission is Denied Unrestricted Access to Chief Hinga Norman' (2004) 2 *Journal of International Criminal Justice* 1100.

[109] *Prosecutor* v. *Samuel Hinga Norman* (Case No. SCSL-03-08-PT-101), Decision on the Request by the Truth and Reconciliation Commission of Sierra Leone to Conduct a Public Hearing with Samuel Hinga Norman, 29 October 2003, para. 10.

[110] *Ibid.*, para. 12.   [111] *Ibid.*, para. 14.

[112] *Prosecutor* v. *Samuel Hinga Norman*, Decision on Appeal by the Truth and Reconciliation Commission for Sierra Leone and Chief Samuel Hinga Norman JP against the Decision of his Lordship, Mr Justice Bankole Thompson to Deny the TRC's Request to Hold a Public Hearing with Chief Samuel Hinga Norman JP, Delivered on 30 October 2003, 28 November 2003, para. 41.

be a 'spectacle' with the appearance of a trial, which might intimidate witnesses, rally dormant forces, have an adverse effect on public perceptions of the indictee's innocence and create anxiety among other indictees as to whether they too ought to give public testimony.[113] It would be dangerous due to the absence of procedural safeguards, the risk of making damaging admissions and the possibility of being condemned in advance by the SLTRC.[114] The Court additionally considered that the SLTRC hearings might create a public expectation that it would pass judgment on indictees, 'whose guilt or innocence it is the special duty of the … Court to determine'.[115]

It is difficult to argue with the Commission's conclusion that these judgments 'constitute poor contributions to the development of transitional justice arrangements in post-conflict societies'.[116] The Bankole Thompson judgment contributes nothing to the dilemmas of how to coordinate the different roles and aims of transitional justice mechanisms. Neither did it offer any solution on how to ease the tension between the Special Court and the Commission in the instant case. Justice Robertson's judgment reveals a simplistic understanding of the contribution of truth commissions to transitional states. He misunderstands the work of truth commissions in bringing about reconciliation,[117] overlooks the key component that perpetrator testimony constitutes in the establishment of a historical record and fails to recognise the need for the populace to feel ownership of the truth-seeking process for it to work most effectively.[118] The reasoning is indicative of a need for those working within transitional justice mechanisms to possess a comprehension of the work and role of other mechanisms.

Both judgments purport to be based on a need to protect the due process and fair trial rights of accused persons. Other than some broad assertions on the potential for self-incrimination, there is no analysis of how those rights would actually have been jeopardised either by the private interview or public hearing with the SLTRC.[119] However, it is difficult to

---

[113] *Ibid.*, para. 30.   [114] *Ibid.*, para. 17.   [115] *Ibid.*

[116] SLTRC, *Witness to Truth*, Chapter 6, para. 211.

[117] *Prosecutor v. Samuel Hinga Norman*, Decision on Appeal by the Truth and Reconciliation Commission for Sierra Leone and Chief Samuel Hinga Norman JP against the Decision of his Lordship, Mr Justice Bankole Thompson to Deny the TRC's Request to Hold a Public Hearing with Chief Samuel Hinga Norman JP, Delivered on 30 October 2003, 28 November 2003, para. 38.

[118] Michael Nesbitt, 'Lessons from the Sam Hinga Norman Decision of the Special Court for Sierra Leone: How Trials and Truth Commissions Can Co-Exist' (2007) 8 *German Law Journal* 977, 1006.

[119] Boister, 'Failing to Get to the Heart of the Matter in Sierra Leone?, 1116.

refute this contention. The participation of detainees in public hearings might have compromised subsequent Special Court proceedings by giving rise to challenges to the fairness of proceedings. As an institution established to bring to justice those who bear the greatest responsibility for the violations committed during the civil conflict, the Special Court had to guard against any potential prejudice of its proceedings. Moreover, both the SLTRC and the Special Court were established to combat impunity within Sierra Leone.[120] It was not, therefore, in the interests of either body that the prosecutions of those responsible for past violations should be compromised, let alone that this should be caused due to the operations of another transitional justice mechanism.

Disappointingly, the judgments do not seek to resolve the legislative tension between the SLTRC's right to obtain information from any person under guarantees of confidentiality and non-disclosure[121] and the Court's power to issue binding orders to all bodies.[122] The solution that detainees could participate in truth seeking only by transmitting information to the SLTRC in writing overlooks that the Commission was endowed in its enacting legislation with the discretion to decide the nature of hearings, whether private or public. These are issues that may well arise again in future transitional contexts as national and international courts and truth commissions seek to fulfil overlapping mandates. It is common practice for truth commissions to be endowed with non-disclosure and confidentiality powers and equally courts routinely possess authority to issue binding orders. The Special Court's judgments represent a wasted opportunity to explore these issues and inform future transitional justice practice.

Nevertheless, this case has created a precedent in international criminal law that permits the restriction of truth-seeking operations in favour of prosecutorial proceedings. The appeal decision, in particular, is founded upon an unquestioning assumption that trials should be prioritised over truth seeking because they render superior results for victims. Trials, Justice Robertson considers, provide the more effective criminal conviction while truth commissions have only the potential of truth and

---

[120] Sierra Leone: Truth and Reconciliation Commission Act 2000, Art. 6(1); Agreement between the United Nations and the Government of Sierra Leone on the Establishment of a Special Court for Sierra Leone, annexed to UN Security Council, Report of the Secretary-General on the Establishment of a Special Court for Sierra Leone, Preamble, para. 1.

[121] Sierra Leone: Truth and Reconciliation Commission Act 2000, Art. 7(3).

[122] Special Court Agreement (Ratification) Act 2002, Art. 21(2).

reconciliation.[123] This assumption is not based on empirical evidence but reflects the prevailing rhetoric on the superiority of trials in traditional transitional justice discourse. There is no attempt to evaluate the benefits of truth commissions, generally or in the Sierra Leonean context, or to engage in any meaningful consideration of how a compromise enabling effective coexistence might have been reached. It may well prove to be the case that truth commission operations have to be limited in favour of ensuring fair trials and due process for accused persons. However, such a conclusion should be reached after examination of all the facts and evaluation of all the interests. There must be consideration of the mandates and powers of truth commissions against those of criminal courts. The need to protect due process rights must be weighed against the need to respect rights to freedom of expression and participation in national truth seeking and against the rights of victims to know the truth. The assumption here is that where there is tension between the operations of a truth commission and criminal court, the truth commission should be compromised in favour of the more important prosecutorial proceedings. The legitimacy of that conclusion is unsubstantiated.

It seems unlikely that interviews, confidential or otherwise, with a small number of indictees of the Special Court would radically have altered the conclusions of the Commission. However, those indicted by the Court occupied positions of authority during the civil war and their input might have provided the SLTRC with unique insights into the conflict. The Court's refusal to allow the Commission to interview the indictees may, therefore, have resulted in important information being excluded from the Commission's investigations and may have led ultimately to the establishment of a narrower truth. In this sense, the Special Court may have undermined the truth commission's ability to operate to its optimum effectiveness.

The issues that arose between the SLTRC and the Special Court suggest that an agreement ought to have been drawn up regulating their relationship. The Commission itself suggested that the problems stemmed from their separate creation and subsequent mutual failure to harmonise their objectives. It concluded that the development of an operational model permitting the objectives of both bodies to be reached in a symbiotic

---

[123] *Prosecutor v. Samuel Hinga Norman*, Decision on Appeal by the Truth and Reconciliation Commission for Sierra Leone and Chief Samuel Hinga Norman JP against the Decision of his Lordship, Mr Justice Bankole Thompson to Deny the TRC's Request to Hold a Public Hearing with Chief Samuel Hinga Norman JP, Delivered on 30 October 2003, 28 November 2003, paras. 33–4.

manner was required,[124] but made no suggestions as to how this can be achieved. It might have been possible to avoid the conflict that arose by regulating the relationship between the two bodies from the outset. The issue was relatively minor and perhaps would have been avoided had there been an agreement in place which stated that: (a) the Commission could not have access to those indicted and awaiting trial by the Court; (b) the Commission could have access to detainees on the condition that any information obtained would be available to the Court; or (c) the Commission had the right to interview detainees on a confidential basis and that the information obtained would not be subject to disclosure. It has also been suggested that an agreement proscribing a division of labour between the TRC and the Special Court, with the TRC assigned to deal only with the 'small fish' and the 'big fish' being dealt with under the prosecutorial jurisdiction of the Special Court, might have avoided the conflict that ensued.[125] However, as Hayner notes, this is unworkable on an operational level and misunderstands the role of a truth commission. She argues convincingly that it would be 'nonsensical' for a commission to compile a record of the past without analysing the roles played by senior figures, as well as practically impossible to ignore them as their names will undoubtedly emerge from other testimony.[126]

The Sierra Leonean experience raises questions as to whether it is possible to regulate the relationship between a truth commission and a prosecutorial institution in a way that enables both bodies to operate to their maximum efficacy. It brings into sharp focus the tension between the powers that enable them to operate at their optimum and suggests that where they operate simultaneously, compromise will be needed on the part of at least one institution if operational conflict between the two is to be avoided. It also shows that where they operate contemporaneously, some perpetrators will be inhibited from offering testimony to the truth commission. This will impede the commission's ability to fulfil its mandate by obtaining perpetrator testimony and establishing the fullest version of the past. The lesson from Sierra Leone is an important one as it suggests that the very presence of a prosecutorial institution will undermine the

---

[124] SLTRC, *Witness to Truth*, Chapter 6, paras. 223–8.

[125] William A. Schabas, 'The Sierra Leone Truth and Reconciliation Commission', in Naomi Roht-Arriaza and Javier Mariezcurrena (eds.), *Transitional Justice in the Twenty-First Century: Beyond Truth versus Justice* (Cambridge University Press, 2006), 21–43, 37.

[126] Priscilla B. Hayner, *Unspeakable Truths: Transitional Justice and the Challenge of Truth Commissions* (2nd edn) (London and New York: Routledge, 2010), 111.

operations of the truth commission to some extent and casts doubt on whether these bodies can truly be considered complementary.

5 Lessons from past practice

The transitional justice models implemented in these states operated neither as unqualified successes or failures. In all three, truth commissions and prosecutorial institutions were able to coexist. Successful prosecutions of at least some past violations were carried out and, at the same time, truth commissions obtained sufficient information to compile reports and provide historical records of the conflicts for affected populations. However, all three models gave rise to operational problems, which should inform future approaches to contemporaneous trial and truth seeking programmes. Their combined experiences suggest that where truth seeking and trials are pursued simultaneously at the national level, the commission and prosecutorial body should operate as distinct but equal institutions, under a regulated relationship and without obligations that link their operations.

The South African experience cautions against the creation of interdependent truth commissions and trials. Using the threat of prosecution as the incentive for perpetrator participation in truth seeking and creating a commission with amnesty-granting powers judicialised the truth-seeking process. This gave rise to regular legal scrutiny before the courts and the imposition of cumbersome procedural requirements to ensure fairness. The adversarial process that resulted from adherence to procedural safeguards intimidated a number of victims, with the likely consequence that many were inhibited from offering testimony. The non-judicial status that often enables truth commissions to gain information from those reluctant to become involved in formal legal processes was undermined. Moreover, the ineffectiveness of the prosecution service in practice impacted negatively on truth seeking by failing to provide the necessary impetus for perpetrators to participate. Where truth seeking and prosecution are closely connected, the success of one will dictate that of the other. The experience of East Timor also counsels against creating closely interconnected truth commissions and prosecutorial institutions. There, creating a Commission with an obligation to refer cases to the Prosecutor limited the truth-seeking powers it could be given and impinged upon the effectiveness of the Community Reconciliation Process. The absence of powers to compel the provision of incriminating information and guarantee confidentiality hampered the Commission's ability to access testimony from both perpetrators and vulnerable victims and witnesses and, ultimately, to fulfil its mandate.

Future commissions and prosecutorial institutions should be created as separate entities, on an equal footing, in recognition of the unique benefits brought to transitional states by each mechanism. The South African and East Timorese models demonstrate that where one mechanism is adopted as the central means of responding to the past, the other is forced to occupy a subsidiary role and operate as a means of bolstering that primary objective. In South Africa, prosecution was a means of incentivising truth seeking and in East Timor the commission was a contributor to the prosecutorial strategy. Naturally, the work of trials and commissions may overlap and contribute to that of the other. The end product of truth seeking may be of use in subsequent trials and the judgments of prosecutorial institutions may enhance national understanding of the past. Both promote accountability. At base level, however, trials and truth commissions have very different roles to play in transitional states. This ought to be reflected in transitional programme design through the creation of equally resourced and robustly equipped institutions. Truth commissions should not be used as a means of furthering prosecutorial investigations and prosecution should not operate as the impetus for perpetrators to participate in truth seeking. Truth commissions should operate with the primary objective of investigating the past and producing an accessible account of it for affected populations. Prosecutorial institutions should have as their focus the prosecution of past crimes. This will ensure the best possibility of transitional states benefiting from the merits of the effective operation of both mechanisms. Equal resourcing does not require that all available resources be divided strictly in half between the commission and prosecutorial body. Carrying out effective prosecutions is likely to be far more financially costly than the operation of a truth commission. It does require, however, that one body is not resourced at the expense of the other.

While the experiences of South Africa and East Timor sound a warning for the creation of interlinked and heavily regulated relationships between truth commissions and prosecutorial institutions, Sierra Leone demonstrates the problems of a lack of regulation. It suggests that the relationship between prosecutorial bodies and commissions should be regulated prior to the commencement of operations. Regulation should have the aim of promoting effective coexistence and ensuring that the operations of one do not undermine those of the other. In order to avoid conflict such as that which arose between the SLTRC and the Special Court, the regulating agreement should prohibit the exercise of truth-seeking powers to obtain testimony from persons indicted by prosecutorial institutions. This will necessitate the loss of some testimony from the truth-seeking process. However, the risk that the involvement of indictees in truth commission proceedings might prejudice the fairness or credibility of future prosecutions must be guarded against.

Equally, commissions should not be under obligations to pass information to prosecutorial bodies and neither should truth commission information be accessible to them. East Timor's experience suggests that the CAVR would have operated more efficiently alongside the prosecutorial institutions had it not been under an obligation to refer information to the prosecutor. There is no necessity for a truth commission to be under an obligation to pass information to national prosecutorial institutions, which are endowed with significant investigatory powers and resources of their own. In both South Africa and Sierra Leone, the disclosure of truth commission information was prohibited. The prosecutorial institutions never sought to access it and did not appear to suffer any direct detriment as a result, although the South African prosecuting authorities expressed frustration at their inability to access it. In any event, the limited benefit that prosecutorial bodies might gain through accessing truth commission information is outweighed by the potential damage to the truth-seeking process should commissions become perceived as investigative arms of prosecutorial bodies. In addition, if there is no obligation for a commission to pass information to a prosecutorial institution and no possibility of information being accessed, this will enable commissions to be endowed with truth-seeking powers of compulsion of testimony and granting confidentiality to maximise the amount of information available in the truth-building process.

Prohibiting the flow of information between commissions and prosecutorial institutions will not dispel all problems, particularly the difficulties truth commissions face in gaining perpetrator testimony. In Sierra Leone, despite the lack of information sharing, the TRC's ability to grant confidentiality, and the Court's focus on only those most responsible for past violations, many perpetrators were reluctant to testify for fear that their information would be passed to the Special Court. It may be that for a myriad of reasons there will be reluctance among perpetrators to offer testimony to a truth commission. The South African experience suggests that the willingness of perpetrators to engage in truth seeking is complex.[127] There, although amnesty was available to perpetrators who made full disclosure of politically motivated crimes, and the passing of TRC information to courts was prohibited, the TRC encountered problems in gaining perpetrator testimony. The Sierra Leonean and East Timorese experiences suggest, however, that inhibition will be increased where there is an information-sharing relationship, or the perception of one, between a commission and a prosecutorial institution and therefore strengthen the argument that they should operate as distinct institutions and should not share information.

Finally, the regulating agreement should make provision for an independent third party to resolve any conflict that arises. The situation that occurred in Sierra Leone, where the Court determined the outcome of the dispute, is unsatisfactory. It is impossible for one transitional justice mechanism to undertake an objective evaluation on an issue in which its powers are challenged and proceedings threatened. Recourse to a neutral and impartial body should be available for the resolution of any emerging conflict.

6   Conclusion

In order for truth commissions and prosecutorial institutions to coexist effectively at the national level, without the work of one undermining that of the other, compromise will be needed on both sides. Ultimately, the contemporaneous operation of these bodies might bring complementary benefits to transitional states, but their overlapping mandates, dependence on the same information and personnel and differing modes of operation can create difficulties in practice. The experiences of South Africa, East Timor and Sierra Leone demonstrate that the extent of these problems can be either exacerbated or minimised by the nature of the relationship implemented between them. States will have to consider carefully how these bodies should cooperate and interact when designing future transitional justice programmes. The temptation to create weak and subordinate truth commissions in an effort to carry out successful prosecutions in accordance with treaty obligations and the ICC rationale should be resisted. A commitment to accountability should not, and need not, require the sacrifice of effective national truth commissions and the important role they play in transitional societies.

---

[127] Pedain, 'Was Amnesty a Lottery?', 813–14.

Of course, the discussion above relates only to domestic-level truth commissions and prosecutions. Where these bodies are established as part of a multifaceted, national level response to past violations, their contemporaneous operation, although not without difficulty, will be much easier to coordinate. Entirely different and more complex challenges are presented by the possibility of prosecution by an international court or a third party state exercising extra-territorial jurisdiction. The remaining sections of this book examine these situations and their likely impact on the realisation of effective truth seeking and successful prosecution.

4

Coordinating truth commissions
and ICC operations

1 Introduction

The ICC Statute is silent on the issue of national truth commissions. Their status under this new prosecutorial regime is unclear and the treatment they are likely to receive uncertain. The Court's proceedings in Kenya represent the first occasion on which it has assumed jurisdiction in a situation that has been or is being investigated by a truth commission.[1] As yet, there has been no interaction between the two and the ICC has given no indication as to how it will treat truth commission operations or information. There is little past practice to inform the Court. The ICTY and ICTR have not had to deal with the contemporaneous operation of truth commissions in the territories under their jurisdiction. No truth commission has been established in Rwanda and the attempts to create commissions in the former Yugoslav states never gave rise to effectively functioning institutions.[2] To date, the Special Court for Sierra Leone remains the only international criminal tribunal that has had to coordinate its operations with those of a contemporaneous truth commission. There, the Prosecutor made clear from the outset that he would respect the autonomy of the TRC and would not seek to access its materials.[3] Whether the ICC will follow this practice remains unknown. Certainly, the Court has not intimated that it intends to adopt this approach.

---

[1] Although a truth commission was established in the Democratic Republic of Congo following the referral of the situation in the DRC to the ICC, the ongoing instability in the country coupled with political interference meant that the truth commission has been unable to operate. As such, the operations of the ICC have not come into contact with those of the planned truth commission.

[2] Neil J. Kritz and Jakob Finci, 'A Truth and Reconciliation Commission in Bosnia and Herzegovina: An Idea Whose Time Has Come' (2001) 3 *International Law Forum* 50; Jelena Pejic, 'The Yugoslav Truth and Reconciliation Commission: A Shaky Start' (2001–2002) 25 *Fordham International Law Journal* 1.

[3] See Chapter 3.

As an international institution, the ICC faces challenges in gaining access to the evidence necessary to discharge its prosecutorial mandate and often has to rely on the information gathered by bodies working on the territory of the state in question.[4] The information collected by a truth commission, and the details of those who provided testimony, may prove of interest to the Court during the course of its investigations and as it builds prosecution cases. However, the prospect of information sharing, while it might prove advantageous to the Court, poses a dilemma for truth commission-holding states. Passing information to a prosecutorial institution could undermine a commission's status as a non-judicial body. Truth commission materials are, additionally, frequently protected from disclosure under domestic legislation and passing them to the Court would require a state to contravene its national law. Nevertheless, the obligatory framework of the ICC Statute appears to make it possible for the Court to require states parties to disclose truth commission information where it is deemed relevant to ICC proceedings. Whether the Court will consider information sharing a means of complementary working, in line with the Office of the Prosecutor (OTP) Policy Paper of 2007,[5] or an unnecessarily invasive strategy in its attempts to fulfil its judicial mandate is unknown. Even the potential exercise of the Court's powers seems likely to impact negatively on the truth-seeking process by inhibiting participation among those who fear involvement in criminal proceedings. It also brings into doubt the compatibility of the exercise of quasi-judicial, truth-seeking powers with ICC orders to disclose information obtained through their use.

This chapter will consider the status of truth commissions under the ICC framework and the potential impact of the ICC cooperation regime upon their operation. It will identify and explore areas of difficulty between commissions and the ICC, focusing particularly on the position of confidential and self-incriminating truth commission materials before the Court. It will demonstrate a potential disharmony between the interests of commissions and those of the Court and show that truth commission powers to grant confidentiality and compel the provision of self-incriminating information may now create conflict situations with the ICC. It will argue that under the current ICC framework, truth

---

[4] Heikelina Verrijn Stuart, 'The ICC in Trouble. Editorial Comment on Stay of Proceedings in Lubanga' (2008) 6 *Journal of International Criminal Justice* 409, 414–15.

[5] ICC, Office of the Prosecutor, *Policy Paper on the Interests of Justice*, September 2007, ICC-OTP-2007, 8.

commissions and the Court can only operate as complements if commissions forego these powers, and the information their exercise yields, in order to avoid requests for disclosure from the ICC.

2   The status of truth commissions under the ICC Statute

The Statute's silence on truth commissions has attracted much scholarly attention. Commentators have deliberated on the place of truth commissions within this new model in light of the provisions of the Statute and the objectives of the Court. It is recorded that national amnesties were discussed by the Preparatory Committee in the context of *ne bis in idem*.[6] However, the Court's relationship with future truth commissions does not appear to have received direct consideration either by the Preparatory Committee or the Rome Conference.[7] This might be explained by the perceived links between truth commissions and amnesty laws at the time of drafting. In June 1998, as the Rome Conference began, South Africa's truth for amnesty process was underway,[8] Guatemala had recently passed an amnesty for human rights crimes and simultaneously established a truth commission[9] and Argentina, Chile and El Salvador had passed controversial sweeping amnesty laws and established truth commissions some years earlier.[10] Truth commissions, such as those of East Timor and Sierra Leone, which operated as complements to prosecution, had not begun to be established. It is therefore possible that truth commissions were viewed as being synonymous with national amnesties and undeserving of independent consideration. However, the suggestion that the Statute's silence on truth commissions is due not to oversight, but a result of irreconcilable, opposing views on how the Court ought to deal with truth

---

[6] *Report of the Preparatory Committee on the Establishment of an International Criminal Court*, vol. 1, p. 40, para. 174 (Proceedings of the Preparatory Committee during March–April and August 1996) GAOR, 51st Sess., Suppl. No. 22 (A/51/22); A/CONF.283/2/Add.1 of 14 April 1998, Art. 19.

[7] See Priscilla B. Hayner, *Unspeakable Truths: Facing the Challenge of Truth Commissions* (New York: Routledge, 2001), 206; John Dugard, 'Possible Conflicts of Jurisdiction with Truth Commissions', in Antonio Cassese, Paulo Gaeta and John R. W. D. Jones (eds.), *The Rome Statute of the International Criminal Court: A Commentary*, 2 vols. (Oxford University Press, 2002), vol. 1, Chapter 18.3, 700.

[8] For a discussion of this process see Kader Asmal, 'Truth, Reconciliation and Justice: The South African Experience in Perspective' (2000) 63 *Modern Law Review* 10.

[9] Ley de Reconciliación Nacional, Decreto No. 145–1996, 18 December 1996.

[10] See Naomi Roht-Arriaza and Lauren Gibson, 'The Developing Jurisprudence on Amnesty' (1998) 20 *Human Rights Quarterly* 843.

and reconciliation efforts,[11] has given rise to considerable speculation. One commentator questions whether the drafters deliberately chose not to codify a comprehensive test to distinguish between acceptable and unacceptable reconciliation measures.[12] Others have wondered whether the provisions of the Rome Statute, particularly Articles 16, 17, 20 and 53, reflect an element of ambiguity that may allow the ICC to defer to national non-prosecutorial programmes.[13]

This author's view that the operation of a truth commission will not render a case inadmissible before the Court under Article 17 is articulated in Chapter 2. It benefits from the direction given by the Trial Chamber's recent admissibility decision on the Kenyan situation. Article 17 is, however, only one of the avenues suggested as a possible means of enabling the ICC to defer to national commissions. It is also argued that where the Security Council has determined that the situation within a particular country amounts to a threat to international peace and security, it may use its Chapter VII and Article 16 powers to temporarily bar investigations or prosecutions by the ICC in order to allow for a national reconciliation process, such as a truth commission.[14] Such an eventuality is not inconceivable. However, the Security Council's reluctance to consider using its powers to delay proceedings in relation to the *Al Bashir* case in the interests of peace and stability in Sudan may suggest that Article 16 will only be used in quite exceptional circumstances.[15] In addition, Article 16 is a temporary device, designed only to delay proceedings by the Court for a period of twelve months to enable the Security Council to coordinate

---

[11] Darryl Robinson, 'Serving the Interests of Justice: Amnesties, Truth Commissions and the International Criminal Court' (2003) 14 *European Journal of International Law* 481, 483; Ruth Wedgwood, 'The International Criminal Court: An American View' (1999) 10 *European Journal of International Law* 93; Mahnoush H. Arsanjani, 'Reflections on the Jurisdiction and Trigger Mechanisms of the ICC', in Herman A. M. von Hebel, Johann G. Lammers and Jolien Schukking (eds.), *Reflections on the International Criminal Court: Essays in Honour of Adriaan Bos* (The Hague: T. M. C. Asser Press, 1999), 57–77, 75.

[12] Robinson, 'Serving the Interests of Justice', 483.

[13] Michael P. Scharf, 'The Amnesty Exception to the Jurisdiction of the International Criminal Court' (1999) 32 *Cornell International Law Journal* 507, 522; Dugard, 'Possible Conflicts of Jurisdiction with Truth Commissions', 701–2.

[14] Scharf, 'The Amnesty Exception to the Jurisdiction of the International Criminal Court', 522.

[15] African Union, Press Release No 119/2010 on the Decision of the Pre-Trial Chamber of the ICC Informing the UN Security Council and the Assembly of States Parties to the Rome Statute about the Presence of President Omar Hassan Al Bashir of the Sudan on the Territories of the Republic of Chad and the Republic of Kenya, Addis Ababa, 29 August 2010.

prosecutions with other measures it may take to restore and maintain peace.[16] The power is not intended as a means by which the Security Council can permanently prevent proceedings by the ICC.[17] Such a power would run contrary to the spirit and purpose of the Statute, by essentially perpetuating a culture of impunity rather than combating it. Thus, even if it is possible to use Article 16 to defer investigations and prosecutions while a truth commission takes place, the truth commission would not be operating as a permanent alternative to criminal prosecutions, as trials would be likely to follow the expiration of the twelve-month period from the date of deferral.

Article 20, which codifies the *ne bis in idem* principle, is another means by which it has been suggested that ICC proceedings might be deferred in favour of the operation of a national truth commission.[18] It is argued that appearance and confession before a truth commission and any attendant penalties could be equivalent to having been tried and convicted, rendering trial before the ICC for the same offence a contravention of that Article.[19] Consideration of the wording and purpose of Article 20, and of the Statute itself, suggests that the protection of the *ne bis in idem* principle will not attach to those who have confessed before national truth commissions. Article 20 is replete with references to formal criminal proceedings. It refers repeatedly to trial by another 'court' and prohibits retrial only where the person concerned has been 'convicted' or 'acquitted' by another court or by the ICC for the same conduct. Truth commissions carry out investigations into many of the crimes that fall within the jurisdiction of the ICC and may in some cases make findings of individual responsibility, although their findings do not have judicial effect. They do not, however, have the power to try, convict or acquit any person for the crimes within the Statute and they cannot impose either criminal or civil penalties. The non-judicial status of commissions therefore makes it unlikely that their proceedings will be considered equivalent to those of criminal courts for the purposes of Article 20.

[16] Luigi Condorelli and Santiago Villalpando, 'Referral and Deferral by the Security Council', in Antonio Cassese, Paulo Gaeta and John R. W. D. Jones (eds.), *The Rome Statute of the International Criminal Court: A Commentary*, 2 vols. (Oxford University Press, 2002), 627–55, 628.

[17] *Ibid.*, 648–9. See also Antonio Cassese, 'The Statute of the International Criminal Court: Some Preliminary Reflections' (1999) 10 *European Journal of International Law* 144, 163–4.

[18] Robinson, 'Serving the Interests of Justice', 499; Scharf, 'The Amnesty Exception to the Jurisdiction of the International Criminal Court', 525.

[19] Scharf, 'The Amnesty Exception to the Jurisdiction of the International Criminal Court', 150.

In addition, Article 20(3) limits the *ne bis in idem* principle in certain situations. Where the ICC determines that national proceedings were conducted for the purpose of shielding the person concerned from international criminal responsibility, were not conducted independently or impartially or were inconsistent with an intent to bring the person concerned to justice, retrial by the Court is permitted. This provides a safeguard against national 'sham' trials and indicates that national proceedings that fall short of independent and impartial trials held with a view to assigning individual criminal responsibility will not attract *ne bis in idem* protection.[20] It is consequently improbable that those who confess before truth commissions will escape prosecution by the ICC on the grounds of *ne bis in idem*. Moreover, it is notable that although a number of commentators have questioned whether Article 20 might provide a means by which a state could hold a truth commission instead of pursuing criminal prosecutions, this provision has received much less consideration than Articles 16 and 17 in this context.[21] While it is acknowledged that Article 20 may, in theory, provide states with a possible means of establishing a truth commission as an alternative to prosecutions, it appears to be accepted that this is improbable.[22]

Article 53 is the final route by which it is advanced that the ICC may defer to non-prosecutorial programmes within states.[23] This Article gives the Prosecutor discretion to decide whether to initiate an investigation,[24] based on a reasonable belief that an ICC crime has or is being committed,[25] the admissibility of the case under Article 17,[26] and the existence of substantial reasons to believe that an investigation or prosecution would not serve the interests of justice.[27] It is this final criterion that arguably may enable the Prosecutor to defer to national truth commission initiatives.

[20] For discussion see Linda E. Carter, 'The Principle of Complementarity and the International Criminal Court: The Role of Ne Bis in Idem' (2010) 8 *Santa Clara Journal of International Law* 165.

[21] See Jessica Gavron, 'Amnesties in the Light of Developments in International Law and the Establishment of the International Criminal Court' (2002) 51 *International and Comparative Law Quarterly* 91; Robinson, 'Serving the Interests of Justice', 499; Scharf, 'The Amnesty Exception to the Jurisdiction of the International Criminal Court', 525.

[22] Gavron, 'Amnesties in the Light of Developments in International Law and the Establishment of the International Criminal Court'; Robinson, 'Serving the Interests of Justice'.

[23] Carsten Stahn, 'Complementarity, Amnesties and Alternative Forms of Justice: Some Interpretive Guidelines for the International Criminal Court' (2005) 3 *Journal of International Criminal Justice* 695, 717; Gavron, 'Amnesties in the Light of Developments in International Law', 110; Robinson, 'Serving the Interests of Justice', 488.

[24] Rome Statute, Art. 53(1).   [25] Rome Statute, Art. 53(1)(a).

[26] Rome Statute, Art. 53(1)(b).   [27] Rome Statute, Art. 53(1)(c) and (2)(c).

In determining whether there are reasons to believe that ICC proceedings would not serve the interests of justice, he must take into account the gravity of the crime and the interests of victims,[28] the age or infirmity of the alleged perpetrator and his or her role in the alleged crime.[29] It is this juxtaposition of traditionally retributive considerations, such as gravity and victims' interests, with the broader concept of the 'interests of justice' that has led to the argument that in some circumstances the 'interests of justice' might be served by mechanisms other than criminal trials.[30] Some have suggested that this provision may enable the ICC to defer to national truth commission initiatives where pursuing prosecutions seems likely to prolong the commission of human rights violations and act as an impediment to peace.[31] It has been countered, however, that the terms of Article 53 are precise in the way that they link the notion of the interests of justice to specific parameters, such as the gravity of the crime, the interests of victims and the age or infirmity of the alleged perpetrator.[32] It is therefore considered that the notion of the interests of justice is linked to justice in a specific case rather than wider policy considerations and that Article 53 does not permit the weighing of general interests of national reconciliation against those of individual accountability.[33] Moreover, it has been argued that the ICC's objectives of ending impunity for the most serious crimes and ensuring that such crimes will not go unpunished but be prosecuted effectively,[34] demonstrate that the drafters of the Rome Statute made a clear choice in favour of prosecution over amnesty and truth commissions.[35]

---

[28] *Ibid.*

[29] Rome Statute, Art. 53(2)(c). The Prosecutor's discretion is not unfettered and decisions are subject to review by the Pre-Trial Camber under Art. 53(3)(b).

[30] Robinson, 'Serving the Interests of Justice', 488.

[31] Thomas Hethe Clark, 'The Prosecutor of the International Criminal Court, Amnesties and the "Interests of Justice": Striking A Delicate Balance' (2005) 4 *Washington University Global Studies Law Review* 389, 409–10; Declan Roche, 'Truth Commission Amnesties and the International Criminal Court' (2005) 45 *British Journal of Criminology* 565; Charles Villa-Vicencio, 'Why Perpetrators Should Not Always Be Prosecuted: Where the International Criminal Court and Truth Commissions Meet' (2000) 39 *Emory Law Journal* 205, 221.

[32] Stahn, 'Complementarity, Amnesties and Alternative Forms of Justice', 718.

[33] *Ibid.* See also Gavron, 'Amnesties in the Light of Developments in International Law', 110.

[34] Rome Statute, Preamble, paras. 4–5.

[35] Hector Olásolo, 'The Triggering Procedure of the International Criminal Court: Procedural Treatment of the Principle of Complementarity and the Role of the Office of the Prosecutor' (2004) 5 *International Criminal Law Review* 121, 136–44.

The ICC's statements and activities to date support the latter position. The *Policy Paper on the Interests of Justice*, issued by the OTP in September 2007, draws a distinction between the interests of justice and the interests of peace, emphasising that the latter falls within the mandate of institutions other than the OTP.[36] Consistent with this policy, the ICC stood firm in its commitment to criminal justice when Lord's Resistance Army (LRA) rebels refused to agree a peace deal with the Government of Uganda unless ICC arrest warrants were withdrawn in 2008.[37] Similarly, the Court has continued its proceedings relating to the situation in Darfur, despite opposition from the African Union, which argues that these activities threaten peace and stability within Sudan.[38] The Policy Paper does not attempt to lay down situations in which an investigation or prosecution would not serve the interests of justice. However, it makes clear that any national political or security initiative must be compatible with the ICC Statute framework.[39] National initiatives that do not ensure the effective prosecution of 'the most serious crimes of concern to the international community'[40] therefore seem unlikely to be acceptable. This would explain why the operation of the Kenyan truth commission and low-level national prosecutions have not prevented the initiation of proceedings by the Court. Indeed, the Paper emphasises that there is a presumption in favour of prosecution where cases are admissible and the standard of proof can be satisfied. Prosecutorial discretion is guided by the objects and purposes of the Statute, namely the prevention of the most serious human rights violations through ending impunity.[41] Thus, where the crimes within the Statute have been committed, criminal trials of those responsible will be required either at the national level or by the ICC itself. National programmes that forego trials in favour of promoting peace through the establishment of truth commissions or other mechanisms are unlikely to prevent the exercise of jurisdiction by the ICC under Article 53 on the grounds that it is not in the interests of justice to pursue prosecution.

---

[36] ICC, Office of the Prosecutor, *Policy Paper on the Interests of Justice*, 1.

[37] Bogonko Bosire, 'ICC Rules out Lifting Ugandan Rebels' Arrest Warrants', Agence France Presse, 22 November 2007; Emma Thomasson, 'Ugandan Rebel Lawyers to Meet with War Crimes Court', Reuters, 10 March 2008; Katy Glassborow and Peter Eichstaedt, 'Ugandan Rebels to Appeal ICC Warrants', Institute for War and Peace Reporting, 12 March 2008.

[38] African Union, Communique on the 3 February 2010 Judgment of the International Criminal Court Appeals Chamber on Darfur, Addis Ababa, 4 February 2010.

[39] ICC, Office of the Prosecutor, *Policy Paper on the Interests of Justice*, 4.

[40] Rome Statute, Preamble, para. 4.   [41] *Ibid.*, paras. 4–5.

The Policy Paper is additionally instructive in its elaboration of the OTP's view of the relationship between the operations of the ICC and those of other transitional justice mechanisms. The Paper notes the need to integrate different approaches and endorses the role that other transitional justice mechanisms, including truth commissions, play in transitional states.[42] It states that the OTP will 'seek to work constructively with and respect the mandates of [other transitional justice bodies] but will pursue its own judicial mandate independently'.[43] Of key importance, however, is the OTP's view that the role played by these mechanisms ought to be *complementary* to that fulfilled by the ICC.[44] Thus, the Paper envisages a future in which a range of initiatives will be implemented in transitional states to respond to past violations. These initiatives, however, must act as a complement to prosecution, not as an alternative to it. From this, it can be concluded that the OTP does not foresee situations in which national truth commissions will operate as an alternative to trials. Rather, prosecution will form an essential component of every transition where the most serious crimes have been committed. The operation of national truth commissions may form an additional component of that transition, but can only ever act as a complement to the trials, which will be the primary response to the commission of the most serious crimes.

3 Truth commissions and the obligations to cooperate and provide assistance to the ICC

Operation as a complement to ICC prosecutions presents a number of challenges for truth commissions, due to the powers of the Court and the obligations imposed on states parties under the Statute to provide assistance in investigations and prosecutions. These powers and obligations appear to enable the Court to obtain almost any form of assistance from its states parties and to attain from them any information deemed relevant to ICC proceedings, including, presumably, that held by national truth commissions. This seems to be the case regardless of the protection from disclosure that some truth commission information may be afforded under national law[45] and the damage that may be done to the non-judicial status of truth commissions if they are used as investigative tools for the ICC.

---

[42] ICC, Office of the Prosecutor, *Policy Paper on the Interests of Justice*, 7–8.
[43] *Ibid.*, 8.   [44] *Ibid.* Emphasis added.   [45] See below.

Cooperation by states parties is required in two main areas: arrest and surrender of persons to the Court[46] and the provision of other forms of assistance that the Court may require in conducting investigations and prosecutions.[47] States parties are required to 'ensure that there are procedures available under their national law for all the forms of cooperation' specified in Part 9 of the Statute.[48] Reservations to the Statute are not permitted.[49] The forms of assistance are listed in Article 93 and include: identifying and locating persons;[50] taking and producing evidence;[51] questioning of persons;[52] serving documents;[53] facilitating the appearance of witnesses and experts;[54] examining sites;[55] executing searches;[56] providing records and documents;[57] protecting victims and witnesses[58] and freezing the proceeds of crime.[59]

It seems that under Article 93(1) truth commission materials, as those of a state institution,[60] will be accessible by the Court, notwithstanding their status under domestic law. A state party may find itself under an obligation to provide records or documents held by its national truth commission to the ICC should the Court consider that the information within them is relevant to an investigation or prosecution. This obligation could extend to non-states parties should the Security Council use its power to refer a situation to the Court under Chapter VII of the UN Charter. Thereafter, all states as members of the UN could be under an obligation to cooperate with the ICC.[61] The Court's jurisdiction may therefore reach

---

[46] Rome Statute, Arts. 89–92 and Arts. 101–102. Surrender is a process distinct from extradition and traditional grounds for refusal of extradition are not legitimate reasons for failure to surrender to the ICC under Art. 102(a) and (b). Under Art. 91(2)(c) national procedures are required to be less burdensome than those used for extradition between states. On the process of surrender see Luisa Vierucci, 'The European Arrest Warrant: An Additional Tool for Prosecuting ICC Crimes' (2004) 2 *Journal of International Criminal Justice* 275, 279; Goran Sluiter, 'The Surrender of War Criminals to the International Criminal Court' (2003) 25 *Loyola of Los Angeles International and Comparative Law Review* 605.

[47] Rome Statute, Arts. 93–96 and Art. 99.   [48] Rome Statute, Art. 88.

[49] Rome Statute, Art. 120.   [50] Rome Statute, Art. 93(1)(a).

[51] Rome Statute, Art. 93(1)(b).   [52] Rome Statute, Art. 93(1)(c).

[53] Rome Statute, Art. 93(1)(d).   [54] Rome Statute, Art. 93(1)(e).

[55] Rome Statute, Art. 93(1)(g).   [56] Rome Statute, Art. 93(1)(h).

[57] Rome Statute, Art. 93(1)(i).   [58] Rome Statute, Art. 93(1)(j).

[59] Rome Statute, Art. 93(1)(k).

[60] See Chapter 1 on the definition of truth commissions as institutions of the state in which they are established.

[61] See Guiseppe Nesi, 'The Obligation to Cooperate with the International Criminal Court and States Not Party to the Statute', in Mauro Polit and Guiseppe Nesi (eds.), *The International Criminal Court: A Challenge to Impunity* (Aldershot: Ashgate, 2001), 222.

beyond the territory of its states parties, bringing it into conflict with non-state party truth commissions. Although some states have implemented Article 93(1) subject to a proviso that assistance will be provided as long as it is not prohibited by national law,[62] the Statute itself does not permit refusal of assistance on this ground. The Statute requires that the national laws of states parties enable all forms of cooperation.[63] General treaty law stipulates that conflicting national laws are not a ground for failure to perform treaty obligations[64] and so prohibitive domestic provisions will not justify the refusal of assistance to the Court. Truth commission materials cannot therefore be kept from the ICC due to protective national laws that prevent their disclosure.

The grounds on which requests for the provision of assistance may be refused are limited. First, any type of assistance that is not listed in Article 93(1)(a–k) must only be provided if it 'is not prohibited by the law of the requested state'.[65] The form of assistance most likely to be requested by the ICC in relation to a truth commission is the provision of information held by the commission. The request is therefore likely to be made under Article 93(1)(i) and involve the production of records and documents. This rules out the refusal of assistance under Article 93(1)(l) as the requested type of assistance will be listed within the Statute.

A request for assistance may also be refused if it concerns the production of documents or disclosure of evidence that relates to a state's national security.[66] The ICC Statute does not define what is meant by a state's 'national security interests'.[67] It is suggested, however, that the term

See also Goran Sluiter, 'Cooperation of States with International Criminal Tribunals', in Antonio Cassese (ed.), *The Oxford Companion to International Criminal Justice* (Oxford University Press, 2009), 187–200, 193 on the doubt in this area following Security Council Resolution 1593 (2005) on the referral of the situation in Sudan to the ICC.

[62] Swiss Federal Law on Cooperation with the International Criminal Court, Art. 30; Belgian Act of 29 March 2004 on Cooperation with the International Court and the International Criminal Tribunals, Art. 22.

[63] Rome Statute, Art. 88.

[64] See also Art. 27 of the Vienna Convention on the Law of Treaties, 1969, 1155 UNTS 331, which states that, 'a party may not invoke the provisions of its internal law as justification for its failure to perform a treaty'.

[65] Rome Statute, Art. 93(1)(l).   [66] Rome Statute, Art. 93(4).

[67] Otto Triffterer, 'Security Interests of the Community of States, Basis and Justification of an International Criminal Jurisdiction versus "Protection of National Security Information", Article 72 Rome Statute', in Herwig Roggerman and Petar Sarcevic (eds.), *National Security and International Criminal Justice* (Dordrecht: Kluwer, 2002) 53–82, 58.

includes more than simply military and defence concerns and extends to encompass sovereignty, independence, structure and/or the protection of inhabitants.[68] It is therefore possible that a truth commission might hold information that could be construed as pertinent to national security given the flexibility of the term and the breadth of sources from where such information might be gleaned. Particular aspects of truth commission work have the potential to render them privy to national security information. Some commissions have been endowed with powers of search and seizure and the authority to compel the provision of information, including records and documents of government authorities.[69] Boraine notes that the South African TRC often exercised its powers of search and seizure to access state department records, particularly those of the South African Defence Force.[70] Commissions may also access information relating to national security through interviews with members of the military, government and security forces. In practice, however, most commissions have encountered significant obstacles in attempting to access information from state institutions. It is common for outgoing regimes to destroy documentary evidence before leaving office, creating a gap in a nation's official documentary memory,[71] and requests to access the information that is available are often resisted by officials.[72] Similarly, while those in positions of authority may agree, or be compelled, to appear before a commission, they do not always disclose the information sought or tell the truth.[73] Thus, while truth commissions may uncover some national

---

[68] Donald K. Piragoff, 'Protection of National Security Information', in Roy S. Lee (ed.), *The International Criminal Court, The Making of the Rome Statute: Issues, Negotiations and Results* (The Hague: Kluwer, 1999), 270–94.

[69] El Salvador, *Annex to the Mexico Agreements: Commission on the Truth*, UN Doc. S/25500, 27 April 1991, Art. 8; South Africa: Promotion of National Unity and Reconciliation Act, No. 34 of 1995, s. 29; Sierra Leone, Truth and Reconciliation Commission Act 2000, s. 8(1)(a); An Act to Establish the Truth and Reconciliation Commission of Liberia, 2005, s. 27(a); Kenya: Truth, Justice and Reconciliation Act 2008, s. 7(2)(a).

[70] Alex Boraine, *A Country Unmasked: Inside South Africa's Truth and Reconciliation Commission* (Oxford University Press, 2001), 200, 272–3.

[71] See *Truth and Reconciliation Commission of South Africa Report* (Cape Town: Truth and Reconciliation Commission, distributed by Juta and Co., 2002), vol. 1, chapter 8 on the problems caused by the destruction of documentary evidence.

[72] *Nunca Más: The Report of the Argentine National Commission on the Disappeared* (New York: Farrar Straus Giroux, 1986), 252–4; *Report of the Chilean National Commission on Truth and Reconciliation* (Notre Dame: University of Notre Dame Press, 1993), 17–20.

[73] Thomas Buergenthal, 'The United Nations Truth Commission for El Salvador' (1994) 27 *Vanderbilt Journal of Transnational Law* 497, 506–7.

security information through their investigations and statement-taking activities, its scope is likely to be limited.

Moreover, Article 93(4), in conjunction with Article 72, allows a state to refuse a request for information only on the grounds that disclosure would 'prejudice' its national security interests.[74] Information held by a truth commission is likely to be published in, or at least used to compile, its final report. It can hardly be argued, therefore, that its disclosure to the ICC would compromise national security as it is likely to imminently enter the public domain. In addition, the ICC Statute requires states parties to take all reasonable steps to resolve such matters by cooperative means in collaboration with the Court[75] and provides a range of methods to enable a satisfactory resolution.[76] Where resolution is not forthcoming and the Court determines that the information requested is necessary to determine the guilt or innocence of an accused, it can refer the matter to the Assembly of States Parties if it concludes that by invoking Article 93(4) the state is not complying with its obligations.[77] It remains possible that in future some information held by truth commissions may remain undisclosed due to its potential to prejudice national security. However, it seems unlikely that Article 93(4) will provide a means of generally preventing the disclosure of truth commission information to the ICC.

The final ground of refusal concerns situations where execution of a request for a particular measure of assistance is prohibited by an 'existing fundamental legal principle of general application'.[78] The Statute provides no guidance on what is meant by the clause and academic commentary reveals no consensus as to its meaning.[79] The validity of this provision in enabling states to refuse to cooperate with or provide assistance to the Court has been questioned. It is argued that Article 88, combined with Articles 89 and 93 of the Statute, makes clear that there must be national procedures in place for all forms of cooperation specified under Part 9. Any prohibition provided for under domestic statutory or constitutional law is not a ground for refusal to comply with requests for cooperation or

---

[74] Rome Statute, Art. 72(1).   [75] Rome Statute, Art. 72(5).
[76] *Ibid.*   [77] Rome Statute, Art. 72(7)(ii).   [78] Rome Statute, Art. 93(3).
[79] David Hunt, 'The International Criminal Court: High Hopes, "Creative Ambiguity" and an Unfortunate Mistrust of International Judges' (2004) 2 *Journal of International Criminal Justice* 56, 69; Claus Kress, 'The Procedural Law of the International Criminal Court in Outline: Anatomy of a Unique Compromise' (2003) 1 *Journal of International Criminal Justice* 603, 615–16.

assistance from the Court.[80] Instead, it is argued that states are under a duty to consult with the Court in an effort to resolve conflicting national laws.[81] However, others, while critical of the provision, consider that it does enable states to refuse a request for assistance by the Court and to impose their own legal order.[82] It could be argued that the word 'existing' suggests that the national legal principle must have been established for some period of time. As the ICC and truth commissions are likely to come into conflict in situations where they are both investigating recent human rights violations, and certainly nothing committed prior to July 2002, which is the date from which the ICC can exercise jurisdiction, it seems unlikely that a state party will be able to withhold truth commission information on the grounds that an existing fundamental legal principle prohibits it. Moreover, Article 93(3) specifies that consideration ought to be given to whether the assistance can be provided in another manner or subject to certain conditions.

Save for the exception of a limited amount of information that may relate to national security interests, the grounds for refusal of assistance under Article 93 do not appear to provide states with a means of preventing the disclosure of truth commission materials to the ICC. The Court's powers and the obligations of its states parties mean that the ICC will be able to access truth commission information where it is considered relevant to investigations or prosecutions. There are, however, some categories of information held by truth commissions, such as information received confidentially and self-incriminating evidence obtained under powers of compulsion, which are generally protected under national and international law from use and disclosure in criminal proceedings. The Statute provides little guidance on how the ICC is likely to treat these materials, whether they will be protected from disclosure or whether they will be subject to scrutiny by the Court under its powers to request assistance from its states parties. Clarification of their status is essential as it is these categories of information and their utility to both truth seeking and prosecution that seem most likely to be the subject of tension between truth commission-holding states and the ICC.

---

[80] Annalisa Ciampi, 'The Obligation to Cooperate', in Antonio Cassese, Paulo Gaeta and John R. W. D. Jones (eds.), *The Rome Statute of the International Criminal Court: A Commentary*, 2 vols. (Oxford University Press, 2002), 1607–8, 1630–1.

[81] *Ibid.*

[82] Goran Sluiter, *International Criminal Adjudication and the Collection of Evidence: Obligations of States* (Antwerp, Oxford and New York: Intersentia, 2002), 162; Kress, 'The Procedural Law of the International Criminal Court in Outline', 615.

4   The status of confidential information

4.1   Truth commissions and the importance of confidentiality

Truth commissions commonly possess the ability to receive testimony under guarantees of confidentiality and prevent its disclosure. South Africa was the first country to regulate its truth commission's information in this way. Where the TRC decided to hold a private hearing, it could also take measures to prevent the information relating to the proceedings, including the identity of any witnesses, being made public.[83] The South African model has been developed by other states establishing truth commissions. The Guatemalan Commission's proceedings were kept 'confidential so as to guarantee the secrecy of the sources and the safety of witnesses and informants'.[84] Peru's Commission on the Truth had powers to withhold the identity of anyone who provided important information or participated in the investigations[85] and was mandated to keep all documentation and testimony confidential during operations and on dissolution.[86] Sierra Leone's TRC was given the power to receive information on a confidential basis and could 'not be compelled to disclose any information given to it in confidence'.[87] It was also instructed to take measures to protect confidential information prior to its dissolution.[88] The East Timorese Commission had similar instructions[89] and Kenya's recently established Truth, Justice and Reconciliation Commission has been given powers to conduct private hearings,[90] withhold the identities of those involved[91] and to take measures to protect confidential information upon dissolution.[92] Where information is given confidentially, the details of the statement-giver will not be included in the commission's final report or in its database,[93] though the statement and identity of its giver are likely

---

[83]   South Africa: Promotion of National Unity and Reconciliation Act, No. 34 of 1995, s. 33.

[84]   Agreement on the establishment of the Commission to clarify past human rights violations and acts of violence that have caused the Guatemalan Population to suffer, Oslo, 17 June 1994, 36 *International Legal Materials* (1997) 283.

[85]   Decreto Supremo No. 065–2001-PCM, Creación de la Comisión de la Verdad en el Perú, Lima, Peru, 2 June 2001, Art. 6(d).

[86]   *Ibid.*, Art. 7.

[87]   Sierra Leone: Truth and Reconciliation Commission Act 2000, s. 7(3).

[88]   *Ibid.*, s. 19(2)(a)(ii).   [89]   UNTAET Regulation No. 2001/10 ss. 44.2 and 43.2(b).

[90]   Kenya: Truth, Justice and Reconciliation Act 2008, s. 25(2).

[91]   *Ibid.*, s. 25(4).   [92]   *Ibid.*, s. 52(2).

[93]   SLTRC, *Witness to Truth: Report of the Sierra Leone Truth and Reconciliation Commission* (Accra: Graphic Packaging Ltd, 2004), vol. 1, chapter 5 'Methodology and Processes', para. 24.

to remain in the commission's archives.[94] There is, therefore, a trend of protecting the information gathered by truth commissions, making it seem likely that states establishing commissions in future will also seek to regulate the use of information gathered through national legislation.

While the ability to conduct confidential hearings may have begun as a means of protecting participants, for more recent commissions it has fulfilled the additional dimension of a truth-seeking tool. The Liberian truth commission began its statement-taking phase with confidential interviews in order to build trust and goodwill with the public before moving to the public hearing stage. It concluded that its careful statement-taking approach aided it in obtaining over 20,000 statements from Liberians in Liberia and the diaspora.[95] The final report of the TRC for Sierra Leone also demonstrates the leverage with which the power to grant confidentiality provides commissions in gaining testimony.[96] In its report, the SLTRC recounts how the power to receive testimony confidentially enabled it to receive information from those who wished their account to remain confidential in order to avoid persecution by perpetrators and from those who required confidentiality due to fear of rejection by their communities should the nature of the violations they had suffered be exposed.[97] It also allowed the Commission to counter the potentially negative impact of the Special Court on the willingness of perpetrators to come forward. By offering confidentiality, the TRC aimed to encourage former perpetrators to reveal their versions of the events of the past.[98] All of the children who gave statements to the TRC did so in confidential sessions.[99] Many women who gave testimony regarding the sexual violence they had experienced did so in closed sessions and in confidential written statements.[100] The sexual violence perpetrated against women and girls during the conflict in Sierra Leone was a striking characteristic of the war,[101] as was the recruitment of child soldiers. It was therefore

[94] See for example, *Final Report of the TRC of Liberia* (Ghana: Twidan Graphics, 2009), vol. 2, 334–5.

[95] *Ibid.* vol. 2, 66.

[96] SLTRC, *Witness to Truth*, vol. 1, chapter 5 'Methodology and Processes', paras. 20–6.

[97] *Ibid.*, para. 22.

[98] *Ibid.*, para. 23. This was made possible by the Special Court Prosecutor's decision not to attempt to access truth commission materials.

[99] *Ibid.*, para. 9. This was also the case in Liberia. See *Final Report of the TRC of Liberia*, 71–2.

[100] SLTRC, *Witness to Truth*, vol. 1, chapter 3 'Women and the Armed Conflict in Sierra Leone', para. 27.

[101] Human Rights Watch, *'We'll Kill You If You Cry': Sexual Violence in the Sierra Leone Conflict*, January 2003, Part V, Sexual Violence against Women and Girls during the Civil War.

important that the TRC was able to gain the testimony of those affected in order to construct an accurate and representative account of the past. The nature of the violations and the stigma that often accompanies them could have made it difficult for many to discuss their experiences publicly. In this instance it is likely that the power to receive information on a confidential basis enabled the TRC to gain information that it would not have received if all truth commission information had to be made public.

The power to grant confidentiality is therefore a useful one. For truth commissions, testimony gained under guarantees of confidentiality can add an otherwise unobtainable account of past events. It also enables those who would be uncomfortable offering testimony publicly to participate in the truth-seeking process. Equally, for the Court, that information may prove of relevance to investigations and prosecutions as it seeks to identify witnesses and amass the evidence necessary to compile cases and bring charges. The ICC Statute envisages situations where states parties may require confidentiality guarantees before providing information to the Court. In conducting investigations, the Prosecutor is empowered to receive information upon the condition of confidentiality and solely for the purpose of generating new evidence.[102] However, this does not provide a solution to the problem of sharing confidential truth commission testimony with the ICC. A commission cannot give a guarantee of confidentiality in good faith if the Court can access the information obtained under that guarantee. It does not matter whether the information is passed on the proviso that it remains confidential and is used solely as a means of generating other evidence. To share the information with any other body would be a breach of the confidentiality guarantee given to the witness and would undermine the integrity of the commission. It has already been shown that states parties cannot generally withhold truth commission information under the Article 93 grounds for refusing assistance. Therefore, only if confidential truth commission information can be considered as privileged under the ICC's Rules of Procedure and Evidence can its disclosure to the Court be prevented.

4.2   Confidentiality and the ICC Statute

Rule 73(2) of the ICC Rules of Procedure and Evidence[103] regulates privileged and confidential information. It provides:

---

[102] Rome Statute, Arts. 54(3)(e) and 93(8).
[103] Rome Statute of the International Criminal Court, Rules of Procedure and Evidence (ICC RPE), ICC-ASP/1/3, adopted by the Assembly of States Parties, First Session, 3–10 September 2002.

communications made in the context of a class of professional or other confidential relationships shall be regarded as privileged, and consequently not subject to disclosure ... if a Chamber decides in respect of that class that:

(a) Communications occurring within that class of relationship are made in the course of a confidential relationship producing a reasonable expectation of privacy and non-disclosure;

(b) Confidentiality is essential to the nature and type of relationship between the person and the confidant; and

(c) Recognition of the privilege would further the objectives of the Statute and the Rules.

Arguably, truth commission information obtained under guarantees of confidentiality fulfils each of these requirements.

4.2.1 Reasonable expectation of privacy and non-disclosure

First, where a commission is endowed with the power to receive information on a confidential basis and gives an undertaking to a witness that their information will remain confidential, that information would seem to be given 'in the course of a confidential relationship producing a reasonable expectation of privacy and non-disclosure' under Rule 73(2)(a).[104] Much will depend, however, on the Court's interpretation of the meaning of this phrase.

The ICTY's jurisprudence on confidentiality provides useful insights into the categories of relationship and information likely to be regarded as privileged by international courts. The Tribunal has held that state officials, International Committee for the Red Cross and Red Crescent (ICRC) officials, Tribunal functionaries and the United Nations Protection Force (UNPROFOR) commander-in-chief, are excluded from being compelled to testify.[105] In some cases, information arising from certain types of relationship has been protected from disclosure in order to ensure confidence in the administration of justice and protect the essential interests of the

---

[104] See William A. Schabas, 'The Relationship between Truth Commissions and International Courts: The Case of Sierra Leone' (2003) 25 *Human Rights Quarterly* 1035, 1056.

[105] *Prosecutor* v. *Blaskic* (Case No IT-95-14-AR), Judgment on the Request of the Republic of Croatia for Review of the Decision of Trial Chamber II of 18 July 1997, 29 October 1997; *Prosecutor* v. *Simic et al.* (Case No IT-95-9-PT), *Ex Parte* Confidential Decision on the Prosecution's Motion under Rule 73 for a Ruling Concerning the Testimony of a Witness, 27 July 1999; *Prosecutor* v. *Delalic et al.* (Case No IT-96-21-T), Decision on the Motion *Ex Parte* by the Defence of Zdravko Mucic Concerning the Issue of a Subpoena to an Interpreter, 8 July 1997.

parties involved.[106] Thus, it has been held that interpreters should not be compelled to testify in relation to situations in which they have provided interpretation services. The need to 'ensure the maintenance of the position of impartiality owed to the parties, which is an essential prerequisite of the interpreter's function', means that it is not in the interests of justice to compel their testimony.[107] Equally, a truth commission's first duty should be to its witnesses and protecting the information they have provided on the understanding that it will remain confidential. The ability to offer a secure environment in which witnesses can account their experiences is 'an essential prerequisite' of the truth commission's function.

Pertinent to this discussion is the reasoning advanced in *Prosecutor v. Brdjanin and Talic*,[108] where the court had to consider whether war correspondents possessed testimonial privilege. The case concerned a subpoena issued to a journalist to give evidence relating to an article he had published which included statements allegedly made by the accused. The journalist sought to have the subpoena set aside on the grounds that there is a recognised public interest privilege that applies to journalists and that to compel them to testify might hinder their ability to obtain information and inform the public.[109] The ICTY dismissed the motion. The Tribunal held that the objectivity and independence required by journalists working in conflict situations was unlikely to be hampered by them being called to testify in cases where they have already published their findings.[110] Distinction was drawn between situations where journalists had published their findings and those where their sources had remained confidential.[111] In discussing the latter situation the Tribunal affirmed the standards laid down in the European Court of Human Rights decision in *Goodwin v. United Kingdom*.[112] In that case it was held that there is a qualified journalistic privilege in cases involving confidential and unpublished information, although it is always subject to an overriding requirement to disclose in the public interest.

The *Brdjanin* decision suggests both good and bad news for truth commissions. On the one hand, the ICTY suggested that where information

---

[106] *Prosecutor v. Delalic et al.* (Case No IT-96–21-T), Decision on the Motion *Ex Parte* by the Defence of Zdravko Mucic Concerning the Issue of a Subpoena to an Interpreter, para. 18.

[107] *Ibid.*, paras. 17–20.

[108] *Prosecutor v. Brdjanin and Talic* (Case No. IT-99–36-T), Decision on Motion to Set Aside Confidential Subpoena to Give Evidence, Trial Chamber, 7 June 2002.

[109] *Ibid.*, para. 10.   [110] *Ibid.*, para. 26.   [111] *Ibid.*, paras. 29–31.

[112] *Goodwin v. United Kingdom* (Application No. 28957/95), Judgment of 11 July 2002, (2002) 35 EHRR 18.

is confidential and unpublished, such as that received under a guarantee of confidentiality by a truth commission, it may attract a form of privilege and protection from disclosure. The reasoning also implies that where testifying before an international court is likely to undermine credibility, it may be necessary to consider information privileged in order to maintain the independence and objectivity necessary for the fulfilment of a particular mandate. Certainly, compelling a truth commission to disclose information that it has guaranteed as confidential will undermine its legitimacy. On the other hand, the Tribunal made clear that privileged information is always subject to an overriding requirement to disclose in the public interest. It stressed that the rights and interests involved in confidentiality cases must be considered within the context of the overriding principle that the withholding of evidence must not unduly impede the course of justice.[113] In the context of truth commission information, that determination will lie with the ICC. Should the Court consider that the disclosure of confidential truth commission materials would assist in prosecution cases and serve the interests of international justice, it may well decide to order disclosure of the information. The reasoning in *Brdjanin* also suggests that a single decision on the status of confidential information held by truth commissions is unlikely and that cases will have to be decided on an individual basis, after a balancing of the interests involved. A requirement that each case is considered on its own merits introduces an element of uncertainty for truth commissions. That uncertainty makes it seem unlikely that future truth commissions will be able to exercise, in good faith, the power to grant confidentiality. Information cannot be received under a guarantee of confidentiality if there is a possibility that it will subsequently be disclosed to the ICC.

4.2.2   Essential to the nature and type of relationship

Secondly, in order for the ICC to consider truth commission information as privileged, the ability of truth commissions to grant confidentiality to witnesses would have to be determined as 'essential to the nature and type of relationship between the person and the confidant', thereby fulfilling Rule 73(2)(b). Again, the jurisprudence of the ICTY provides guidance in this area. In *Prosecutor* v. *Simic et al.*,[114] the Tribunal had to

---

[113] *Prosecutor* v. *Brdjanin and Talic* (Case No. IT-99-36-T), Decision on Motion to Set Aside Confidential Subpoena to Give Evidence, Trial Chamber, 7 June 2002, para. 27.

[114] *Prosecutor* v. *Simic et al.* (Case No. IT-95-9), Decision on the Prosecution Motion under Rule 73 for a Ruling Concerning the Testimony of a Witness, Trial Chamber, 27 July 1999.

consider whether a former employee of the ICRC could be called to give evidence of facts that came to his knowledge by virtue of his employment. The ICRC opposed his giving testimony on the grounds that confidentiality was necessary in the performance of its functions to win the trust of warring parties, without which it would not be able to perform the tasks assigned to it under international humanitarian law.[115] In particular, concerns were raised that national authorities might deny ICRC personnel access to places where persons protected by the Geneva Conventions are located if they consider that ICRC personnel might subsequently testify in criminal proceedings about what they have seen and heard in those places.[116] The Tribunal held that 'the right to non-disclosure of information relating to the ICRC's activities in the possession of its employees in judicial proceedings is necessary for the effective discharge by the ICRC of its mandate'.[117] It considered that the parties to the Geneva Conventions and their Protocols must 'be taken as having accepted the fundamental principles on which the ICRC operates, that is impartiality, neutrality and confidentiality, and in particular as having accepted that confidentiality is necessary for the effective performance by the ICRC of its functions'.[118] The Tribunal concluded that the ICRC has a right under customary international law to non-disclosure of its information.[119]

The ICTY's reasoning that non-disclosure and confidentiality is necessary for the effective discharge of the ICRC's mandate may prove relevant in any future decisions on whether truth commission information ought to be subject to disclosure. The ICRC's argument that the ability to maintain confidentiality is essential to gain the trust of warring parties which in turn allows the ICRC access to those in need to carry out its mandate, is equally applicable to truth commissions. The ability to receive information on a confidential basis is necessary for commissions to gain information from former perpetrators and vulnerable witnesses.

---

[115] *Ibid.*, para. 14.

[116] *Ibid.* For a thorough discussion of the arguments advanced see Stéphane Jeannet, 'Recognition of the ICRC's Long-standing Rule of Confidentiality – An Important Decision by the International Criminal Tribunal for the former Yugoslavia' (2000) 82 *International Review of the Red Cross* 403.

[117] *Prosecutor v. Simic et al.* (Case No. IT-95–9), Decision on the Prosecution Motion under Rule 73 for a Ruling Concerning the Testimony of a Witness, Trial Chamber, 27 July 1999, para. 73.

[118] *Ibid.*

[119] This decision was upheld on appeal. See *Prosecutor v. Simic et al.* (Case No. IT-95–9), Decision Denying Request for Assistance in Securing Documents and Witnesses from the International Committee of the Red Cross, Appeal Chamber, 7 June 2000.

This in turn allows them to fulfil their mandates to establish the most representative record of the past and enables them to involve all sectors in the truth-seeking process. Although the work of the ICRC and that of truth commissions broadly complements the objectives of international courts,[120] both have interests in maintaining a division between their roles and those of prosecutorial institutions. For truth commissions, their primary role of providing an inclusive, victim-centred truth-seeking process is distinct from the judicial mandate of the ICC. That distinction will be blurred if truth commission materials become a means of supporting prosecution cases. While it has been suggested that some witnesses may feel encouraged by the prospect of their testimony contributing to criminal justice initiatives,[121] many may not. The prospect of their testimony being disclosed to a prosecutorial institution may persuade them not to offer information to the commission, denying them the opportunity to participate and excluding their account from the historical record.

4.2.3   Furthering the objectives of the Statute

Thirdly, in order for the ICC to recognise the confidentiality of truth commission information, the Court would have to consider that such recognition would further the objectives of the Statute under Rule 73(2)(c). Piragoff lists the objectives of the ICC as including:

> the need to ensure that the most serious crimes to the international community do not go unpunished, that the rights of accused persons are guaranteed, that the safety, physical and psychological well-being, dignity and privacy of victims and witnesses are protected, that trials are conducted fairly and the testimony of witnesses evaluated fairly, that the human rights and equality of all participants are respected, that persons convicted are fairly punished, that victims receive reparations, including restitution, compensation and rehabilitation and that the jurisdiction of the Court is complementary to that of national legal systems.[122]

Truth commissions and the ICC share many of the same objectives. Both aim to respond to past human rights violations, uncover the truth surrounding them, expose those responsible, provide acknowledgement of

---

[120] Toni Pfanner, 'Cooperation between Truth Commissions and the International Committee of the Red Cross' (2006) 88 *International Review of the Red Cross* 363.

[121] Priscilla B. Hayner, *Unspeakable Truths: Transitional Justice and the Challenge of Truth Commissions* (2nd edn) (New York and London: Routledge, 2010), 113.

[122] Donald K. Piragoff, 'Evidence', in R. S. Lee (ed.), *The International Criminal Court: Elements of Crimes and Rules of Procedure and Evidence* (New York: Transnational Publishers, 2001) 349–401, 361.

the suffering of victims and bring a measure of accountability. Viewed in this way, the work of truth commissions may well be considered as furthering the objectives of the Statute. The OTP has stated that it endorses the role played by other transitional justice mechanisms and will seek to work constructively with them and respect their mandates.[123] It may therefore consider that to compel the disclosure of information received by truth commissions under guarantees of confidentiality would undermine, rather than respect, the mandate of truth commissions. It may also consider that to use information provided under guarantees of confidentiality contravenes the objective of protecting the dignity and privacy of victims and witnesses by using their testimony in a way to which they did not consent. Indeed, the Prosecutor is under an obligation to respect the interests and personal circumstances of victims and witnesses and to have particular regard to the nature of the crime, particularly where it relates to sexual violence or violence against children.[124] Often, the confidential information possessed by commissions involves crimes of these natures. Equally, the OTP has stated that it will pursue its own judicial mandate independently.[125] Central to that mandate is the objective of ending impunity and ensuring that the most serious crimes do not go unpunished. The Prosecutor has obligations to investigate all facts and evidence relevant to the determination of criminal responsibility under the Statute.[126] Should he consider that confidential truth commission information would assist in prosecution cases he may well seek an order for its disclosure.

In sum, the Court has discretion to decide how to treat confidential truth commission information. The jurisprudence of the ICTY suggests that case-by-case decisions are the most likely means of resolution. Certainly, it seems unlikely that the Court will implement a blanket prohibition on accessing confidential truth commission materials and will seek to preserve some means of accessing information in particular cases. This introduces an element of uncertainty for truth commissions and casts doubt on whether future commissions should be created with powers to grant confidentiality while such uncertainty persists. In the absence of clear policy from the ICC on this issue, it may be better to forego powers to grant confidentiality, and the information their exercise brings, than risk orders for disclosure and damage to the credibility of the truth-seeking process.

[123]   ICC, Office of the Prosecutor, *Policy Paper on the Interests of Justice*, 8.
[124]   Rome Statute, Art. 54(1)(b).
[125]   ICC, Office of the Prosecutor, *Policy Paper on the Interests of Justice*, 8.
[126]   Rome Statute, Art. 54(1)(a).

4.3   Defence applications for witness testimony

Defence counsel may also seek to access confidential truth commission testimony. They may seek exculpatory evidence or evidence to ascertain whether prosecution witnesses are giving the same account of events before the commission and the ICC. Should there be discrepancies between the testimonies, it is possible that defence counsel could use these discrepancies to challenge the credibility of prosecution witnesses.[127] Unlike the ICC, defence counsel have no authority to compel truth commissions to disclose information. Where information has been received on a confidential basis it seems likely that commissions will rely on their powers to guarantee confidentiality to withhold information. In order to gain access to truth commission information, defence counsel will, therefore, be dependent on obtaining an order from the ICC instructing a state to produce information held by its commission.

In considering this situation in the context of Sierra Leone, Schabas concluded that the most likely outcome, should a court refuse to order a truth commission to disclose information, was that the defence would apply for a stay of proceedings, arguing a violation of fundamental rights.[128] The Trial Chamber's decision in the *Lubanga* case[129] lends support to Schabas's contention. Although the context is different, in that case the inability of the defence to access potentially exculpatory materials resulted in a stay of proceedings.[130] The Trial Chamber confirmed that the right to disclosure of potentially exculpatory material is an integral aspect of the fundamental right to a fair trial.[131] This point has also been stressed by the Special Court for Sierra Leone on numerous occasions.[132]

---

[127] Schabas has also considered the possibility of defence applications for truth commission testimony in the context of Sierra Leone. See Schabas, 'The Relationship between Truth Commissions and International Courts', 1054–7.

[128] *Ibid.*,1054.

[129] *Prosecutor* v. *Thomas Lubanga Dyilo* (Case No. ICC-01/04-01/06–1401), Decision on the Consequences of Non-disclosure of Exculpatory Materials Covered by Article 54(3)(e) Agreements and the Application to Stay the Prosecution of the Accused, ICC Trial Chamber I, 13 June 2008.

[130] Kai Ambos, 'Confidential Investigations, (Article 53(4)(e) ICC Statute) vs. Disclosure Obligations: The Lubanga Case and National Law' (2009) 12 *New Criminal Law Review* 543.

[131] Matthew E. Cross and Sarah Williams, 'Recent Developments at the ICC' (2009) 9 *Human Rights Law Review* 267, 270.

[132] *Prosecutor* v. *Charles Ghankay Taylor* (SCSL-03-1-T), Decision on Public with Confidential Annexes A–D Defence Motion for Disclosure of Exculpatory Information Relating to DCT-032, 20 October 2010, note 36, for a list of the cases in which this issue has been discussed.

While the *Lubanga* case concerns disclosure by the Prosecution to the defence, as does the relevant jurisprudence of the Special Court, a similar argument might be raised in relation to the inability of defence counsel to access confidential truth commission materials. It is conceivable that even if it does not ultimately give rise to a stay of proceedings, it will significantly delay them.

Schabas has argued that one solution to the issue of defence applications for truth commission testimony is to allow the judges alone to examine it.[133] If they are satisfied that the information is not relevant or that it is essentially the same as the testimony given to the Court, it would not be disclosed to the prosecution or defence or be made public.[134] He concedes, however, that if the testimony is not the same, or pertains directly to the guilt of the accused, the judges would presumably have to admit it in evidence and allow the defence to utilise it.[135] Schabas's proposal does not therefore provide a solution for the difficulties posed to truth commissions by the threat of requests for disclosure of their information from the ICC. It remains the case that should there be discrepancies between the testimony given by a witness to a truth commission and that given to prosecutorial institutions, or should a commission possess exculpatory evidence, the information held by the truth commission could be used as evidence in criminal proceedings. In such circumstances, the guarantee given by the commission to the witness is therefore worthless and the credibility of the commission undermined.

This situation further highlights the fundamental tension between the proceedings of truth commissions and criminal trials. In practice, there is no solution to this dilemma that satisfies both bodies. There is an operational incompatibility between the interests of truth commissions to grant confidentiality and maintain the secrecy of information related to serious human rights violations and those of prosecutorial institutions to have access to all relevant information to support criminal trials. While truth commissions continue to be endowed with powers to guarantee confidentiality, one body will operate at the expense of the other should conflict arise. Given the ICC's powers to enlist national cooperation and to access information, it is likely that the pursuit of its judicial mandate will, in practice, be prioritised over the interests of national truth seeking. There may be options to enable a limited number of parties to view

---

[133] Schabas, 'The Relationship between Truth Commissions and International Courts', 1054.
[134] *Ibid.*   [135] *Ibid.*

confidential information as a first step, in line with Schabas's proposal. Ultimately, however, commission information might be admitted as evidence if it pertains to prosecution cases, compromising the perceived legitimacy of the truth commission. The fundamental question is therefore whether truth commissions should continue to grant confidentiality where there is a possibility that the ICC will initiate investigations and prosecutions. In reality, this seems to be a power that commissions cannot exercise in good faith, as there will be a possibility that the information obtained through its exercise will be subject to disclosure in line with the obligations of states to provide assistance to the Court.

5   The status of self-incriminating evidence

Another area that may create tension between truth commissions and the ICC is the possibility of requests by the Court for disclosure of self-incriminating testimony held by commissions. The testimony of former perpetrators forms a significant component of the truth-seeking process. Some commissions have been mandated to provide a forum for both victims and perpetrators to share their experiences to facilitate healing and reconciliation.[136] Perpetrator testimony also enables the construction of a more representative report. Some perpetrators offer testimony willingly to truth commissions, despite the fact that this may involve providing evidence of their own involvement in the commission of serious human rights violations.[137] Others, particularly higher ranking perpetrators, are often less forthcoming.[138] In order to ensure the capability of truth commissions to access perpetrator testimony, a number of past commissions have been given powers to compel the provision of self-incriminating perpetrator testimony.

Under Section 29(1)(c) of the Promotion of National Unity and Reconciliation Act 1995, the South African TRC was given authority to 'call upon any person to appear before the Commission and to give

---

[136] An Act to Establish the Truth and Reconciliation Commission of Liberia 2005, s. 4(b); Sierra Leone: Truth and Reconciliation Commission Act 2000, s. 6(2)(b); Kenya: Truth, Justice and Reconciliation Act 2008, s. 5(1)(g) and (i).

[137] Hayner, *Unspeakable Truths: Transitional Justice and the Challenge of Truth Commissions*, 117.

[138] Antje Pedain, 'Was Amnesty a Lottery? An Empirical Study of the Decisions of the Truth and Reconciliation Commission's Committee on Amnesty' (2004) 121 *South African Law Journal* 785, 806–7 on the difficulties of the South African TRC in obtaining testimony from high-ranking officials.

evidence or to answer questions relevant to the subject matter of the hearing'. The Commission was further empowered to 'require any person who in compliance with the terms of this section appears before it to take the oath or to make an affirmation'.[139] Refusal to be sworn or to make an affirmation or failure or refusal to answer the questions asked is an offence and renders the person concerned liable to a fine or imprisonment or both.[140] Subsequent commissions have been established following this model. Ghana,[141] Liberia,[142] East Timor,[143] Sierra Leone[144] and Kenya[145] created truth commissions with powers to issue subpoenas and compel the provision of self-incriminating information. These powers have seen varying degrees of use. The South African TRC used the power of subpoena primarily as a threat to incentivise appearance before the Commission,[146] whereas the TRC for Sierra Leone issued subpoenas against serving ministers, leaders of government and the Attorney General.[147] In many of these states prosecution for past crimes remained a possibility. In order to ensure the protection of fair trial rights and uphold the credibility of the commissions, most of the enacting legislation for these commissions stipulated that self-incriminating evidence obtained under powers of compulsion could not be used in subsequent criminal proceedings.[148]

This situation presents additional dilemmas in the relationship between truth commissions and the ICC. Incriminating evidence given

---

[139] South Africa: Promotion of National Unity and Reconciliation Act, No. 34 of 1995, s. 29(4).

[140] *Ibid.*, s. 39.   [141] Ghana: National Reconciliation Commission Act 2002, s. 13.

[142] An Act to Establish the Truth and Reconciliation Commission of Liberia 2005, s. 27(d).

[143] UNTAET Regulation 2001/10, s. 14.1(c).

[144] Sierra Leone: Truth and Reconciliation Commission Act 2000, s. 8(1)(g).

[145] Kenya: Truth, Justice and Reconciliation Act 2008, s. 7(2)(d),(e) and (g).

[146] Boraine, *A Country Unmasked*, 273. For a discussion of some of the subpoenas that the TRC did issue, particularly that relating to former President P. W. Botha, see *Truth and Reconciliation Commission of South Africa Report*, vol. 1, Chapter 7.

[147] SLTRC, *Witness to Truth*, vol. 1, Chapter 4, para. 38.

[148] South Africa: Promotion of National Unity and Reconciliation Act, No. 34 of 1995, s. 31(3); Ghana, National Reconciliation Commission Act 2002, s. 15(2); An Act to Establish the Truth and Reconciliation Commission of Liberia 2005, s. 30; Kenya: Truth, Justice and Reconciliation Act 2008, s. 24(3). The legislation enacting the Sierra Leonean TRC did not contain a similar provision, perhaps because no prosecutions were envisaged at the time of its enactment. However it did state that the Commission could receive information on a confidential basis and that the Commission could not be compelled to disclose information given to it in confidence; Sierra Leone: Truth and Reconciliation Commission Act 2000, s. 7(3).

by a perpetrator to a truth commission could be of significant interest to the Court. The Court's powers to obtain records and documents from its states parties will enable it to access self-incriminating commission information should it be deemed relevant to investigations or prosecutions of core crimes. Where a perpetrator has voluntarily offered self-incriminating testimony to a truth commission, there is unlikely to be any bar to that information being used as evidence in a prosecution case. However, if that information has been obtained under a truth commission's powers of subpoena and a perpetrator has been compelled to incriminate himself, the use of such evidence in subsequent prosecutorial proceedings raises questions concerning the right against self-incrimination and consequently, the right to a fair trial.

The right against self-incrimination in criminal investigations and proceedings is well established in international law as a fundamental facet of the right to a fair trial. It is enshrined in numerous international statutes and conventions,[149] as well as in many national legal systems.[150] It is protected within the Statutes for the ad hoc tribunals[151] and in those of some of the hybrid courts.[152] The ICC Statute protects extensively the right against self-incrimination at both the investigation stage and following

---

[149] International Covenant on Civil and Political Rights, 16 December 1966, 999 UNTS 171, Art. 14(3)(g); American Convention on Human Rights, 22 November 1969, 1144 UNTS 123, Art. 8(2)(7). While the European Convention on Human Rights, 4 November 1950, 213 UNTS 221, does not explicitly mention the right against self-incrimination, it has been recognised in the jurisprudence of the European Court of Human Rights on Art. 6. See for example *Murray* v. *United Kingdom* (Application No. 18731/01), Judgment of 25 January 1996, (1996) 22 EHRR 29 and *Saunders* v. *United Kingdom*, (Application No. 19187/91), Judgment of 29 November 1996, (1997) 23 EHRR 313.

[150] See for example, the Constitution of the United States of America, Amendment 5; Canadian Charter of Rights and Freedoms, s. 11(c).

[151] International Criminal Tribunal for the Prosecution of Persons Responsible for Serious Violations of International Humanitarian Law Committed on the Territory of the former Yugoslavia since 1991, established pursuant to Security Council Resolution 827, UN Doc. S/RES/ 827 (1993), Art. 21(4)(g); International Criminal Tribunal for the Prosecution of Those Responsible for Genocide and Other Serious Violations of International Humanitarian Law Committed in the Territory of Rwanda and Rwandan Citizens Responsible for Genocide and Other Such Violations Committed in the Territory of Neighbouring States between 1 January 1994 and 31 December 1994, established pursuant to Security Council Resolution 955, UN Doc. S/RES/955 (1994), Art. 20(4)(g).

[152] Statute of the Special Court for Sierra Leone, appended to the Report of the Secretary-General on the Establishment of a Special Court for Sierra Leone, S/2000/915, 4 October 2000, Art. 17(4)(g); Law on the Establishment of Extraordinary Chambers in the Courts of Cambodia for the Prosecution of Crimes Committed during the Period of Democratic Kampuchea, 27 October 2004, Art. 35(g).

any indictment, at the trial stage. Article 55(1)(a) provides that during an investigation 'a person shall not be compelled to incriminate himself or herself or to confess guilt'. Similarly, Article 67(1)(g) states that, 'in the determination of any charge, the accused shall be entitled ... not to be compelled to testify or to confess guilt and to remain silent, without such silence being a consideration in the determination of guilt or innocence'. The Statute also contains provisions that enable the Court to provide assurances to witnesses who might provide incriminating evidence that their information 'will be kept confidential and will not be disclosed to the public or any State' and 'will not be used either directly or indirectly against [them] in any subsequent prosecution by the Court'.[153] In addition, witnesses do not have to answer questions that might lead them to make statements that would incriminate a spouse, child or parent.[154] These provisions, however, apply only to those subject to investigations and proceedings carried out by the Court. There are no legal guarantees that self-incriminating evidence obtained by another body will not be used against an accused in a prosecution by the ICC.[155]

The prospect of use by the ICC of self-incriminating information obtained under another body's powers of compulsion seems at odds with the jurisprudence of other international courts and inconsistent with international human rights standards. The ICTY has taken what has been described as an 'over-protective'[156] approach to the right against self-incrimination, interpreting it broadly[157] and excluding evidence where it considers that the right has not been adequately protected.[158] The Special Court for Sierra Leone emphasised the importance of protecting the right against self-incrimination in the *Norman* case, refusing to allow a detainee to testify before the TRC for fear that his fair trial rights and the

---

[153] ICC RPE, r. 74(3)(c).   [154] ICC RPE, r. 75.

[155] This issue has also been raised by Schabas in relation to the TRC for Sierra Leone and the Special Court. See Schabas, 'The Relationship between Truth Commissions and International Courts', 1052.

[156] Goran Sluiter and Alexander Zahar, *International Criminal Law* (Oxford University Press, 2008), 305.

[157] *Prosecutor* v. *Delalic et al.* (Case No. IT-96–21), Decision on the Prosecution's Oral Requests for the Admission of Exhibit 155 into Evidence and for an Order to Compel the Accused, Zdravko Mucic, to Provide a Handwriting Sample, 19 January 1998.

[158] *Prosecutor* v. *Delalic et al.* (Case No. IT-96–21), Decision on the Prosecution's Oral Requests for the Admission of Exhibit 155 into Evidence and for an Order to Compel the Accused, Zdravko Mucic, to Provide a Handwriting Sample, 19 January 1998; *Prosecutor* v. *Halilovic* (Case No. IT-01–48-T), Decision on Motion for Exclusion of Statement of Accused, 8 July 2005.

integrity of the Court would be jeopardised as a result.[159] The European Court of Human Rights has held that the right against self-incrimination was infringed by the use of compelled, incriminating statements made by the accused in a subsequent trial.[160] In accordance with this line of reasoning, the ICC may consider that using self-incriminating material obtained under compulsion in proceedings before the Court is contrary to the notion of a fair trial under Article 67 of the Statute.

However, the parameters of the right against self-incrimination remain unsettled. It is by no means certain that the right is absolute.[161] Some are in fact critical of the high level of protection the right against self-incrimination has been afforded in international criminal law and question whether it might actually impede investigations and prosecutions in some circumstances.[162] In respect of truth commission testimony, Freeman proposes a compromise. He argues that investigative authorities should be able to use compelled statements to further investigations regarding the underlying offences to which each relates, provided that they can ultimately prove that the evidence offered at a future trial could reasonably have been discovered in the absence of the compelled testimony.[163] This suggestion may well provide the ICC with a solution to the problem of balancing the rights of the accused with the interests of the Court in using all relevant information and evidence to build prosecution cases. However, it does not provide a satisfactory solution for truth commissions. The prospect of using truth seeking powers to compel the provision of self-incriminating information for use in subsequent prosecution cases seems fundamentally unjust. It does not sit easily with the notions of leaving behind past injustice and the promotion of a human rights culture

---

[159] *Prosecutor v. Samuel Hinga Norman* (Case No. SCSL-03-08-PT-101), Decision on the Request of the Truth and Reconciliation Commission of Sierra Leone to Conduct a Public Hearing with Samuel Hinga Norman, 29 October 2003, para. 14; *Prosecutor v. Samuel Hinga Norman* (Case No. SCSL-03-08-PT-122-I and II), Decision on Appeal by the Truth and Reconciliation Commission of Sierra Leone and Chief Samuel Hinga Norman JP against the Decision of His Lordship Justice Bankole Thompson to Deny the TRC's Request to Hold a Public Hearing with Chief Norman, 28 November 2003, para. 41.

[160] *Saunders v. United Kingdom*, Application No. 19187/91, (1997) 23 EHRR 313.

[161] The ECHR in *Saunders* did not make any statement on whether the right is absolute or whether it might be subject to qualification in certain circumstances. See, *ibid.*, paras. 71–4.

[162] Sluiter and Zahar, *International Criminal Law*, 305.

[163] Mark Freeman, *Truth Commissions and Procedural Fairness* (Cambridge University Press, 2006), 253.

that truth commission establishment is meant to represent. Moreover, it raises practical difficulties, as commissions will be faced with the additional problem of mitigating the negative impact of such an arrangement on the overall willingness of perpetrators to give testimony.[164]

6 Access to detainees

Another issue that is unresolved is whether truth commissions will be permitted to interview detainees in the custody of the ICC and if so, what form those interviews will take. Almost all commissions are established to construct a complete and comprehensive account of the past,[165] implying that it is not only victim testimony that is relevant to the commission's proceedings but the accounts of all parties. Many commissions are additionally tasked with identifying those responsible for the commission of abuses.[166] In order to determine responsibility for past crimes and create the most representative version of the past, the testimony of those indicted by the ICC, who will be high-ranking perpetrators, may well be of relevance. Some commissions name those they consider responsible for past abuses,[167] leading to the argument that those persons should be afforded the opportunity to provide their account before any final report is published.[168]

The domestic powers of truth commissions to subpoena any person to appear and to testify, to decide whether a hearing should be public or private and to maintain the confidentiality of information provided will have no influence with the ICC. Commissions will be dependent on the Court

---

[164] On the difficulties caused in Sierra Leone due to the perception of information sharing between the TRC and the Special Court, see Letter from PRIDE to ICTJ, cited in, Marieke Wierda, Priscilla B. Hayner and Paul van Zyl, *Exploring the Relationship between the Special Court and the Truth and Reconciliation Commission of Sierra Leone*, International Center for Transitional Justice, New York, 24 June 2002, 8.

[165] See for example: Chile: Supreme Decree No. 355, Creation of the Commission on Truth and Reconciliation, Santiago, 25 April 1990, Art. 1(a); South Africa: Promotion of National Unity and Reconciliation Act, No. 34 of 1995, s. 3(1)(a); An Act to Establish the Truth and Reconciliation Commission of Liberia, 2005, s. 4(f); Kenya: Truth, Justice and Reconciliation Act, 2008, s. 5(a)

[166] South Africa: Promotion of National Unity and Reconciliation Act, No. 34 of 1995, s. 4(a)(iii)–(v); Sierra Leone: Truth and Reconciliation Commission Act 2000, s. 6(2)(a) and 7(1)(a); An Act to Establish the Truth and Reconciliation Commission of Liberia, 2005, s. 4(a)

[167] Hayner, *Unspeakable Truths: Transitional Justice and the Challenge of Truth Commissions*, chapter 10.

[168] *Ibid.*, 141.

for access to detainees. Decisions on the nature of any interview and the use of material generated will be at the discretion of the Court. Past practice, although limited, has shown international tribunals to be cautious in their approach to the possibility of such a close overlap between truth commission and prosecutorial activities. The suggestion of establishing a Bosnian truth commission[169] was met with opposition from the ICTY in the early stages of its operation.[170] The Tribunal was concerned that the commission would interfere in the judicial activity of the Tribunal, infringe upon the activities of the Prosecutor and prove prejudicial to the Court.[171] There was anxiety that the commission's findings of responsibility would differ from those of the Tribunal and give rise to unreasonable demands for prosecution. It was also argued that evidence could be 'contaminated' by the commission, particularly through the repeated interviewing of witnesses.[172] To mitigate these concerns, it was suggested that a truth commission should be expressly prohibited from interfering in the judicial activity of the Tribunal. In addition, the Tribunal proposed that the commission should have provisions inserted within its enacting legislation obligating it to provide to the Tribunal all public or confidential information and documents on request, to maintain close contacts with prosecutorial investigators and to authorise a liaison officer from the Tribunal to attend its hearings.[173]

A few years later, a similar approach was taken by the Special Court for Sierra Leone, when it refused to allow the TRC to conduct a public hearing with Sam Hinga Norman for fear that it would jeopardise fair trial and due process rights.[174] Requests to hold private hearings, in accordance with the SLTRC's powers, were restricted much in line with the ICTY's proposals of 2001. The Special Court would only permit interviews if they were supervised by a legal officer, transcribed and available to any party to legal proceedings upon order of the Court.[175] The Special Court looked

---

[169] Kritz and Finci, 'A Truth and Reconciliation Commission in Bosnia and Herzegovina'.

[170] Hayner, *Unspeakable Truths: Transitional Justice and the Challenge of Truth Commissions*, 112.

[171] ICTY, Press release, 'The ICTY and the Truth and Reconciliation Commission in Bosnia and Herzegovina', The Hague, 17 May 2001.

[172] Hayner, *Unspeakable Truths: Transitional Justice and the Challenge of Truth Commissions*, 112.

[173] ICTY, Press release, 'The ICTY and the Truth and Reconciliation Commission in Bosnia and Herzegovina'.

[174] See Chapter 3.

[175] The Revised Practice Direction makes additional provision for material covered by a confidentiality order, which can only be disclosed if it is in the interests of justice to so.

likely to follow this approach again in 2008, when it received a request from the TRC of Liberia to interview Charles Taylor.[176] In that case, however, the Court allowed Taylor to decide whether to testify before the TRC. His refusal to do so meant that the issues of how the interview would be conducted, and whether the TRC would be permitted to broadcast it in Liberia as it wished to, were left unanswered.[177]

This practice, while sparse, nevertheless suggests that the ICC is likely to take a restrictive approach to the possibility of truth commissions interviewing detainees. It would seem most unlikely that the Court will allow public hearings with detainees. As in the *Norman* case, the risk to fair trial standards seems likely to outweigh any individual rights to freedom of expression and to participate in national truth-seeking and societal rights to know the truth about past events. It also seems unlikely that the Court will be content to allow a truth commission to privately interview a detainee, without the possibility of accessing the information obtained. In Sierra Leone that approach led the TRC to abandon any attempts at private interviews as it considered it at odds with its spirit and purpose.[178] The result was that the accounts of those deemed to bear the greatest responsibility for the crimes committed in Sierra Leone did not contribute to the TRC process. Likewise, in Liberia the TRC's failure to include testimony from Charles Taylor in its final report is seen by some as a considerable omission.[179]

Without a guarantee of confidentiality, it seems unlikely that a detainee, in custody and awaiting trial for the most serious international crimes, will offer information of major significance to a truth commission. Charles Taylor indicated that he would not testify before the TRC for Liberia before the conclusion of his trial at the Special Court.[180] Even

---

See Practice Direction on the procedure following a request by a State, the Truth and Reconciliation Commission, or other legitimate authority to take a statement from a person in the custody of the Special Court for Sierra Leone, adopted 9 September 2003, Amended 4 October 2003, para. 4(3).

[176] Special Court for Sierra Leone, Press Statement, 'Statement by Registrar Herman von Hebel regarding the request by the Liberian Truth and Reconciliation Commission for an audience with Charles Taylor', Freetown, Sierra Leone, 5 September 2008.

[177] Matiangai Sirleaf, 'Regional Approaches to Transitional Justice? Examining the Special Court for Sierra Leone and the Truth and Reconciliation Commission for Liberia' (2009) 21 *Florida Journal of International Law* 209.

[178] SLTRC, *Witness to Truth*, chapter 6 'The TRC and the Special Court for Sierra Leone', para. 87.

[179] See Sirleaf, 'Regional Approaches to Transitional Justice?', 264.

[180] *Ibid.*, 268.

where an accused is willing to meet with a commission in order to give their account of events, as was the situation with Norman, defence counsel seem likely to caution against offering testimony to guard against self-incrimination. Indeed, in Liberia Taylor's lawyers sought a court order prohibiting all testimony about the former president being heard before the TRC as it had the potential to prejudice his trial before the Special Court.[181] Hayner argues that interviews with detainees may be useful even if defendants do not provide testimony of their own involvement in past events as they may offer broader contextual information. This may be the case in some situations. However, in many, the information offered is likely to be so limited by the need to safeguard future trials and protect against self-incrimination, that it will become vague and superficial. This leads to the conclusion that there may be no real benefit for truth commissions to have access to detainees. In practice, it seems likely that any information obtained through interviews with detainees will be so restricted as to remove any worthwhile additional dimension that it might otherwise have made to the truth commission's findings. This may also have the repercussion that truth commissions will be unable to name those they consider responsible for past abuses. However, the practice of 'naming names' is by no means universally accepted as a positive or beneficial aspect of truth commission work.[182] The task of assigning individual responsibility is probably best left to courts, which are designed for that purpose and do so after rigorous analysis of all the evidence and on a higher standard of proof. The inability of truth commissions to obtain full and frank testimony from detainees will, of course, narrow the account of the past they are able to compile. However, trials also contribute to the establishment of the truth about past human rights violations. When it comes to the individual role played by the highest ranking perpetrators, victims' and society's right to know the truth about the past may have to be delivered by the criminal justice process.

7 Charting a way forward

The discussion above demonstrates that the overlap in truth commission and ICC operations is likely to lead to some difficult legal and policy issues.

---

[181] Amnesty International, 'Full Participation and Support Necessary for the Success of the Truth and Reconciliation Commission', 21 December 2006.

[182] Hayner, *Unspeakable Truths: Transitional Justice and the Challenge of Truth Commissions*, 139–40; Freeman, *Truth Commissions and Procedural Fairness*, chapter 7.

Such dilemmas are no longer purely academic. The ICC is operational alongside a national truth commission in Kenya and the Court is monitoring the situation in Cote d'Ivoire,[183] which has recently announced its intention to establish a truth commission.[184] It is therefore essential to find a means of coordinating the operations of these bodies that minimises the potential for conflict.

7.1 Information sharing

One possible basis for the relationship between truth commissions and the ICC is for information to be shared. The possibility of truth commissions sharing information with prosecutorial institutions received greatest attention in the Sierra Leonean context. A number of NGOs formulated proposals on how and when SLTRC information should be shared. Three models were identified: the firewall model in which no information would be shared; the 'free access' model in which all SLTRC information would be available to the Court; and the conditional sharing model in which some information would be shared subject to certain conditions.[185]

The conditional sharing model emerged as the favoured approach. Human Rights Watch proposed that the Special Court should obtain information from the TRC only where (1) the information or evidentiary material sought could only be obtained from the TRC and (2) the evidentiary material requested was essential for the conviction or acquittal of the accused.[186] The International Center for Transitional Justice (ICTJ) suggested that information be made available by the SLTRC to the Special Court following an application for specific information by the prosecution or defence to the Trial Chamber.[187] If the information requested was essential to the fair determination of the case and could not reasonably be obtained from another source, the Trial Chamber would order its disclosure. The ICTJ contended that a statement given to the SLTRC should be accorded immunity from use in Special Court proceedings against the

---

[183] ICC, Office of the Prosecutor, 'Statement of the Deputy Prosecutor of the ICC on the Situation in Cote d'Ivoire', 2 December 2010.

[184] Stephanie Nebehay, 'Ivory Coast's Outtara Pledges Human Rights Body', Reuters, 8 April 2011.

[185] Wierda *et al.*, *Exploring the Relationship between the Special Court and the Truth and Reconciliation Commission of Sierra Leone*, 8.

[186] Human Rights Watch, *Policy Paper on the Interrelationship between the Sierra Leone Special Court and Truth and Reconciliation Commission*, 18 April 2002, 2.

[187] Wierda *et al.*, *Exploring the Relationship between the Special Court and the Truth and Reconciliation Commission of Sierra Leone*, 12.

person who made it, although it could be used in evidence against others. It also suggested that the SLTRC warn persons coming before it that while there would be no general information sharing with the Special Court, in exceptional circumstances the Court may require it to disclose statements, even if taken confidentially.[188] This arrangement, the ICTJ concluded, would preserve the 'autonomous nature of each institution'.[189] Amnesty International, while also in favour of truth commissions sharing information with prosecutorial institutions, does not consider that commissions should provide those compelled to offer testimony with use immunity.[190] It offers no explanation as to whether or how this position can be reconciled with fair trial rights but justifies it on the basis of the need to combat impunity.[191] It suggests that if those compelled to offer testimony are later prosecuted and convicted, the court could take account of their disclosure as a mitigating factor.[192]

These proposals approach the need to coordinate truth commissions and trials from a prosecutorial perspective. In each of them, the work of truth commissions is viewed as a means of aiding prosecutorial proceedings. None of the proposals supported the idea of the Court sharing information with the Commission, for fear that it would prejudice fair trial proceedings.[193] They are indicative of the elevated importance of prosecution within the transitional justice framework and the perceived inferiority of truth commissions. While the ICTJ and Human Rights Watch proposals limit the circumstances in which information can be accessed, they are based on the assumption that where truth commissions possess information pertinent to prosecution cases, the interests of the prosecutorial institution to access that material should trump the commission's interests in maintaining its confidentiality. On balance, that may prove to be the resolution should a situation arise where a commission possesses information which is of real significance to a prosecution case. However, the consequences of information-sharing arrangements should also be considered from a truth commission perspective. The assumption that truth commission interests should yield to those of prosecutorial institutions should not be automatic.

---

[188] *Ibid.*, 12–13 and Attachment A, Orders for the Disclosure of Information to the Truth and Reconciliation Commission.

[189] *Ibid.*, 13.

[190] Amnesty International, *Truth, Justice and Reparation: Establishing an Effective Truth Commission*, AI Index: POL 30/009/2007, 11 June 2007, 32.

[191] *Ibid.*   [192] *Ibid.*, note 62.

[193] On this point see Wierda *et al.*, *Exploring the Relationship between the Special Court and the Truth and Reconciliation Commission of Sierra Leone*, 115.

In reality, conditional sharing models will create uncertainty for truth commissions. There will always be a threat of requests for disclosure of information, making it impossible to guarantee with certainty the confidentiality of witness testimony. The ICTJ's suggestion that confidentiality be given with the caveat that in some circumstances testimony may have to be disclosed, significantly weakens the guarantee and may dissuade perpetrators and vulnerable witnesses from offering their account. Requests for disclosure of information under such an arrangement may damage the perception of the commission as an independent, non-judicial investigatory body and inhibit the participation of those who do not wish to become involved in prosecutorial proceedings. The commission's ability to conduct an inclusive process that provides all sectors of society with the opportunity to offer their story will be hampered. Thus, the uncertainty and blurring of the distinction between truth commissions and courts caused by conditional sharing models do not provide a satisfactory solution to the problem of how to coordinate the operations of truth commissions with those of the ICC. In short, these arrangements do not 'preserve the autonomy of each institution' but serve the needs of prosecution at the expense of the credibility and efficacy of truth commissions.

7.2 Limiting truth-seeking powers

Another means of reducing the potential for conflict between truth commissions and the ICC over access to information is to limit the powers of truth commissions. Powers to grant confidentiality, compel the provision of information and prevent disclosure of testimony were given to truth commissions to assist with the fulfilment of their mandates. Ironically, they now appear the most likely aspect of truth commission operation to generate areas of tension and conflict with prosecutorial proceedings. At national levels it may be possible to coordinate the operations of truth commissions and prosecutorial institutions in enacting legislation or in subsequent regulating agreements. Where the ICC is involved this is not an option; the ICC is a treaty institution with an international mandate that cannot be moulded around the operation of domestic truth commissions. In the absence of an ICC policy to the contrary, truth commission information will be accessible to the Court under its powers to request cooperation and assistance from its states parties, regardless of the status of that information under national law. Under current conditions, the answer is for states establishing truth commissions to tailor their powers in light of the ICC's capabilities. If truth commissions do not possess powers to compel the provision of testimony or grant confidentiality, it follows that they will not hold confidential information and any incriminating information in their files will have been offered voluntarily, making its disclosure less problematic. The need for national laws that protect truth commission information is therefore dispelled and the potential for conflict between these and the ICC's powers to access information diminished.

Removing powers to grant confidentiality and compel the provision of self-incriminating evidence will likely hamper truth seeking to some extent. Without either the ability to offer confidentiality or the power of compulsion, it will be more difficult to obtain perpetrator testimony. Witnesses who fear social stigma or reprisals and those who are reluctant to become involved in prosecutorial proceedings may decide not to participate in the truth-seeking process if the confidentiality of their account cannot be guaranteed. This will impede the truth commission's ability to provide an open and inclusive process and hamper the compilation of the broadest and most representative version of the past.

However, the impact of limiting truth-seeking powers, while significant, is unlikely to be catastrophic to the overall process. Many offer testimony voluntarily, without the protection of confidentiality or the inducement of subpoena. Early truth commissions, many of which published robust and extensive reports, were not endowed with these powers but attracted witness testimony in large numbers regardless. Moreover, truth commissions came to be endowed with a range of truth-seeking powers at a time when they operated largely as a substitute for trials, rather than as a complement to them. These powers were intended to enhance the efficacy of the truth commission process because it was the primary, and sometimes sole, method of responding to past abuses. This is no longer the case. While truth commissions can contribute to a culture of accountability, they no longer have to provide the only means of calling perpetrators to account. Powers of compulsion are less vital. The loss of powers to grant confidentiality is more significant as this very often protects not perpetrators, but the truth commission's primary focus group, their victims. While the loss of this power does not preclude the possibility of a private, rather than public, hearing or the exclusion of identifying details from the final report, it does make an absolute guarantee of confidentiality impossible. However, it would seem preferable for truth commissions to be endowed with fewer powers and suffer a slight limitation in their truth-seeking abilities than to be given a range of powers which will give them access to sensitive information but may in turn give rise to requests for disclosure of that protected information from the ICC. Ultimately, those powers may create more harm than good by discrediting the commission and casting doubt on its credibility if it cannot uphold the guarantees it makes in order to obtain information or becomes perceived as an investigative arm of the ICC.

7.3   Extending Rule 73(4) protections

A final means of regulating the potential for conflict between truth commissions and the ICC is to extend the Rule 73(4) protections of the ICC Rules of Procedure and Evidence to encompass truth commission information. These currently pertain exclusively to the ICRC and reflect the ICTY's decision in *Simic*. Rule 73(4) provides that information, documents and other evidence obtained by the ICRC through the performance of its functions under its statutes shall be regarded by the Court as privileged. This includes the testimony of employees, past and present. This rule does not serve, however, to prevent the disclosure of all ICRC material in all circumstances. Rule 73(6) provides for consultations between the Court and the ICRC should the Court consider that information held by the ICRC is of 'great importance for a particular case'. The aim of these consultations is to resolve the matter on cooperative grounds, bearing in mind the circumstances of the case, the relevance of the evidence sought, whether the evidence could be obtained from another source, the interests of justice and of victims, and the performance of the Court's and the ICRC's functions. This provision suggests that while there may be a general rule that ICRC information is privileged, it is not absolute and in some cases, on balance, the significance of the information to prosecution cases may trump the ICRC's need to maintain confidentiality.

The system laid down in Rule 73(4) and (6) provides an imperfect but workable solution to the practical difficulties of balancing the interests of institutions that require the guarantee of confidentiality to conduct their operations optimally with the Court's interests in having access to all relevant information. It carries with it the risk that in some instances supposedly confidential information will be disclosed and used in prosecution cases, thereby undermining the credibility of the institution that disclosed it. Conversely, its tethers the Court's powers and may actually prevent access to all relevant materials by requiring agreement for the disclosure of confidential information. Nevertheless, it offers some flexibility and a middle way between the opposed and absolutist positions that either all information is available to the Court or that no confidential information is accessible regardless of the circumstances.

Although Rules 73(4) and (6) apply exclusively to the ICRC, the rationale could provide some resolution to the dilemma of how the Court should treat confidential truth commission materials. As a general rule, confidential information held by truth commissions, including that obtained under powers to compel self-incriminating evidence, would be privileged and protected from disclosure. In the event that it was suspected to be 'of great importance' to a particular case, a consultative process based on consideration of all relevant factors between the commission and the ICC could be undertaken to ascertain whether disclosure would be possible. The Court would have no absolute right of access to materials but there would be no blanket prohibition on the use of truth commission materials in ICC proceedings. This consultative process acknowledges the worth of the work of truth commissions and the ICC, viewing them as equal institutions, rather than elevating prosecution to a position of superiority.

This solution is not entirely satisfactory from the viewpoint of either truth commissions or the Court. For truth commissions, the possibility remains that the Court will request access to protected information and that in certain circumstances guarantees of confidentiality will be broken due to the significance of the information to prosecution cases. Problems of credibility and integrity arise. Equally, for the Court there is a possibility that it will not gain access to information that it considers of significance if a truth commission cannot be convinced of the need to disclose it. Again, the tension between the operations of truth commissions and prosecutorial institutions emerges.

8 Conclusion

The ICC regime has the potential to impact significantly upon the operation of future truth commissions. The extensive powers of the Court and the obligations imposed upon states parties to cooperate and provide assistance mean that should the ICC seek to access confidential and self-incriminating information held by truth commissions, it will be able to do so. Whether the ICC will use its powers to compel the disclosure of such information remains uncertain. However, even the potential exercise of these powers must impact the design of future truth commissions, the powers they are endowed with and, therefore, their modes of operation. Indeed, it would be naive to create truth commissions in situations where the ICC's jurisdiction may also be active, without taking into account the need to coordinate operations and avoid conflict between the two bodies.

In an ideal world, it is tempting to suggest that the ICC should issue a policy paper stating that it will not attempt to access truth commission materials to further investigations and will fulfil its mandate using its own resources. However, practice to date demonstrates that the Court is experiencing real difficulties in obtaining the information necessary to build prosecution cases. Although the OTP has expressed a determination to reduce reliance on the information gathered by other bodies,[194] it would seem impossible for the ICC to guarantee absolutely that it will never seek access to truth commission materials. It must be remembered that the Court has its own judicial mandate to fulfil. Excluding, as a matter of policy, the possibility of accessing information that may assist in the investigation and prosecution of the most serious international crimes seems at odds with its purposes. Nevertheless, clarification by the Court of the status of truth commissions and their materials within the ICC framework is essential to enable a more informed truth commission establishment.

For the time being, the uncertainty created by the ICC's silence on the likely treatment of truth commission information and its powers to access information should it be deemed relevant to prosecutorial proceedings makes limiting the powers of truth commissions the best way forward. Without powers to grant confidentiality and compel the provision of testimony, future commissions simply will not possess confidential or compelled self-incriminating information. The problems of violating national laws that afford such information a protected status will be removed and potential for conflict with the ICC will be diminished. In addition the integrity of commissions will not be threatened by the use of guarantees that may not be upheld in the long term. The Court may still seek access to truth commission information, but if all information has been given freely and openly, its disclosure will prove less problematic.

This proposal is not a perfect solution. It requires compromising truth commissions and makes them weaker than they have come to be. It risks curtailing their ability to fulfil their mandates of providing an opportunity for all interested parties to participate in the truth-seeking process and jeopardises their capacity to provide a forum in which the most vulnerable witnesses can share their experiences. For proponents of truth

---

[194] International Criminal Court, Office of the Prosecutor, *Prosecutorial Strategy 2009–2012*, The Hague, 1 February 2010, para. 34(b).

commissions, it may well represent another example of the subjugation of truth commissions in favour of criminal prosecutions. Yet there cannot be a perfect solution in the current situation. The overlapping mandates of prosecutorial bodies and truth commissions and their reliance on the same information and evidence makes difficulties inevitable and the need for compromise unavoidable. In reality, perfectly balanced, harmonious coexistence is unachievable. Where truth commissions operate alongside the ICC, the powers of the Court and its status as an international treaty institution make truth commissions the weaker party. The limitation of their powers provides a workable solution. It enables the maintenance of truth commissions as legitimate, autonomous bodies, with a specific victim-centred, truth-seeking mandate within the transitional justice framework, while minimising the risk of them becoming investigative tools for the ICC.

5

Truth commissions and prosecutions
in bystander states

1 Introduction

The possibilities for the prosecution of the most serious human rights crimes are not limited simply to domestic trials or, where those are not undertaken, proceedings by the ICC. Particularly where these first two avenues are not pursued, bystander states may initiate criminal proceedings. All states possess the right to assert universal jurisdiction over genocide, war crimes, crimes against humanity and torture, as crimes defined under customary law.[1] Some additionally belong to treaty regimes that require either prosecution of specific crimes or extradition to a state willing to prosecute.[2] Recently, the likelihood of third country prosecutions has increased. A number of states parties to the ICC have enacted legislation implementing their obligations under the Statute that also extends existing jurisdictional competence and authorises the prosecution of genocide, crimes against humanity and war crimes wherever they occur. The potential for overlap between bystander state prosecutions and national truth commissions in the state of territoriality is therefore also greater.

A key issue arising in any prosecution by a bystander state is the absence of any obligation per se on the state of territoriality or nationality to provide judicial assistance.[3] This is the case even where the crimes concerned are international in character. The provision of assistance in such cases is dependent upon existing methods of inter-state cooperation in international law. However, states' treaty obligations to provide information under existing judicial assistance arrangements may conflict with national legislative provisions which protect truth commission

---

[1] Claus Kress, 'Universal Jurisdiction over International Crimes and the *Institut de Droit International*' (2006) 4 *Journal of International Criminal Justice* 561.

[2] See Chapter 2.

[3] Bruce Broomhall, *International Justice and the International Criminal Court: Between State Sovereignty and the Rule of Law* (Oxford University Press, 2003), 119–23.

material from disclosure, creating genuine difficulties in the sharing of some information and evidence. Moreover, the traditional grounds for refusal of assistance under mutual legal assistance and extradition treaties may enable an obstructive truth commission-holding state to withhold information or refuse extradition of those who have offered testimony before a commission.

Chapter 5 focuses on the difficulties that may arise where a bystander state exercises jurisdiction in relation to violations that are being/have been investigated by a truth commission. It will show that, in some instances, the operation of a national truth commission on the state of territoriality may impede the effective prosecution of international crimes by a bystander state due to reliance on existing cooperation arrangements. Equally, it will argue that attempts by bystander states to access truth commission materials will hamper truth seeking by inhibiting those who are reluctant to become involved in criminal proceedings from offering testimony. The chapter will therefore demonstrate a disharmony between truth commissions and prosecutorial proceedings when pursued in this way, and argue that, under current arrangements, in some situations their contemporaneous operation will make it impossible to achieve either full and effective truth seeking or successful criminal trials.

2 Bystander state prosecutions and the expansion of jurisdiction

National prosecutions for serious human rights violations have been sparse. For a variety of reasons, states often encounter difficulties in pursuing a policy of prosecution following conflict or regime change.[4] Third states, even when possessing the capability, have been traditionally reluctant to interfere in the internal affairs of another. Thus, prosecutorial practice concerning serious human rights crimes at the national level is haphazard and patchy. The Second World War gave rise to a number of trials, although prosecution was often for 'ordinary' crimes under domestic law rather than for international crimes, with jurisdiction exercised on nationality, territoriality or passive personality grounds.[5] Prosecutions by

---

[4] See Chapter 1.
[5] Alex Marschik, 'The Politics of Prosecution: European National Approaches to War Crimes', in Timothy L. H. McCormack and Gerry J. Simpson (eds.), *The Law of War Crimes: National and International Approaches* (The Hague: Kluwer, 1997), 65–101. On the French experience, see Leila Sadat Wexler, 'Prosecutions for Crimes against Humanity in French Municipal Law: International Implications' (1997) *American*

third states on the grounds of universality were rare, the Israeli trial of Adolf Eichmann being a notable exception.[6] The serious human rights abuses of the cold war period regimes went largely unpunished in the states of territoriality at the time.[7] Attempts by third states to exercise jurisdiction on the grounds of protective and passive personality jurisdiction over torture and enforced disappearance committed by members of foreign regimes amounted, at best, to *in absentia* convictions.[8]

Prosecutions by third states, and the important role they can play in ensuring accountability for past violations, came to attention in the 1990s following the conflicts in the former Yugoslavia and Rwanda. Austria,[9] Belgium,[10] Denmark,[11] Germany,[12] the Netherlands,[13] and Switzerland[14] undertook trials of a number of those responsible for international crimes who had fled to their territory as a result of the conflicts. In many cases, these states exercised jurisdiction over the crimes concerned under the universality principle, without the traditional territoriality or nationality links to the crimes, the defendant or the victims.[15] These prosecutions,

---

Society of International Law Proceedings 270. For practice in Italy, see Pier Paulo Rivello, 'The Prosecution of War Crimes Committed by Nazi Forces in Italy' (2005) 3 *Journal of International Criminal Justice* 422. On the Canadian experience, see Sharon A. Williams, 'Laudable Principles Lacking Application: The Prosecution of War Criminals in Canada', in Timothy L. H. McCormack and Gerry Simpson (eds.), *The Law of War Crimes: National and International Approaches* (The Hague: Kluwer, 1997), 151–71.

[6] *Attorney General of Israel v. Eichmann* (1968) 36 ILR 5; *Attorney General of Israel v. Eichmann* (1968) 36 ILR 227.

[7] Naomi Roht-Arriaza, 'The New Landscape of Transitional Justice', in Naomi Roht-Arriaza and Javier Mariezcurrena (eds.), *Transitional Justice in the Twenty-First Century: Beyond Truth versus Justice* (Cambridge University Press, 2006), 1–16, 3–4.

[8] Amnesty International, *Universal Jurisdiction: The Duty of States to Enact and Enforce Legislation*, chapter 2 'The History of Universal Jurisdiction', AI Index: IOR 53/004/2001, 1 September 2001.

[9] *Public Prosecutor v. Cvjetkovic*, discussed in Luc Reydams, *Universal Jurisdiction: International and Municipal Legal Perspectives* (Oxford University Press, 2003), 99–100.

[10] Damien Vandermeersch, 'Prosecuting International Crimes in Belgium' (2005) 3 *Journal of International Criminal Justice* 400; Luc Reydams, 'Belgium's First Application of Universal Jurisdiction: The Butare Four Case' (2003) 1 *Journal of International Criminal Justice* 428.

[11] *The Prosecutor v. Saric*, Eastern Division of the High Court (Third Chamber), 25 November 1994. See also Reydams, *Universal Jurisdiction*, 129–30.

[12] See Ruth Rissing-van Saan, 'The German Federal Supreme Court and the Prosecution of International Crimes Committed in the Former Yugoslavia' (2005) 3 *Journal of International Criminal Justice* 381; Reydams, *Universal Jurisdiction*, 147–57.

[13] *Public Prosecutor v. Knesevic*, discussed in Reydams, *Universal Jurisdiction*, 171–2.

[14] See for example, Luc Reydams, 'International Decisions: Niyonteze v. Public Prosecutor' (2002) 96 *American Journal of International Law* 231.

[15] Reydams, *Universal Jurisdiction*, 220–2.

and the emerging international commitment to combat impunity, gave rise to a small spate of attempts by third states to prosecute international human rights crimes on the basis of universal jurisdiction.[16] A number of European states became involved in the *Pinochet* litigation of the late 1990s,[17] Belgium issued a series of indictments against high-profile foreign political figures[18] and Spain initiated proceedings against members of Latin America's former regimes.[19] While the Belgian and Spanish parliaments have since imposed limits upon the circumstances in which their courts can exercise universal jurisdiction,[20] the possibility of third states undertaking prosecutorial proceedings for international crimes is once again an issue of international debate. Ratification of the ICC Statute has stimulated a wave of domestic legislative activity in which universal jurisdiction in respect of genocide, war crimes and crimes against humanity has been incorporated into national law.

Many states parties have passed implementing legislation ensuring that they are capable of fulfilling their obligations under the treaty. Some of the legislation contains provisions that enable the assertion of universal jurisdiction over core crimes and, therefore, the prosecution of these crimes wherever they occur. Some states have asserted absolute universal jurisdiction over ICC crimes. For example, New Zealand's International Crimes and International Criminal Court Act 2000 asserts absolute universality over genocide, crimes against humanity and war

---

[16] For an overview see Wolfgang Kaleck, 'From Pinochet to Rumsfeld: Universal Jurisdiction in Europe 1998–2008' (2009) 30 *Michigan Journal of International Law* 927.

[17] Richard Wilson, 'Prosecuting Pinochet: International Crimes in Spanish Domestic Law' (1999) 21 *Human Rights Quarterly* 927.

[18] Steven R. Ratner, 'Belgium's War Crimes Statute: A Post-Mortem' (2003) 97 *American Journal of International Law* 888.

[19] On the Guatemalan Generals cases, see Hervé Ascensio, 'Are the Spanish Courts Backing Down on Universality?: The Supreme Tribunal's Decision in Guatemalan Generals' (2003) 1 *Journal of International Criminal Justice* 690; Hervé Ascensio, 'The Spanish Constitutional Tribunal's Decision in Guatemalan Generals: Unconditional Universality is Back' (2006) 4 *Journal of International Criminal Justice* 586. On the extradition of Cavallo, see Luis Benavides, 'Introductory Note to the Supreme Court of Mexico's Decision on the Extradition of Ricardo Miguel Cavallo' (2003) 42 *International Legal Materials* 884. On the Scilingo case, see Christian Tomuschat, 'Issues of Universal Jurisdiction in the Scilingo Case' (2005) 3 *Journal of International Criminal Justice* 1074.

[20] Spain: Ley Orgánica 1/2009, de 3 de noviembre, complementaria de la Ley de reforma de la legislación procesal para la implantación de la nueva Oficina judicial, por la que se modifica la Ley Orgánica 6/1985, de 1 de julio, del Poder Judicial. Luc Reydams, 'Belgium Reneges on Universality: The 5 August 2003 Act on Grave Breaches of International Humanitarian Law' (2003) 1 *Journal of International Criminal Justice* 679.

crimes, without limitation on grounds of nationality, citizenship, the place of commission of the offence or the location of the accused, either at the time of commission or charge.[21] Germany has enacted similar legislation. Under the Code of Crimes against International Law 2002, jurisdiction can be exercised over all the criminal offences contained within the Code, which include the core crimes, even if the crime was committed abroad and bears no relation to Germany.[22] There are few limitations to this wide jurisdiction. The Prosecutor may decline to prosecute if the accused is not present in Germany and must not proceed where there is no link with Germany and the offence is being prosecuted either by an international court or a state with closer links to the offence or the accused.[23] Other states, including Australia,[24] Canada,[25] the Netherlands[26] and South Africa,[27] have asserted conditional universal jurisdiction over core crimes. These states require the presence of the accused on their territory before jurisdiction can be exercised. It is likely that this more cautious approach results from the continuing uncertainty around the international legality of the exercise of universal jurisdiction *in absentia* and the conflicting judgments in the International Court of Justice (ICJ)'s consideration of the Arrest Warrant case.[28]

[21] New Zealand: International Crimes and International Criminal Court Act 2000, ss. 8–11. Juliet Hay, 'Implementing the Rome Statute in New Zealand' (2004) 2 *Journal of International Criminal Justice* 533. Trinidad and Tobago's International Criminal Court Act 2006, s 8. provides for similar jurisdiction.

[22] Germany: Code of Crimes against International Law 2002, s. 1.

[23] Strafprozessordnung, S153(f). See also Kai Ambos, 'International Core Crimes, Universal Jurisdiction and ss153f of the German Criminal Procedure Code. A Commentary on the Decisions of the Federal Prosecutor General and the Stuttgart Higher Regional Court in the Abu Ghraib/Rumsfeld Case' (2007) 18 *Criminal Law Forum* 43.

[24] See Reydams, *Universal Jurisdiction*, 88–9; Gideon Boas, 'An Overview of Implementation by Australia of the Statute of the International Criminal Court' (2004) 2 *Journal of International Criminal Justice* 179.

[25] Canada: Crimes against Humanity and War Crimes Act 2000, ss. 6 and 8, requires that the accused has some form of link with Canada before prosecution can be pursued, or that a person is present in Canada after the commission of the crime.

[26] Netherlands: International Crimes Act 2003, s. 2(1)(a).

[27] South Africa: Implementation of the Rome Statute of the International Criminal Court Act 27 of 2002, s. 4(3)(c).

[28] Case Concerning the Arrest Warrant of 11 April 2000 *(Democratic Republic of Congo v. Belgium)*, Judgment of 14 February 2002, International Court of Justice, General List. Contrast the Separate Opinion of President Guillaume, para. 12, and the Declaration of Judge Ranjeva, para. 6, with Joint Separate Opinion of Judges Higgins, Kooijmans and Buergenthal. For analysis of the case see Case Comment, 'Arrest Warrant of 11 April 2000 *(Democratic Republic of the Congo v. Belgium)*, Preliminary Objections and Merits, Judgment of 14 February 2002' (2003) 52 *International and Comparative Law Quarterly* 775.

Nevertheless, it seems that even a conditional construction of universal jurisdiction does not, per se, preclude the initiation of criminal investigations against those not present on a state's territory or a request for their extradition.[29] In general terms, the enactment of this implementing legislation increases the possibility that where ICC crimes are committed, third states with the willingness and requisite domestic legislation to do so may attempt to exercise jurisdiction.

Whether there is any obligation under the Statute for states to enact such legislation remains a moot point.[30] The ICC Statute itself makes no mention of universal jurisdiction. There is, however, an emerging argument based on pragmatism that the exercise of universal jurisdiction by states parties over core crimes is an essential element of the complementarity regime envisaged by the Statute. This argument is founded on the notion that without national courts exercising universal jurisdiction there will be an unacceptable source of impunity in the cases in which the ICC is unable to exercise jurisdiction.[31] Current practice at the ICC suggests that the cases in which the Court will be unable to exercise jurisdiction may not only be those in which states are not party to the Statute or are not referred by the Security Council. The current volume of cases and budgetary constraints suggest that demand may exceed the capability and resources of the Court.[32] Thus, action by third states may be necessary if international crimes are to be prosecuted effectively. This has led to proposals that the ICC Prosecutor should encourage bystander state prosecutions where the states of nationality or territoriality are unable

---

[29] Kress, 'Universal Jurisdiction over International Crimes', 576.

[30] For a comprehensive account of reasons supporting an obligation to implement domestic legislation, see Jann K. Kleffner, 'The Impact of Complementarity on National Implementation of Substantive International Criminal Law' (2003) 1 *Journal of International Criminal Justice* 86, 90–4. For argument that the Rome Statute contains no such obligation, see Daryl Robinson, 'The Rome Statute and Its Impact on National Law', in Antonio Cassese, Paulo Gaeta, and John R. W. D. Jones (eds.), *The Rome Statute of the International Criminal Court: A Commentary*, 2 vols. (Oxford University Press, 2002), vol. 2, Chapter 47, 1860–1. On the general debate surrounding the exercise of universal jurisdiction in light of the Rome Statute, see Cedric Ryngaert, 'The International Criminal Court and Universal Jurisdiction: A Fraught Relationship?' (2009) 12 *New Criminal Law Review* 498; Christian Tomuschat, 'The Duty to Prosecute International Crimes Committed by Individuals', in Hans-Joachim Cremer *et al.* (eds.), *Tradition und Weltoffenheit des Rechts: Festschrift für Helmut Steinberger* (Berlin: Springer, 2002), 315–39.

[31] Dissenting Opinion of Judge ad hoc Van den Wyngaert, Case Concerning the Arrest Warrant of 11 April 2000 *(Democratic Republic of Congo* v. *Belgium)*, Judgment of 14 February 2002, International Court of Justice, General List, para. 65.

[32] Aaron Gray Block, 'ICC Budget "Under Pressure" to Fund Libya Probe', Reuters, 14 April 2011.

or unwilling to pursue trials[33] and should determine a case inadmissible where a bystander state is willing and able to prosecute under the principle of complementarity.[34] It is submitted that under a 'positive' construction of the complementarity principle, the ICC may even assist bystander states through the sharing of information and evidence from its own investigations.[35] Another option is for the Court to divide labour with a bystander state to share the burden of providing accountability for core crimes.[36] It has even been suggested that states parties draw up an Optional Protocol to the ICC Statute, providing for an *aut dedere, aut judicare* regime in relation to core crimes.[37] Whether any of these proposals will find enunciation in the OTP's forthcoming policy paper on positive complementarity remains to be seen. Nevertheless, it seems that the potential role for bystander states in prosecuting international crimes is receiving increased attention. Certainly, much of the national ICC implementing legislation provides for the possibility that in future, states may more frequently exercise jurisdiction on the basis of universality in accordance with the ICC Statute objective of ending impunity.

3 Mutual legal assistance, truth commissions and areas of potential conflict

3.1 *The use and protection of truth commission information*

In theory, prosecutions by bystander states appear to provide an effective means of plugging the impunity gap. In practice, bystander states may face difficulties in obtaining the necessary information and evidence to build cases against those who have committed core crimes in another country. The distance at which they will operate means that, like the ICC, they may be dependent on information compiled by other bodies to facilitate investigations and bolster cases. A truth commission operating in the state of territoriality may be one such body. Where there is a mutual assistance treaty in place between the state of territoriality and the prosecuting state,

---

[33] William W. Burke-White, 'Proactive Complementarity: The International Criminal Court and National Courts in the Rome System of Justice' (2008) 49 *Harvard International Law Journal* 53, 101–2.

[34] Ryngaert, 'The International Criminal Court and Universal Jurisdiction'.

[35] *Ibid.*, 509.   [36] Burke-White, 'Proactive Complementarity', 104.

[37] Payam Akhaven, 'Whither National Courts: The Rome Statute's Missing Half' (2010) 8 *Journal of International Criminal Justice* 1245.

information held by the truth commission may be subject to requests for disclosure due to its potential utility to investigating institutions in a third state attempting to build a prosecution case. As discussed in Chapter 1, in constructing a historical record, truth commissions examine official government, security forces and military records,[38] in addition to interviewing large numbers of victims, witnesses and perpetrators and recording their versions of events.[39] This allows detailed accounting of the patterns of violence across time and regions. It enables commissions to gather vast amounts of varied information from a number of different sources and outline broad patterns of institutional responsibility.[40] The usefulness of such materials to prosecution cases can be seen in Spain's references to the Chilean and Guatemalan commission reports in the international arrest warrants issued for General Pinochet[41] and the Guatemalan Generals.[42] In both cases, the reports were used as evidence of the nature and scale of the violations committed under the military regimes and state complicity in their commission. Similarly, the Chadian commission report was presented as evidence of the political killings, torture and disappearances carried out by the Habré regime in the victims' action to bring a prosecution against Hissène Habré.[43] It was also used by NGOs assisting with the case to provide leads to victims and other witnesses who could be used in a trial.[44] More recently, the Prosecution used extracts from the report of the TRC for Sierra Leone to provide contextual evidence and to support establishment of the *chapeau* elements of the crimes charged in the trial of Charles Taylor before the Special Court for Sierra Leone.[45] As

---

[38] Mark Freeman, *Truth Commissions and Procedural Fairness* (Cambridge University Press, 2006), 276–80.

[39] *Ibid.*, 168–71.

[40] Priscilla B. Hayner, *Unspeakable Truths: Confronting State Terror and Atrocity* (New York: Routledge, 2001), 24–5.

[41] Ampliación y funadamentación del Auto ordenando la prisión provisional incondicional de AUGUSTO PINOCHET y su detención, (Amplification and Foundation for an Order of Unconditional Provisional Arrest of Augusto Pinochet and his Detention), Madrid, 18 October 1998. See also *Re Pinochet Ugarte* [1998] 3 All ER (D) 629, para. 57.

[42] Rights Action/NISGUA (Network in Solidarity with Guatemala), 'Arrest Warrants against Former Military Officials', 12 November 2006.

[43] Human Rights Watch, 'The Case against Hissène Habré, An African Pinochet', May 2006.

[44] See interviews with Reed Brody and Genoveva Hernandez of Human Rights Watch cited in Hayner, *Unspeakable Truths: Confronting State Terror and Atrocity*, 59.

[45] *Prosecutor* v. *Charles Ghakay Taylor* (SCSL-03-1-T), Decision on Prosecution Motion for Admission of Extracts of the Report of the Truth and Reconciliation Commission of Sierra Leone, 19 February 2009.

Argentina returns to a policy of prosecution for the violations committed by the military regime of the 1970s and 1980s, it has revisited the materials of its truth commission.[46]

However, it is clear that truth commission-holding states can be unwilling to provide judicial assistance to others for the purposes of prosecuting crimes that were committed on their territory or by their nationals. Attempts by third states to prosecute may be viewed as an unjustified interference in internal affairs and a threat to sovereignty.[47] Guatemala refused numerous assistance and extradition requests from Spain in relation to the involvement of former officials in the commission of human rights violations during the Guatemalan civil war,[48] despite the existence of a judicial cooperation treaty between the two.[49] Argentina maintained a twenty-year refusal to cooperate with France, Italy and Spain in their attempts to prosecute the violations committed by members of the Argentinean military junta.[50] The Argentinean authorities maintained that foreign courts could not prosecute human rights violations that occurred in Argentina due to the principle of territoriality.[51] They stressed that the violations concerned had been subject to a domestic process, in that case investigation by a truth commission and amnesty or pardon for those responsible.[52] Although a slightly different scenario, Kenya is proving hostile to the ICC's attempts to prosecute international crimes

---

[46] Priscilla B. Hayner, *Unspeakable Truths: Transitional Justice and the Challenge of Truth Commissions* (2nd edn) (London and New York: Routledge, 2010), 94–5.

[47] Decree 111 of 26 January 1998, published in the Official Gazette of Argentina on 9 February 1998, with the signatures of Minister of Foreign Affairs Guido Di Tella, and Minister of Justice Raúl Granillo Ocampo, stating that Spanish attempts to prosecute violations committed in Argentina during the period of military dictatorship were a violation of Argentinean sovereignty.

[48] See Rights Action/NISGUA, 'Arrest Warrants against Former Military Officials', and 'Rechazan Resolución de la CC en Caso España', *Prensa Libre*, 18 December 2007.

[49] Extradition Treaty between Spain and Guatemala, Guatemala, 7 November 1895.

[50] Roseann M. Latore, 'Coming out of the Dark: Achieving Justice for Victims of Human Rights Violations by South American Military Regimes' (2002) 25 *Boston College International and Comparative Law Review* 419; Maria Fernanda Pérez Solla, 'Enforced Disappearances before Argentinean Tribunals: New Developments in an Endless Fight for Justice' (2003) 19 *South African Journal on Human Rights* 691.

[51] Rebecca Lichtenfeld, 'Accountability in Argentina: 20 Years Later Transitional Justice Maintains Momentum', International Center for Transitional Justice, August 2005, 5. This is no longer the position in Argentina. See 'Argentina: President Allows Extraditions', *New York Times*, 26 July 2003.

[52] Human Rights Watch, *Argentina: Reluctant Partner: The Argentine Government's Failure to Back Trials of Human Rights Violators*, December 2001, Part VII, Transnational Justice.

committed on its territory and has stated that prosecution by the Court constitutes a violation of its sovereignty, despite its status as a state party to the ICC Statute.[53] It may not, therefore, be easy for bystander states to gain the necessary information or evidence where the requested state is hostile to the notion of prosecution by a third state. Where states have decided to establish a truth commission rather than pursuing prosecution, they may well view bystander state attempts to prosecute as an unwanted intrusion into domestic affairs. The hostile state may not only be one that decides not to prosecute out of negative motivation and with the aim of avoiding accountability. States that have established truth commissions as a first step towards dealing with past violations and are open to the prospect of national trials in the future, such as Liberia and perhaps Kenya, may also oppose attempts by bystander states to prosecute.

A further problem lies in the fact that, as discussed in Chapter 4, some truth commission information is typically protected from disclosure under domestic legislation.[54] Using a truth commission report to provide contextual evidence of the types of violations committed, as in the Pinochet, Guatemalan Generals and Taylor cases, is unlikely to prove problematic. These reports are generally published and, therefore, widely available. Judicial assistance from the truth commission-holding state will not be required to use a report in this way. However, a more complex situation is that which arose in relation to the prosecution of Hissène Habré, where the information held by the commission was used to provide leads to specific victims and witnesses. These details are not always publicly available and may be protected from disclosure under national law.

Truth commissions have adopted various approaches in their reports to the inclusion of information relating to those who have provided testimony. The South African TRC report contained a 900-page list of the names of victims and the violations they had suffered[55] and the Peruvian TRC report contained an annex of cases in which individual victims were named.[56] However, El Salvador's Commission divided its list of victims into categories of those whose identities were confidential and those

---

[53] ICC, Press Release, 'Pre-Trial Chamber II Receives Application from Kenyan Government', 4 April 2011.

[54] This is discussed in detail below.

[55] *Truth and Reconciliation Commission of South Africa Report* (Cape Town: Truth and Reconciliation Commission, distributed by Juta and Co., 2002), vol. 7, Victim Findings: Summaries, 10–920.

[56] *Informe Final de la Comisión de la Verdad y Reconciliación* (Lima: CVR, 2003), Anexo 4: Casos y víctimas registradas por la CVR.

whose were not.[57] The TRC for Sierra Leone listed some of its victims by initial, age and region only, to protect their privacy,[58] and listed the full names and the violations suffered by others. The report also included transcripts from public hearings in an annex.[59] Details of victims and witnesses published in a truth commission report might provide a prosecutorial institution in another state with valuable leads. However, should an investigating state seek access to the statements of particular victims and witnesses or seek details of those whose identity was kept confidential, the situation becomes more complicated. The ability to gain access to information of this nature is dependent upon the cooperation of the state holding the truth commission. Many of these states have drawn up national legislation that enables commissions to grant confidentiality and protects their information from disclosure and use in subsequent criminal proceedings.

There do not appear to be any instances, thus far, where information held by commissions has been requested by prosecutorial institutions in other states and withheld on the basis of these protective provisions. At the national level, the Peruvian prosecutor's office requested access to the Commission's files while operations were still underway, leading to a court ruling that materials were privileged due to the Commission's status as a branch of the executive.[60] However, the expansion of national jurisdiction under ICC implementing legislation, and the ICC Statute objective of ending impunity through the complementarity regime, may inspire a previously unseen vigour in attempts to prosecute serious human rights violations, even when they are committed on the territory of another state. What effect, if any, the confidentiality and non-disclosure provisions contained within national truth commission legislation are likely to have on requests for judicial assistance from third states remains unclear. Prima facie, there appears to be a direct conflict between national legislation that prevents the disclosure of information relating to human rights crimes and international agreements which oblige states to provide information to another for use in a criminal investigation or prosecution. Whether the protection of national truth commission information will be a valid

---

[57] *From Madness to Hope: The 12-year War in El Salvador: Report of the Commission on the Truth for El Salvador*, UN Doc. S/25500, Annex, 1993, Annex 6.

[58] SLTRC, *Witness to Truth: Report of the Sierra Leone Truth and Reconciliation Commission* (Accra: Graphic Packaging Ltd, 2004), vol. 2, chapter 5 'List of Victims'.

[59] *Ibid.*, Appendix 3, 'Transcripts of TRC Public Hearings'.

[60] Hayner, *Unspeakable Truths: Transitional Justice and the Challenge of Truth Commissions*, 95–6.

ground for refusing the provision of assistance under a judicial assistance treaty is uncertain.

There are therefore two problems that arise in relation to the possibility of bystander states seeking information under judicial assistance treaties from truth commission-holding states. The first is that the truth commission-holding state may view this as an unwarranted interference in domestic affairs and seek to obstruct trials by manipulating judicial assistance treaty provisions to withhold information. The second is that national laws that protect truth commission information may create genuine obstacles to the provision of evidence and information under mutual legal assistance treaty provisions. The next sections will explore in greater detail these areas of potential conflict and their likely impact on the ability to undertake effective truth seeking and to carry out successful criminal trials.

3.2   Truth commissions and the grounds for refusing assistance

Should states be reluctant to cooperate, there are a number of provisions within mutual legal assistance treaties which may allow the refusal of assistance. These include: where the offence in question is political;[61] where the provision of assistance would cause the requested state to act incompatibly with national laws[62] or contravene principles of *ne bis in idem*;[63] or where compliance with the request would prejudice national sovereignty, security or public order.[64]

---

[61] States are entitled to refuse mutual legal assistance on the grounds that the offence for which assistance is requested is political under a number of treaties: European Convention on Mutual Assistance in Criminal Matters 1959, ETS 30, Art. 2(a), United Nations Model Treaty on Mutual Assistance in Criminal Matters 1990, 30 ILM 1419 (1991), Art. 4(1)(b); Scheme Relating to Mutual Assistance in Criminal Matters within the Commonwealth 1986, Commonwealth Secretariat, London, Art. 8(1)(b); Inter-American Convention on Mutual Assistance in Criminal Matters 1992, OASTS 75, Art. 9(c); EU Convention on Mutual Assistance in Criminal Matters 2000, OJ C197/01, Art. 9.

[62] United Nations Model Treaty on Mutual Assistance in Criminal Matters 1990, Art. 4(1)(e); Scheme Relating to Mutual Assistance in Criminal Matters within the Commonwealth 1986, para. 8(2)(a).

[63] United Nations Model Treaty on Mutual Assistance in Criminal Matters 1990, Art. 4(1)(d); Scheme Relating to Mutual Assistance in Criminal Matters within the Commonwealth 1986, para. 8(1)(d); Inter-American Convention on Mutual Assistance in Criminal Matters 1992, Art. 9(a). This will be discussed in detail below.

[64] European Convention on Mutual Assistance in Criminal Matters 1959, Art. 2; United Nations Model Treaty on Mutual Assistance in Criminal Matters 1990, Art. 4(1)(a); Scheme Relating to Mutual Assistance in Criminal Matters within the Commonwealth 1986, para. 8(2)(a); Inter-American Convention on Mutual Assistance in Criminal Matters, Art. 9(e).

3.2.1   The political offence exception

One ground of refusal on which a truth commission-holding state might seek to rely is the political offence exception. Under a number of treaties, states are entitled to refuse mutual legal assistance on the grounds that the offence for which assistance is requested is 'political'.[65] The classification of even the most serious human rights violations as political can be seen in the practice of some states that have established truth commissions. The Chilean commission was mandated to investigate, among other things, *political* kidnappings.[66] The South African TRC was tasked with investigating gross violations of human rights,[67] 'the commission of which was advised, planned, directed, commanded or ordered by any person acting with a *political* motive'.[68] The East Timorese Commission also had a mandate to investigate violations that had 'taken place in the context of the *political* conflicts in East Timor'.[69] All of these commissions documented the perpetration of international crimes among the violations committed. The Chilean Commission attributed a policy of state torture to the Pinochet regime.[70] The South African TRC concluded that the system of apartheid, although not actually included within its investigatory mandate, amounted to a crime against humanity[71] and the East Timorese CAVR found that the Indonesian security forces had committed

---

[65] European Convention on Mutual Assistance in Criminal Matters 1959, Art. 2(a); United Nations Model Treaty on Mutual Assistance in Criminal Matters 1990, Art. 4(1)(b); Scheme Relating to Mutual Assistance in Criminal Matters within the Commonwealth 1986, Art. 8(1)(b); Inter-American Convention on Mutual Assistance in Criminal Matters 1992, Art. 9(c); EU Convention on Mutual Assistance in Criminal Matters 2000, OJ C197/01, Art. 9; Caribbean Mutual Legal Assistance Treaty in Serious Criminal Matters, 2000, Art. 7(b); Southeast Asia Treaty on Mutual Assistance in Criminal Matters, 2004, Art. 3(1)(a); South Asian Association for Regional Cooperation (SAARC) Convention on Mutual Assistance in Criminal Matters 2008, Art. 5(1)(vi).

[66] Chile: Supreme Decree No. 355, Creation of the Commission on Truth and Reconciliation, Santiago, 25 April 1990, Art. 1.

[67] South Africa: Promotion of National Unity and Reconciliation Act, No. 34 of 1995, Preamble.

[68] *Ibid.*, s. 1(1)(ix). See Anurima Bhargava, 'Defining Political Crimes: A Case Study of the South African Truth and Reconciliation Commission' (2002) 102 *Columbia Law Review* 1304.

[69] UN Transitional Administration in East Timor Regulation No. 2001/10 on the Establishment of a Commission for Reception, Truth and Reconciliation in East Timor, UN Doc. UNTAET/REG/2001/10, 13 July 2001, s. 3.1(a).

[70] *Report of the Chilean National Commission on Truth and Reconciliation* (University of Notre Dame Press, 1993), Part 3.

[71] *Truth and Reconciliation Commission of South Africa Report*, vol. 1, chapter 4, 94.

war crimes and crimes against humanity.[72] This suggests that in future there may be tension between the state of territoriality's classification of past crimes as political, internal matters and the perceptions of bystander states, which may rightly consider crimes international in character and prosecution a necessary response.

Whether international human rights crimes fall legitimately within the ambit of the political offence exception is questionable. The exception emerged in the development of extradition law and, historically, served to protect revolutionaries from unfair, retaliatory trials in the state that had been the target of the political crime.[73] It enabled states to remain neutral in relation to the internal affairs of others and, traditionally, was justified on the grounds that states did not have mutual interest in the suppression of political crimes as they did not threaten international public order.[74] Extending this protection to armed groups or government actors for human rights violations committed, commonly, against civilian populations seems a long way removed from the initial rationale behind the exception.[75] It is now generally accepted that the most serious human rights crimes are the concern of all nations[76] and do, indeed, threaten international public order.[77]

However, there is no international agreement on what constitutes a 'political offence'.[78] Under extradition law, national courts have developed different tests for determining whether an offence can be deemed 'political',[79] distinguishing between 'pure' and 'relative' political offences,[80] but an unambiguous, universal definition remains

---

[72] *Chega!* Final Report of the Commission for Reception, Truth and Reconciliation in East Timor, January 2006, Part 8, 5.

[73] Christine Van Den Wijngaert, *The Political Offence Exception to Extradition: The Delicate Problem of Balancing the Rights of the Individual and the International Public Order* (Deventer: Kluwer, 1980), 2–4.

[74] *Ibid.,* 3.

[75] On the disconnect between the current use of the political offence exception and its origins, see Aimee J. Buckland, 'Offending Officials: Former Government Actors and the Political Offence Exception to Extradition' (2006) 94 *California Law Review* 423.

[76] Rome Statute, Preamble, para. 9.

[77] Security Council Resolution 827 on the establishment of the ICTY, S/Res/827, 25 May 1993, Preamble, para. 4; Security Council Resolution 955 on the establishment of the ICTR, S/Res/955, 8 November 1994, Preamble, para. 4.

[78] Van den Wijngaert, *The Political Offence Exception to Extradition,* chapter 3.

[79] On these different approaches see Michael R. Littenburg, 'The Political Offence Exception: An Historical Analysis and a Model for the Future' (1990) 64 *Tulane Law Review* 1195.

[80] Geoff Gilbert, *Aspects of Extradition Law* (Dordrecht: Martinus Nijhoff, 1991), 140.

elusive.[81] Extradition law does provide some instruction on the ambit of the political offence exception. The Norgaard principles, developed to define political crimes in the Namibian transition, undertook an extensive examination of the factors considered by states under extradition law in determining whether a crime is political. It was concluded that weight is attached to the following criteria: the motive behind the act; the context in which it was committed; the legal and factual nature of the act, including its gravity; the object or objective of the act; whether it was committed on behalf of, on the approval of or under an order of an institution of which the person concerned is a member; the relationship between the act and the political objective and the proportionality of the act.[82] These principles suggest that where a crime is particularly grave, disproportionate in its severity to the objective pursued and targeted at individuals, rather than state actors, the likelihood of it being considered political is diminished. When viewed in this manner, the use of the political offence exception to refuse judicial assistance for the commission of core crimes appears less justifiable, particularly where those crimes have been committed against civilian populations.

It would appear that there is a growing international consensus that certain crimes are so serious that doctrines such as the political offence exception cannot properly be applied to them. Some national courts have stated that the normal protections under extradition law do not apply where international human rights crimes have been committed.[83] The ICTY and ICTR Rules of Procedure and Evidence stipulate that states must surrender an accused to the jurisdiction of the Courts regardless of any impediment under national law or extradition treaties.[84] In accordance, most states passed national legislation to enable them to transfer suspects to the Tribunals without the impediments normally found in

---

[81] Lloyd W. Grooms and Jane M. Samson, 'The Political Offence Exception to Extradition: A 19th Century British Standard in 20th Century American Courts' (1984) 59 *Notre Dame Law Review* 1005, 1009.

[82] Listed in Faustin Z. Ntoubandi, *Amnesty for Crimes against Humanity under International Law* (Leiden: Martinus Nijhoff, 2007), 162.

[83] See the decision of the French Chambre d'Accusation in the Barbie case, Cass Crim [Crim Chamber], 20 December 1985, translated in 78 ILR (1985) 125. P. 130 and the US decision in *Quinn v. Robinson* 783 F.2d 776, (9th Circuit), 1986, 800.

[84] International Criminal Tribunal for Rwanda, Rules of Procedure and Evidence, UN Doc. ITR/3/Rev.1, adopted on 29 June 1995, R. 58; International Criminal Tribunal for the former Yugoslavia, Rules of Procedure and Evidence, UN Doc. IT/32/Rev.44 (2009), R. 58.

extradition treaties.[85] The ICC Statute requires states parties to surrender suspects to the Court[86] and does not permit refusal on the grounds that the request relates to a political crime. In mutual assistance arrangements too, the political offence exception is being excluded. Under the Commonwealth Scheme, it does not apply where the offence falls within the scope of an international Convention to which both states are party and which imposes on them an obligation to prosecute or extradite the crime.[87] Neither does the EU Convention on Mutual Assistance in Criminal Matters 2000 allow states to refuse a request for assistance on the grounds that the offence concerned is political.

Nevertheless, under many multilateral and bilateral treaties the categorisation of an offence as political remains a ground for refusing assistance in relation to it. In this context, the lack of an unequivocal and widely accepted definition of a political offence remains problematic and leaves the exception open to manipulation. The classification of offences as 'political' under domestic law may therefore present an obstructive state with grounds for refusing assistance without contravening international treaty obligations. The refusal of assistance on these grounds may, however, thwart attempts by other states to carry out effective prosecutions.

3.2.2 Threats to sovereignty, national security and public order

Another ground for refusal that could be relied upon is that the provision of assistance might prejudice sovereignty, national security or public order in the requested state.[88] It has already been shown that

---

[85] International Law Association, Committee on Extradition and Human Rights, Third Report, February 1998, in Report of the 68th Conference (Taipei: International Law Association, 1998), 132.

[86] Rome Statute, Arts. 88 and 89.

[87] Commonwealth Scheme, Art. 8(4). Thus, under the Scheme the political offence exception would not apply to grave breaches of the Geneva Conventions or torture, providing that the states concerned were both parties to the Geneva Conventions and the Convention against Torture. For further discussion of the *aut dedere aut judicare* provisions of these Conventions, see M. Cherif Bassiouni and Ernest M. Wise, *Aut Dedere, Aut Judicare: The Duty to Extradite or Prosecute in International Law* (Dordrecht: Martinus Nijhoff Publishers, 1995), chapter 2.

[88] European Convention on Mutual Assistance in Criminal Matters 1959, Art. 2(b); United Nations Model Treaty on Mutual Assistance 1990, Art. 4(1)(a); Inter-American Convention on Mutual Assistance in Criminal Matters 1992, Art. 9(e); Caribbean Mutual Legal Assistance Treaty in Serious Criminal Matters 2000, Art. 7(3)(a); Southeast Asia Treaty on Mutual Assistance in Criminal Matters 2004, Art. 3(1)(f); South Asian

Argentina considered the Italian, French and Spanish attempts to prosecute Argentineans for crimes committed in Argentina a violation of its sovereignty and exclusive right to exercise jurisdiction over its territory and population. It refused judicial assistance on this ground.[89] Where a state has established a truth commission as a response to past violations, or indeed where it has not, it may consider attempts by a bystander state to prosecute those violations as an infringement of its sovereignty and refuse judicial assistance on that ground. A move away from the use of the prejudice of national sovereignty as a justification for the refusal of judicial assistance can be seen in the cooperation regimes between states and international courts prosecuting international crimes. In international criminal law, the broad assertion of national sovereignty is no longer an acceptable ground for refusing assistance where international crimes are concerned. Thus, while cooperation with the ad hoc tribunals may infringe a state's sovereignty, it has been held that sovereignty-related grounds cannot be unilaterally invoked as a ground for refusing assistance to the Tribunals and that such infringement is justified by Article 2(7) of the UN Charter.[90] Neither does the ICC Statute permit its states parties to refuse a measure of assistance on the grounds that sovereignty may be infringed. However, there is no corresponding regime in place to facilitate cooperation between states in the prosecution of international crimes. Where prosecutions of international crimes are undertaken by third states, cooperation will be dependent on existing bilateral and multilateral treaty arrangements in which the prejudice of national sovereignty remains as a ground for refusing assistance.

National security is one aspect of sovereignty that is generally considered a legitimate concern and attracts protection. International courts have sought to find a balance between their own interests in carrying out effective prosecutions with all relevant evidence and the interests of states to protect certain types of information and prevent its public disclosure. The ICTY Appeal Chamber has stated that states' legitimate national security concerns ought to be accommodated through

---

Association for Regional Cooperation (SAARC) Convention on Mutual Assistance in Criminal Matters 2008, Art. 5(1)(i).

[89] See above, section 3.1.

[90] *Prosecutor* v. *Blaskic* (Case No. IT-95–14-AR108BIS), Judgment on the Request of the Republic of Croatia for Review of the Decision of Trial Chamber II of 18 July 1997, 29 October 1997, para. 65. See also *Prosecutor* v. *Kanyabashi* (Case No. ICTR-96–15-T) Judgment on the Defence Motion on Jurisdiction, 18 June 1997.

the provision of practical arrangements.[91] The ICC Statute lays down a cooperative procedure through which states and the Court seek to resolve issues relating to disclosure of national security information.[92] The potential for truth commissions to come into possession of national security information was discussed in Chapter 4, making it a possibility that requests for truth commission information by third states might legitimately be refused on this ground. However, while the cooperation regimes between states and international courts allow for consideration of national security interests, they do not permit states to unilaterally refuse disclosure.[93] Instead, states are expected to reach agreement with the courts on the conditions under which sensitive information can be disclosed. This is not the case under mutual assistance treaties. Some treaties provide for the provision of assistance subject to conditions,[94] but the decision as to whether national security interests would be prejudiced by the disclosure of information to a third state lies at the discretion of the requested state. The breadth of information covered by the term and the ease with which states can classify categories of information as relating to national security[95] means that even the requirement that the requested state give reasons for the refusal of assistance[96] is no real impediment to using this ground. The absence of scrutiny mechanisms leaves it open to manipulation. In some cases the disclosure of requested information, including that held by truth commissions, might prejudice national security interests. It is also possible that this

---

[91] *Ibid.* See also Salvatore Zappala, 'Blaskic Subpoena Proceedings', in Antonio Cassese (ed.), *The Oxford Companion to International Criminal Justice* (Oxford University Press, 2009), 613–15.

[92] Rome Statute, Art. 72.

[93] See *Prosecutor v. Blaskic* (Case No. IT-95-14-AR108BIS), Judgment on the Request of the Republic of Croatia for Review of the Decision of Trial Chamber II of 18 July 1997, 29 October 1997.

[94] See for example the United Nations Model Treaty on Mutual Assistance in Criminal Matters 1990, Art. 4(4)

[95] David Banisar, 'Freedom of Information, International Trends and National Security', Geneva Centre for the Democratic Control of Armed Forces, October 2002. On the US system see Christina E. Wells, '"National Security" Information and the Freedom of Information Act' (2004) 56 *Administrative Law Review* 1195; David Pozen, 'The Mosaic Theory, National Security and the Freedom of Information Act' (2005) 115 *Yale Law Journal* 628. On the UK's Freedom of Information Act, which is heavily qualified in the interests of national security, see John Wadham and Kavita Modi, 'National Security and Open Government in the United Kingdom', in Campbell Public Affairs Institute (ed.), *National Security and Open Government: Striking the Right Balance* (Syracuse: Campbell Public Affairs Institute, 2003), 75–101.

[96] United Nations Model Treaty on Mutual Assistance in Criminal matters 1990, Art. 4(5).

ground of refusal may be open to abuse and used as a tool by uncooperative states to prevent the disclosure of requested information.

A final ground of refusal related to sovereignty is that the provision
of assistance would threaten public order within the requested state. It
has been suggested that this ground is rarely invoked and serves only as
a protection in principle for states.[97] However, in the aftermath of mass
human rights violations it is often argued that, as a matter of policy,
prosecution should not be pursued where it threatens the peaceful transition to democracy.[98] In Chile, it was argued that the former military
regime would oppose any attempt at prosecution and that trials should
be foregone in an effort to maintain peace and democracy.[99] Likewise,
in Argentina the government's policy of prosecution was abandoned in
the face of military hostility. It was considered more sensible to forego
prosecution than to risk a *coup d'état* and a return to military rule.[100]
Both of these states opted instead to respond to past violations by establishing truth commissions. The trial of Charles Taylor before the Special
Court for Sierra Leone was held in The Hague due to concerns that trial
in Freetown would threaten regional stability.[101] Arguments on the need
to secure stability over pursuing criminal prosecutions were advanced
in response to the ICC's issuance of arrest warrants for Ugandan LRA
rebels.[102] Bigombe, the lead peace negotiator, condemned the ICC for

[97] Kimberly Prost, 'Toward Meaningful Adherence to Multilateral Instruments for International Cooperation: The Challenges to Effective Mutual Legal Assistance', in Rodrigo Yepes-Enríquez and Lisa Tabassi (eds.), *Treaty Enforcement and International Cooperation in Criminal Matters with Special Reference to the Chemical Weapons Convention* (The Hague: T. M. C. Asser Press, 2002), 480–91, 484.

[98] Carlos S. Nino, 'The Duty to Punish Past Abuses of Human Rights Put into Context: The Case of Argentina' (1991) 100 *Yale Law Journal* 2619; Jose Zalaquett, 'Balancing Ethical Imperatives with Political Constraints: The Dilemma of New Democracies Confronting Past Human Rights Violations' (1992) 43 *Hastings Law Journal* 1425.

[99] Zalaquett, 'Balancing Ethical Imperatives with Political Constraints', 1432–3.

[100] Nino, 'The Duty to Punish Past Abuses of Human Rights Put into Context', 2627–9.

[101] Special Court for Sierra Leone, Press Release, 'Special Court President Requests Charles Taylor be Tried in the Hague', Freetown, Sierra Leone, 30 March 2006.

[102] In 2004 the head of the Ugandan Government's Amnesty Commission joined mem-bers of parliament and religious leaders from northern Uganda in opposing the ICC investigation. See 'Kony: Amnesty, Not Arrest', All Africa News, 16 February 2004. See also Refugee Law Project, 'Whose Justice? Perceptions of Uganda's Amnesty Act 2000: The Potential for Conflict Resolution and Long Term Reconciliation', Working Paper No. 15, 2005. See also Abigail H. Moy, 'The International Criminal Court's Arrest Warrants and Uganda's Lord's Resistance Army: Renewing the Debate over Amnesty and Complementarity' (2006) 19 *Harvard Human Rights Journal* 267, 269–72.

jeopardising the peace process.[103] Kony, leader of the LRA, stated that he would not sign a peace agreement with the Ugandan government until the ICC withdrew its charges, claiming that the arrest warrants are an obstacle to lasting peace.[104] The warrants issued for Sudanese officials prompted similar statements. The Sudanese government called the ICC Prosecutor an 'impeder of the peace process' and an enemy of peace and stability in the country.[105]

Of course, a contrary argument can be advanced. In response to the Ugandan criticism, the ICC Deputy Prosecutor stated that it is those who have committed atrocities that are an impediment to lasting peace. The warrants, she considered, had been a significant factor in bringing the perpetrators into peace negotiations with the government in Uganda and have therefore contributed to the promotion of peace and stability in the country.[106] The International Criminal Tribunals have mandates to contribute to the restoration and maintenance of peace in the regions in which they are established through the prosecution of those responsible for past violations,[107] as does the Special Court for Sierra Leone.[108] It is reported that the arrest of Charles Taylor had a 'calming affect' in Liberia as worries over his potential to play a covert destabilising role in the country were removed.[109] Thus, there is an argument that, rather than threatening stability, pursuing a prosecutorial policy may enhance it. Indeed, prosecution by a third state may reduce the likelihood of instability by removing both the trial and those likely to cause disruption from the state of territoriality.

Again, however, the issue is not whether assisting another state in prosecutions would, in reality, threaten public order but whether an uncooperative state might be able to exploit this ground to refuse assistance. It

---

[103] 'Uganda Aide Criticises Court over Warrants', *New York Times*, 9 October 2005.

[104] Bogonko Bosire, 'Uganda War Crimes Suspects Must Face Justice: UN', *Agence France Presse*, 14 November 2007.

[105] John Heilprin, 'International Criminal Court and UN Tested by Strength of Response to Darfur Crimes', *Associated Press*, 2 December 2007.

[106] *Ibid.*

[107] Security Council Resolution 827 (1993), UN Doc S/RES/827 (1993), 25 May 1993, Preamble; Security Council Resolution 955 (1994), UN Doc. S/RES/955 (1994), 8 November 1994, Preamble.

[108] Security Council Resolution 1315 (2000), UN Doc. S/RES/1315 (2000), 14 August 2000, Preamble.

[109] Priscilla B. Hayner, 'Negotiating Peace in Liberia: Preserving the Possibility for Justice', Report for the Center for Humanitarian Dialogue and the International Center for Transitional Justice, November 2007, 24.

would seem that where a state does not want to assist another in prosecutions, under the majority of treaties[110] it will be able to refuse on the grounds that doing so might threaten public order and point to the establishment of a truth commission as a compromise which contributes to justice without threatening stability.

3.2.3   Incompatibility with national law

A further ground of refusal under some treaties is that the provision of assistance would require the requested state to act in a way that is incompatible with its national laws.[111] As described in Chapter 4, the laws of many truth commission-holding states protect the information gathered by commissions, particularly confidential information, and prevent its disclosure to third parties. In some cases their enacting legislation has stipulated that proceedings must be conducted confidentially to protect the identities and guarantee the safety of those who give testimony.[112] Other commissions have been given discretion to grant confidentiality.[113] To protect that information truth commission legislation also now often contains provisions preventing the disclosure of confidential materials on

[110] An example of a treaty which does not allow states to refuse assistance on the grounds that it would present a threat to security or public order is the EU Convention on Mutual Assistance in Criminal Matters 2000.

[111] United Nations Model Treaty on Mutual Assistance in Criminal Matters 1990, Art. 4(1)(e); Scheme Relating to Mutual Assistance in Criminal Matters within the Commonwealth 1986, Art. 8(3); South Asian Association for Regional Cooperation (SAARC) Convention on Mutual Assistance in Criminal Matters 2008, Art. 5(1)(ii).

[112] Agreement on the Establishment of the Commission to Clarify Past Human Rights Violations and Acts of Violence that have caused the Guatemalan Population to Suffer, Oslo, 17 June 1994, (1997) 36 *International Legal Materials* 283, which established the Guatemalan Commission, stated that 'the Commission's proceedings shall be confidential so as to guarantee the secrecy of the sources and the safety of witnesses'. Similarly, the legislation that established the Peruvian TRC, Decreto Supremo No. 065–2001-PCM, Creación de la Comisión de la Verdad en el Perú, Lima, Peru, 2 June 2001, Art. 7, stated that all testimony collected by the Commission was to remain confidential. This was also the situation in El Salvador. See Mexico Peace Agreements, Mexico City, 27 April 1991, Art. 7.

[113] Peru: Decreto Supremo No. 065–2001-PCM, Creación de la Comisión de la Verdad en el Perú, Lima, Peru, 2 June 2001, Art. 6(d); An Act to Establish the Truth and Reconciliation Commission of Liberia, 2005, Art. 27(c); Sierra Leone: Truth and Reconciliation Commission Act 2000, s. 7(3); Kenya: Truth Justice and Reconciliation Act 2008, s. 7(2)(c). The South African Promotion of National Unity and Reconciliation Act, No. 34 of 1995, s. 33, enabled the TRC to hold hearings in private and prevent the disclosure of any information obtained during that hearing.

dissolution.[114] Should a state receive a request for assistance relating to confidential information held by its commission, it might refuse to provide assistance on the grounds that disclosing such information would be inconsistent with national laws.

Other difficulties are posed in relation to the rights against self-incrimination and to a fair trial by the possibility of requests for self-incriminating information obtained under a truth commission's powers of compulsion.[115] The right against self-incrimination is not only protected under international and regional human rights instruments,[116] it is often constitutionally protected at the national level.[117] If that is the case, it may be incompatible with national law to pass self-incriminating evidence to another state for use in prosecutorial proceedings, or at least there may be an argument that to do so would violate national standards. Equally, the use of such information in a subsequent prosecution may be incompatible with the laws of the requesting state, depending, particularly, on how the testimony was obtained by the commission within the requested state. While many treaties now stipulate that evidence be gathered in accordance with the laws of the requesting state,[118] this will not be possible where information has already been obtained under a truth commission's powers of compulsion. Much may rest on the scope of the protection afforded under national law and there is variation in national recognition of the principle. Some states limit the right to the giving of testimony at trial,[119] while others recognise it from the time of arrest.[120] Within the EU, the laws of the Member States generally grant the right not to give evidence

---

[114] Sierra Leone: Truth and Reconciliation Commission Act 2000, s. 19(2)(a)(ii); Kenya: Truth Justice and Reconciliation Act 2008, s. 52(2)(a). The Liberian TRC's Final Report contains thorough discussion on the need to protect TRC materials following dissolution. See *Final Report of the TRC of Liberia*, (Ghana: Twidan Graphics, 2009), vol. 2. 334–5.

[115] See Chapter 4 on these powers.   [116] See Chapter 4.

[117] See M. Cherif Bassiouni, 'Human Rights in the Context of Criminal Justice: Identifying International Procedural Protections and Equivalent Protections in National Constitutions' (1993) 3 *Duke Journal of Comparative and International Law* 235, fn. 138 for a list of states that protect the right against self-incrimination in their constitutions.

[118] See, for example, European Convention on Laundering Search, Seizure and Confiscation of the Proceeds of Crime, 1990 ETS 141, 2000 EU Convention on Mutual Assistance in Criminal Matters 2000, Art. 4.

[119] Bassiouni, 'Human Rights in the Context of Criminal Justice', 265.

[120] Constitution of the Republic of South Africa 1996, s. 35(1)(c) and *Miranda* v. *Arizona*, Case No. 759, 384 US 436 (1966) on the rights under the Fifth Amendment to the US Constitution.

against oneself only to a person charged with an offence in criminal proceedings,[121] although there is discrepancy within the individual laws as to which stage of proceedings the protection becomes available.[122]

It may therefore appear that self-incriminating evidence obtained pre-charge will not always attract the protection of the right against self-incrimination and that information obtained under a commission's powers of compulsion will not fall within its ambit. However, national and regional courts have held that where self-incriminating evidence is obtained under the powers of compulsion of a body established by law, that evidence will not be admissible in subsequent criminal proceedings against the accused.[123] It has also been held that statements obtained by compulsion which are not directly incriminating but which are used to discredit the accused in future criminal proceedings constitute an infringement of the right.[124] Of course, this does not rule out the possibility that third states might seek disclosure of self-incriminating information in order to further their investigations, while ruling out reliance upon it at trial.[125] Nevertheless, authorities in a requested state may conclude that to provide any evidence adduced under a commission's powers of compulsion is inconsistent with national laws on the right against self-incrimination.

Generally, requested states may refuse to provide truth commission information, and particularly self-incriminating evidence obtained under powers of compulsion, on the grounds that to do so would be incompatible with national law. Unlike with the political offence exception and potential threats to national security and public order, there seems to be more scope for genuine conflict between national laws and human rights protections and international assistance treaty obligations under this ground. At a general level, the provision of any truth commission information may conflict with national laws that protect it from disclosure. However, to provide self-incriminating information obtained under a commission's powers of compulsion may contravene not only national laws but international human rights standards as well.

---

[121] Case 374/87, *Orkem SA* v. *Commission of the European Communities* [1989] ECR 3283, para. 29.

[122] *Ibid.*, para. 111. See also Canadian Charter of Rights and Freedoms, 1982, s.11(c); Constitution of the United States of America, Fifth Amendment.

[123] *Ferreira* v. *Levin and Others*, Judgment of 6 December 1995 [1995] ZACC 13; *Saunders* v. *UK* (Application No. 19187/91), Judgment of 29 November 1996, (1997) 23 EHRR 313.

[124] *Saunders* v. *United Kingdom*, Application No. 19187/91, (1997) 23 EHRR 313, paras. 71–4.

[125] Freeman, *Truth Commissions and Procedural Fairness*, 252.

3.3 The incompatibility of truth seeking and bystander state prosecutions

Where a third state attempts to prosecute the violations committed on the territory of a truth commission-holding state there may be negative consequences for both truth commissions and prosecutorial institutions. Arrangements such as the 2000 EU Convention on Mutual Assistance in Criminal Matters are indicative of a narrowing of the traditional grounds for refusal of assistance in favour of greater cooperation, particularly where serious human rights violations are concerned. However, the traditional grounds for refusal continue to apply in many bilateral and multilateral mutual assistance treaties. As discussed, these may pose a significant obstacle to states seeking to prosecute crimes that have occurred on the territory of a truth commission-holding state. On the one hand, a state seeking to obstruct potential prosecutions might exploit the grounds of refusal to withhold relevant information. For other states, there may be a genuine conflict between fulfilling obligations under mutual legal assistance treaties to provide assistance and abiding by national laws, which seek to protect the information held by truth commissions. Regardless of the motivation behind the refusal of assistance, it will likely have the result of hindering investigations and hampering the compilation of prosecution cases.

A truth commission-holding state would have to consider carefully before refusing a request for evidence relating to violations already investigated by a commission or for information specifically held by it. Where the crimes concerned fall within the jurisdiction of the ICC, refusal by a state party to the ICC to provide information to a state seeking to prosecute might be determined by the Court as unwillingness or inability to prosecute and render the case admissible before the ICC.[126] The traditional grounds for refusal of requests for judicial assistance do not apply between the ICC and states parties, which are under international treaty obligations to provide assistance to the Court when requested.[127] The situation differs where states are not party to the Statute. Where human rights violations are committed in a non-party state the case will not be admissible before the Court, unless the Security Council refers the situation[128] or the

---

[126] Rome Statute, Art. 17. See John T. Holmes, 'The Principle of Complementarity', in Roy S. Lee (ed.), *The International Criminal Court: The Making of the Rome Statute – Issues, Negotiations, Results* (The Hague: Kluwer, 1999), 41–79.

[127] Rome Statute, Art. 93. See Chapter 4.

[128] Rome Statute, Art. 13(b).

state of territoriality accepts the Court's jurisdiction.[129] Prosecution will be dependent on action either by the state of territoriality or by another state with the requisite domestic legislation exercising jurisdiction. In the latter situation, even presuming that there is a mutual legal assistance treaty in place between the prosecuting and truth commission-holding states, the traditional grounds for refusing the provision of information will be valid. Reliance on these existing methods of cooperation may therefore make it difficult, if not impossible, for states parties to effectively prosecute human rights crimes.

Equally, however, requests for assistance and attempts to access truth commission information are likely to impede the work of the truth commission by inhibiting those who are reluctant to become involved in criminal proceedings from offering testimony. Support for this contention can be seen in the experience of the South African TRC and the difficulties it experienced in obtaining testimony from former members of the South African Defence Force (SADF). The number of amnesty applications received by the Commission from this group was extremely low.[130] It is generally considered that this was due to concerns regarding potential prosecution by third states for crimes committed outside South Africa in accordance with apartheid government policy.[131] As part of the security policy of the apartheid era, the SADF was involved in extra-territorial assassinations and abductions in Southern Africa and Western Europe, attacks on the infrastructure of other states and attempts to overthrow the governments of other countries.[132] Although the TRC had the power to grant individualised amnesty, this was only effective within South Africa. It was not recognised under international law and could not preclude a foreign state from exercising jurisdiction to prosecute. The SADF therefore advised its members not to apply for amnesty and thereby disclose information relating to acts committed outside South African territory.[133] As a result, the TRC could not access testimony on this significant dimension of the violations committed under the apartheid system. Although the South African example relates to the commission of crimes on the territory of other states, it demonstrates that where there is a threat of prosecution by a third state, perpetrators 'in particular' will be reluctant to offer testimony relating to those crimes to a truth commission.

---

[129] Rome Statute, Art. 12(3).
[130] *Truth and Reconciliation Commission of South Africa Report*, vol. 6. Section 3, chapter 1, 263.
[131] *Ibid.*, 185.   [132] *Ibid.*, vol. 2, chapter 2.
[133] *Ibid.*, vol. 6. Section 3, chapter 1, 185.

There is, therefore, an incompatibility between these two transitional justice mechanisms when they operate in this manner. Admittedly, the number of instances in which such a situation is likely to arise is probably limited. However, in the cases which will arise where the ICC is overstretched or does not have jurisdiction and the state of territoriality does not hold trials, successful prosecution will be dependent on a third state exercising jurisdiction.[134] There is potential, then, for the operation of a national truth commission in the requested state to act as an impediment to the provision of the judicial assistance required to carry out criminal trials in the requesting state. Despite the efforts of many states parties to ensure that they have the necessary domestic legislation to prosecute human rights crimes wherever they occur, the impunity gap will remain. It is frustrating that uncooperative requested states may be able to prevent successful prosecution in another state by manipulating the grounds for refusal of assistance under judicial cooperation treaties. However, it is unthinkable that human rights crimes may go unpunished as a result of national laws protecting from disclosure the information uncovered in the operations of another transitional justice mechanism, one which is also designed to contribute to justice in the aftermath of human rights crimes.[135] Neither, of course, is it desirable that the operation of truth commissions be compromised as a result of prosecutions in third states.

As suggested in Chapter 4, some of this tension might be resolved by limiting the powers of future truth commissions. Removing the powers to grant confidentiality and compel the provision of self-incriminating testimony would alter the nature of the information held by commissions, in that all testimony would have been given freely and voluntarily. It would therefore require less stringent protection under national law, making it easier to disclose under judicial assistance treaties. At the same time, if truth commissions hold less controversial evidence and do not possess confidential or incriminating information, it may be of less interest to prosecuting authorities. Limiting powers would necessarily reduce the scope of information available to a truth commission in compiling its historical record and exclude some sectors from the truth-seeking process. However, it is questionable whether this situation is any worse than the

---

[134] Broomhall, *International Justice and the International Criminal Court*, 116.

[135] Martha Minow, 'The Hope for Healing: What Can Truth Commissions Do?', in Robert I. Rotberg and Dennis Thompson (eds.), *Truth v. Justice: The Morality of Truth Commissions* (Princeton University Press, 2000), 235–61; James Gibson, 'On Legitimacy Theory and the Effectiveness of Truth Commissions' (2009) 72 *Law and Contemporary Problems* 123.

damage that may be done to the commission's credibility if information obtained under truth-seeking powers is subject to requests for disclosure and subsequently accessed by prosecuting authorities in a third state.

Problems surrounding exploitation of the grounds for refusal by states determined to deny assistance would of course remain. Limiting the powers of truth commissions would only alleviate the tension between protective national laws and treaty obligations to disclose information. While existing mutual legal assistance treaties remain the only means of gaining information and evidence from another state, the grounds for refusal of assistance will continue to present an obstacle to states seeking to prosecute violations that took place outside their territory. The problems seem likely only to be exacerbated by the operation of a truth commission in the state of territoriality.

4 Truth commissions and extradition

The operation of a national truth commission might additionally create difficulties for a third state attempting to gain custody of alleged perpetrators for the purposes of prosecution under extradition proceedings. There is no rule of international law that requires a state to surrender fugitive offenders. Most states extradite on the basis of bilateral or multilateral treaties, which set down obligations to extradite subject to mandatory and discretionary grounds of refusal. On first consideration, there appear to be fewer potentially problematic areas as regards truth commissions under extradition treaties than there are under those on mutual legal assistance. Most extradition treaties require satisfaction of the double criminality rule[136] and contain reciprocal speciality provisions.[137]

---

[136] European Convention on Extradition 1957, 1960 ETS 24, Art. 2; UN Model Treaty on Extradition, General Assembly Resolution 45/116, (1990) 30 ILM 1410, Art. 5; Inter-American Convention on Extradition, (1981) OASTS 60, Art. 3. For a discussion of this rule see Ivan Shearer, *Extradition in International Law* (Manchester University Press, 1971), 137–8 and Ivor Stanbrook and Clive Stanbrook, *Extradition Law and Practice* (2nd edn) (Oxford University Press, 2000), 21–36.

[137] European Convention on Extradition 1957, Arts. 14 and 15; UN Model Treaty on Extradition 1990, Art. 14; Inter-American Convention on Extradition 1981, Art. 13. The rule has customary international law status and therefore applies to all extraditions, regardless of their legal basis. A strict definition of this rule is now rare and many modern treaties allow for standard exceptions. For instance, under the European Convention on Extradition 1957, Art. 14(1)(a) and (b), the extradited person can be proceeded against for an offence other than that for which he was extradited if the requested state consents or where the person, having had an opportunity to leave the territory of the party to which he was surrendered does not do so, or having left, voluntarily returns.

Many do not require the requested state to extradite to states that enforce the death penalty, unless the requesting state gives an undertaking not to implement it.[138] There is traditional reluctance to extradite for military crimes[139] and for fiscal offences.[140] In addition, a number of treaties give parties the right to refuse extradition of nationals.[141] There is sometimes a provision that where extradition is refused on the grounds that the person concerned is a national, at the request of the requesting state the requested state must submit the case to its competent authorities.[142] These conditions may well create difficulties for third states in obtaining custody of a requested person but those difficulties are not related to the operation of a truth commission in the requested state.

As under mutual assistance treaties, extradition was traditionally refused where it was sought, or where the alleged offence was committed, for political reasons.[143] The scope of the exception has been reduced with regard to international human rights crimes. The Genocide Convention provides that the acts enumerated within the treaty shall not be considered political crimes for the purposes of extradition.[144] The 1975 Additional Protocol to the 1957 European Extradition Convention

See M. Cherif Bassiouni, *International Criminal Law: Procedural and Enforcement Mechanisms* (New York: Transnational Publishers, 1999), 236.

[138] See UN Model Treaty on Extradition 1990, Art. 4; European Convention on Extradition 1957, Art. 1. See also the decision of the European Court of Human Rights in *Soering* v. *United Kingdom* (Application No. 14038/88), Judgment of 7 July 1989, (1989) 11 EHRR 439 which considered the death penalty in relation to the prohibition of torture and inhumane or degrading treatment or punishment and makes clear that states parties to the European Convention for the Protection of Human Rights and Fundamental Freedoms are under an obligation to refuse a request for extradition where there are substantial grounds for believing that a person would face a real risk of being subjected to torture or ill-treatment in the receiving state.

[139] European Convention on Extradition 1957, Art. 4; UN Model Treaty on Extradition 1990, Art. 3.

[140] European Convention on Extradition 1957, Art. 5.

[141] European Convention on Extradition 1957, Art. 6; UN Model Treaty on Extradition 1990, Art. 4(a); Inter-American Convention on Extradition 1981, Art. 7.

[142] European Convention on Extradition 1957, Art. 6(2); UN Model Treaty on Extradition 1990, Art. 4(a). On the attempts to do away with the nationality ground of refusal in the EU, see Zsuzsanna Deen-Racsmany and Rob Blextoon, 'The Decline of the Nationality Exception in European Extradition? The Impact of the Regulation of (Non) Surrender of Nationals and Dual Criminality under the European Arrest Warrant' (2005) 13 *European Journal of Crime, Criminal Law and Criminal Justice* 317.

[143] European Convention on Extradition 1957, Art. 3; UN Model Treaty on Extradition 1990, Art. 3; Inter-American Convention on Extradition 1981, Art. 4.

[144] UN Convention on the Prevention and Punishment of the Crime of Genocide, 9 December 1948, 78 UNTS 227, Art. 7.

excludes genocide and a number of war crimes from the political offence exception.[145] The European Arrest Warrant scheme applies to the crimes within the jurisdiction of the ICC[146] and does not include the political offence exception for the prevention of their extradition. These instruments indicate a determination that the perpetrators of these violations should not escape punishment through the manipulation of the political offence exception. Thus, unlike under most mutual legal assistance treaties, the classification of violations as 'political' under the national laws of a truth commission-holding state will not prevent extradition under many treaties. Nevertheless, the Guatemalan Constitutional Court recently refused the extradition to Spain of former military officers on the grounds that the crimes they committed were of a political nature,[147] despite the inclusion of the crimes of genocide and torture in the arrest warrants.[148] The Court gave no consideration to its obligations as a state party to the Genocide or Torture Conventions. It simply ruled that under the treaty in place between Spain and Guatemala extradition for political crimes was not possible. Thus, while the inclusion of the political offence exception as a ground for refusing extradition may be declining within treaty arrangements,[149] its use has not entirely ceased in extradition practice.

The traditional link between truth commissions and national amnesty laws may, however, present an obstacle to requests for extradition. Many treaties contain provisions that allow a request to be refused where amnesty has been granted in respect of the offence in the requested state. For example, the Second Additional Protocol to the 1957 European Convention on Extradition prohibited extradition where amnesty had been granted for the offence in the requested state and that state had

---

[145] Additional Protocol to the 1957 European Convention on Extradition 1975, 1979 ETS 86, Art. 1.

[146] Council Framework Decision of 13 June 2002 on the European Arrest Warrant and the Surrender Procedures between Member States, OJ L190, 1–20, Art. 2(2).

[147] Amnesty International, 'Guatemala: Inconsistent Ruling by the Constitutional Court Rejects Extraditions Sought by Spain', AI Index: AMR 34/026/2007, 21 December 2007; NISGUA, 'Constitutional Court Verdict Consolidates Impunity in Guatemala', 18 January 2008; Centre for Justice and Accountability, 'Judge Pedraz Takes Testimony of CJA Clients, Despite Refusal of Guatemalan Court to Extradite Defendants', 5 February 2008.

[148] 'Spanish Judge Orders Guatemalan Ex-Rulers Arrested', New York Times, 7 July 2006.

[149] Under the European Arrest Warrant a state cannot refuse to surrender on the grounds that the offence in question is of a political nature.

competence to prosecute under its own criminal law.[150] The UN Model Treaty on Extradition also states that extradition shall not be granted 'if the person whose extradition is requested has ... become immune from prosecution or punishment for any reason, including ... amnesty'.[151] A similar provision can be found within the Inter-American Convention on Extradition.[152] Even the Framework Decision on the European Arrest Warrant, which abolishes and narrows many of the traditional grounds for refusal of requests for extradition, contains a provision that prevents extradition where the offence is covered by amnesty in the executing Member State.[153]

A number of truth commissions have been established prior to or following the passing of national amnesty laws[154] or have had the power to grant individualised amnesty as part of their mandate.[155] Amnesties for international crimes have received strong criticism.[156] The ICTY has held that amnesty for torture is illegitimate because of the *jus cogens* nature of the crime.[157] The Inter-American Court of Human Rights considers that amnesties for non-derogable international human rights are invalid.[158] The Human Rights Committee stated that 'generally' amnesties for state officials responsible for torture are incompatible with duties to investigate, prosecute and prevent human rights violations.[159] At the national level,

---

[150] Second Additional Protocol to the European Convention on Extradition, 1978 ETS 98, Art. 4.

[151] UN Model Treaty on Extradition 1990, Art. 3(e).

[152] Inter-American Convention on Extradition 1981, Art. 4(1).

[153] Council Framework Decision of 13 June 2002, Art. 3(1).

[154] See Louise Mallinder, *Amnesty, Human Rights and Political Transitions: Bridging the Peace and Justice Divide* (Oxford: Hart Publishing, 2008), 165–73.

[155] Under the South African Promotion of National Unity and Reconciliation Act, No. 34 of 1995, s. 3(1)(b), the South African TRC was endowed with the power to grant individualised amnesty in exchange for truthful testimony.

[156] For discussion of the status of amnesty laws see, Ben Chigara, *Amnesty in International Law: The Legality under International Law of National Amnesty Laws* (Harlow: Pearson Education Ltd, 2002). On the challenges to amnesty laws, see Mallinder, *Amnesty, Human Rights and Political Transitions*, Part 2.

[157] *Prosecutor* v. *Furundzija* (Case No. IT-95-17/1-T), Judgment, 10 December 1998, para. 155. See also *Ould Dah* v. *France* (Application No. 13113/03), Judgment of 30 March 2009, [2009] ECHR 532, 17.

[158] *Barrio Altos Case* (*Chumbipuma Aguirre et al.* v. *Peru*) Inter-American Court of Human Rights, Series C, No. 75, 14 March 2001.

[159] General Comment 20, Compilation of General Comments and General Recommendations Adopted by Human Rights Treaty Bodies, UN Doc. HRI/GEN/1/Rev.1, 30 (1994).

too, amnesty laws for international crimes are being ruled inapplicable. In recent times, courts in Argentina and Chile have restricted the application of these laws.[160] However, there is no general rule of international law that prohibits national amnesty laws for international crimes. As such, the Special Court for Sierra Leone has held that 'there is a crystallising international norm that a government cannot grant amnesty for serious violations of crimes under international law'.[161] That norm is developing, rather than established.[162]

Recent practice in the use of truth commission and amnesty programmes is in line with the development of international jurisprudence. Since 2000, commissions have been established in conjunction with limited amnesty programmes, which exclude amnesty for the most serious human rights crimes. In East Timor, the truth commission operated the Community Reconciliation Process, which allowed perpetrators of low-level crimes to gain immunity from prosecution by admitting responsibility for their crimes and carrying out some form of community service.[163] However, the programme did not extend to serious criminal offences, which included genocide, crimes against humanity and war crimes.[164] The Liberian TRC, established in 2005, was given the power to make recommendations for the granting of amnesty to individuals who gave full disclosure of their wrongs and expressed remorse for their actions. Again, such a recommendation could not apply to violations of international humanitarian law or crimes against humanity.[165] Kenya's Truth, Justice and Reconciliation Commission was recently endowed with the power to recommend the granting of conditional amnesty to those who committed crimes during the 2007 post-election violence. This is not possible in cases involving genocide, crimes against humanity and other gross violations of human rights.[166]

---

[160] Fannie Lafontaine, 'No Amnesty or Statute of Limitation for Enforced Disappearances: The Sandoval Case before the Supreme Court of Chile' (2005) 3 *Journal of International Criminal Justice* 469; Christine Bakker, 'A Full Stop to Amnesty in Argentina' (2005) 3 *Journal of International Criminal Justice* 1106.

[161] *Prosecutor v. Kallon and Kamara* (SCSL-2004–15-AR72(E)), Decision on Challenge to Jurisdiction: Lomé Accord Amnesty, 13 March 2004, para. 82.

[162] *Ibid.*

[163] UN Transitional Administration in East Timor Regulation No. 2001/10, s. 3.1(h).

[164] UNTAET Regulation No. 2000/11 on the Organisation of Courts in East Timor, UNTAET/REG/2000/11, 6 March 2000, s. 10.1.

[165] An Act to Establish the Truth and Reconciliation Commission of Liberia, 2005, s. 26(g). See also Hayner, 'Negotiating Peace in Liberia', 25.

[166] Kenya: Truth, Justice and Reconciliation Act 2008, s. 34(3).

However, as discussed in Chapter 2, the issue of granting amnesty for the most serious human rights crimes has not disappeared. Of recent times, Sierra Leone, [167] Algeria[168] and Uganda[169] have considered or enacted national amnesty laws for core crimes. Most recently, the Liberian TRC recommended that those who had cooperated fully with the TRC should not be prosecuted, rather granted some form of de facto amnesty, despite having committed war crimes and serious violations of international humanitarian law.[170] It therefore remains possible that some states may, in future, decide to pass national amnesty laws for international crimes and establish truth commissions as an alternative to pursuing prosecution. Where that state is a party to the ICC Statute, this will not prevent the Court exercising jurisdiction.[171] Neither does the existence of a national amnesty law constitute a ground for refusing to surrender a suspect to the Court.[172] Thus, for states parties the enactment of a national amnesty in relation to international crimes will not prevent their criminal prosecution. As with the provision of mutual legal assistance, the situation will become more complex where the state in which a national amnesty law is enacted is not a party to the ICC Statute. The existence of a national amnesty cannot oust the extra-territorial jurisdiction of bystander states. As in the South African example above, national amnesty laws apply only within the state concerned. However, in this situation the bystander state

---

[167] Peace Agreement between the Government of Sierra Leone and the Revolutionary United Front of Sierra Leone, Lomé, 3 June 1999, Articles IX and XXVI. This idea was later abandoned when renewed fighting caused the government to rethink its position. It should also be noted that the UN refused to support the amnesty provision. See *Seventh Report of the Secretary-General on the United Nations Observer Mission in Sierra Leone*, Security Council, UN Doc. S/1999/836.

[168] Laura Scully, 'Neither Justice Nor Oasis: Algeria's Amnesty' (2008) 33 *Brooklyn Journal of International Law* 975.

[169] 'War Crimes Amnesty for Rebels Is Necessary, Uganda Tells UN General Assembly', UN News Service, 20 September 2006. See also Kathleen E. MacMillan, 'The Practicability of Amnesty as a Non-Prosecutory Alternative in Post Conflict Uganda' (2007) 6 *Cardozo Public Law, Policy and Ethics Journal* 199, Alexander K. A. Greenawalt, 'Complementarity in Crisis: Uganda, Alternative Justice and the ICC' (2009) 50 *Virginia Journal of International Law* 107; Alex K. Kriksciun, 'Uganda's Response to ICC Arrest Warrants: A Misguided Approach?' (2007) 16 *Tulane Journal of International and Comparative Law* 213.

[170] *Republic of Liberia, Truth and Reconciliation Commission, Consolidated Final Report* (Ghana: Twidan Graphics, 2009), 353.

[171] See Chapter 4 and ICC, Office of the Prosecutor, *Policy Paper on the Interests of Justice*, September 2007, ICC-OTP-2007, 3-4, 8-9.

[172] Rome Statute, Arts. 89 and 102. See Goran Sluiter, 'The Surrender of War Criminals to the International Criminal Court' (2003) 25 *Loyola of Los Angeles International and Comparative Law Review* 605.

will be dependent on existing extradition arrangements in order to gain custody of suspected perpetrators. Where a national amnesty law has been passed in relation to the crimes for which extradition is sought, extradition treaty provisions relating to amnesty make it likely that assistance will be refused.

Truth commissions themselves may not pose particular problems to the extradition process, other than perhaps indicating unwillingness on the part of the state in which they are established to cooperate in prosecutions. However, the national amnesty laws with which they are sometimes associated may act as an impediment to successful prosecution by preventing the execution of extradition requests. Where effective prosecution is dependent on a third state obtaining custody of suspected perpetrators under existing extradition agreements, the operation of a truth and amnesty programme in the state of territoriality may prevent the execution of extradition requests and impede the pursuit of criminal justice. Equally, the possibility of extradition and prosecution by another state may have a negative impact on national truth seeking generally, much in the way that requests for mutual legal assistance may. Extradition requests are likely to impact most significantly on the willingness of perpetrators to offer testimony. Former perpetrators will be reluctant to appear before a truth commission and testify in relation to the commission of human rights crimes where there is a possibility that another state might seek their extradition to stand trial for those same crimes. Again, however, without their testimony, it will not be possible for truth commissions to establish a full and balanced account of the past. There is, therefore, a tension between the operation of truth commissions and prosecutions when they occur in different states, which raises doubts as to whether they truly are complementary mechanisms. The above discussion suggests that where a truth commission is established in one state and prosecutorial proceedings are commenced within another, the operation of each mechanism may impede the other, ultimately compromising both processes.

5   Judicial cooperation, truth commissions and the principle of *ne bis in idem*

The final area in which truth commissions might create problems for bystander states seeking to prosecute surrounds the principle of *ne bis in idem*. Scharf has suggested that it may be possible for an accused to argue that a confession before a truth commission is the functional equivalent of having been tried and convicted of an offence and that therefore the *ne bis in idem* principle offers protection to those who have confessed before a truth commission.[173] Many mutual legal assistance and extradition treaties contain mandatory or discretionary provisions that allow for a request for assistance or extradition to be refused on the grounds of *ne bis in idem*. If protection does attach to those who have testified before a truth commission, such a confession could then act as an obstacle to the provision of assistance and extradition under existing arrangements. While this may initially appear unlikely and an overstretching of the principle, the different versions of the principle included in existing treaties make it difficult to determine definitively whether such a scenario is out of the question.

The UN Model Treaty on Mutual Assistance in Criminal Matters provides that assistance may be refused if 'the request relates to an offence that is subject to investigation or prosecution in the requested State or the prosecution of which in the requesting State would be incompatible with the requested State's law on double jeopardy (*ne bis in idem*)'.[174] This provision is broad and under it a truth commission-holding state might refuse a request for assistance on the grounds that the offence is being investigated by a truth commission or that having been investigated by a national truth commission, provision of assistance relating to the same crimes would be contrary to national laws on *ne bis in idem*. The Commonwealth Scheme for Mutual Assistance in Criminal Matters allows for requests to be refused where they concern 'conduct for which the person accused or suspected of having committed an offence has been acquitted or convicted by a court in the requested country'.[175] Similarly, the Inter-American Convention on Mutual Assistance in Criminal Matters states that a request may be refused where it 'is being used in order to prosecute a person on a charge with respect to which that person has already been sentenced or acquitted in a trial in the requesting or requested state'.[176] In contrast to the UN Model Treaty, under these provisions it seems unlikely that a state could successfully refuse requests for assistance on the grounds of *ne bis in idem*. The Commonwealth Scheme refers to acquittal and conviction by a court and the Inter-American Convention refers to having been sentenced or acquitted in a trial. These are clear references to formal

---

[173] Michael P. Scharf, 'The Amnesty Exception to the Jurisdiction of the International Criminal Court' (1999) 32 *Cornell International Law Journal* 507, 525.

[174] UN Model Treaty on Mutual Assistance in Criminal Matters 1990, Art. 4(4).

[175] Scheme Relating to Mutual Assistance in Criminal Matters within the Commonwealth 1986, Art. 8(1)(d).

[176] Inter-American Convention on Mutual Assistance in Criminal Matters 1992, Art. 9(a).

criminal proceedings. It seems unlikely that a truth commission, which is a non-judicial body and incapable of acquitting, convicting or sentencing, would fall within the scope of these provisions.

Extradition treaties contain similar *ne bis in idem* provisions. The 1957 European Convention on Extradition states that, 'extradition shall not be granted if final judgment has been passed by the competent authorities of the requested Party upon the person claimed in respect of the offence or offences for which extradition is requested'.[177] The clause goes on to state that extradition may also be refused 'if the competent authorities of the requested Party have decided either not to institute or to terminate proceedings in respect of the same offence or offences'.[178] Under this provision, a truth commission-holding state could legitimately refuse a request for extradition on the grounds that it has decided not to initiate proceedings and has, instead, established a national truth commission. The UN Model Treaty on Extradition prohibits extradition where 'there has been a final judgement rendered against the person in the requested State in respect of the offence for which ... extradition is requested'.[179] The Council Framework Decision on the European Arrest Warrant states that a Member State shall refuse to execute the Warrant where 'the requested person has been finally judged by a Member State in respect of the same acts'.[180] However, this provision is qualified by the requirement that where there has been a sentence, it has or is being served, or can no longer be executed under the law of the sentencing Member State.[181] There appears to be less scope for refusing extradition on the grounds of having held a national truth commission under these provisions. Again, the references to 'final judgment' and, under the Framework Decision, to a 'sentence' suggest that these provisions refer to criminal proceedings.

The different national approaches towards the *ne bis in idem* principle do not offer clarification in this area and, in international law, have prevented the crystallisation of a customary rule and the recognition of a general principle of law.[182] While it is an internationally recognised

---

[177] European Convention on Extradition 1957, Art. 9.   [178] *Ibid.*

[179] UN Model Treaty on Extradition 1990, Art. 3(d).

[180] Council Framework Decision of 13 June 2002 on the European Arrest Warrant and the Surrender Procedures between Member States, Art. 3(2).

[181] *Ibid.*

[182] Gerard Conway, 'Ne Bis in Idem in International Law' (2003) 2 *International Criminal Law Review* 217.

human right, the relevant instruments do not provide international *ne bis in idem* protection but limit themselves to the national level.[183] Despite widespread acceptance of the principle, it is defined and interpreted differently between states.[184] There are differences between the approaches taken by civil law and common law systems in their assessment of when a judgment is 'final'. Many Continental European countries allow the state to appeal against an acquittal due to errors of law or questions of fact,[185] whereas other states, including the United States, which have common law systems, do not allow the state to appeal an acquittal.[186] Other countries limit the *ne bis in idem* principle to punishment only and do not prohibit repeated prosecutions.[187]

Most states do not recognise foreign judgments unconditionally for the purposes of the *ne bis in idem* principle and only give a *res judicata* effect to judgments by their own courts.[188] The Netherlands is perhaps the only example of a state that recognises foreign judgments without any limitations.[189] In contrast, the United States does not recognise any.[190] Most states give some recognition to foreign judgments, subject to certain limitations. For instance, some crimes, typically bribery and treason, are excluded from the *ne bis in idem* principle.[191] Some states distinguish between foreign judgments for territorial and extraterritorial crimes and do not extend the *ne bis in idem* protection to foreign convictions or acquittals for crimes committed on their own territory.[192] In addition,

---

[183] International Covenant on Civil and Political Rights 1966, Art. 14(7); European Convention on Human Rights 1950, Protocol 7, Art. 4; American Convention on Human Rights 1969, Art. 8(4); Arab Charter on Human Rights, adopted by the League of Arab States 15th September 1994, reprinted in (1997) 18 *Human Rights Law Journal* 151.

[184] Michele N. Morosin, 'Double Jeopardy and International Law: Obstacles to Formulating a General Principle' (1995) 64 *Nordic Journal of International Law* 261, 262–3.

[185] Bassiouni, 'Human Rights in the Context of Criminal Justice', 288.

[186] Morosin, 'Double Jeopardy and International Law', 262.

[187] Bassiouni, 'Human Rights in the Context of Criminal Justice', 289.

[188] Christine Van den Wyngaert and Guy Stessens, 'The International *non bis in idem* Principle: Resolving Some of the Unanswered Questions' (1999) 48 *International and Comparative Law Quarterly* 779, 783.

[189] See Peter Baauw, 'Ne Bis in Idem', in Bert Swart and Andre Klip (eds.), *International Criminal Law in the Netherlands* (Freiburg im Breisgau: Max-Planck-Institut für ausländisches und internationales Strafrecht, 1997), 75–84.

[190] Morosin, 'Double Jeopardy and International Law', 86.   [191] *Ibid.*

[192] Christine Van den Wyngaert and Tom Ongena, 'Ne Bis In Idem Principle, Including the Issue of Amnesty', in Antonio Cassese, Paulo Gaeta, and John R. W. D. Jones (eds.), *The Rome Statute of the International Criminal Court: A Commentary*, 2 vols. (Oxford University Press, 2002), chapter 18.4, 712–13.

many states insist that the foreign sentence must have been enforced for the *ne bis in idem* principle to apply, otherwise another prosecution will not be excluded.[193] This again raises questions as to whether truth commission proceedings fall within the application of the *ne bis in idem* principle. As non-judicial bodies, commissions do not have the power to sentence those who testify before them. Where the only response to the commission of serious human rights violations is a national truth commission, there is unlikely to be any sentence to enforce. This suggests that appearance before a truth commission will not attract the protection of the *ne bis in idem* principle and will not exclude future prosecution by another state.

Moreover, most states only give a *ne bis in idem* effect to acquittals and convictions.[194] It is argued that in order for the *ne bis in idem* protection to attach, 'the defendant must be acquitted or convicted on the merits by a court of competent jurisdiction.'[195] Decisions not to prosecute or to discontinue prosecutions will not have a *res judicata* effect and will not necessarily prevent new prosecutions. This again suggests that truth commission proceedings fall outside the scope of the *ne bis in idem* principle. However, in some jurisdictions out-of-court settlements cause the right to prosecute to lapse.[196] Therefore, while such settlements do not have the same legal status as judgments, they may ultimately have the same result. The status of out-of-court settlements, decisions not to prosecute and deals with criminals are unclear under the *ne bis in idem* rule.[197]

It is impossible to determine definitively whether confession before a truth commission might give rise to protection under the *ne bis in idem* principle. It appears that much may depend on the content and phrasing of the individual treaty provisions. However, it is possible that a state that has decided not to pursue prosecution and establish a national truth commission might attempt to use the *ne bis in idem* provisions of mutual legal assistance and extradition treaties to argue that confession before a truth commission is equivalent to trial and conviction and thereby obstruct prosecution by refusing requests for assistance.

---

[193] *Ibid.*, 712.   [194] *Ibid.*, 713.

[195] Morosin, 'Double Jeopardy and International Law', 263.

[196] In Belgium, France, Luxembourg, Netherlands and Italy, out-of-court settlements cause the right to prosecute to elapse. See Christine Van den Wyngaert *et al.*, *Criminal Procedure Systems in the European Community* (London: Butterworths, 1993).

[197] Van den Wyngaert and Ongena, 'Ne Bis In Idem Principle', 713–14.

6 Coordinating truth commissions and bystander state prosecutions

The possibility of bystander state prosecutions in relation to crimes that are being, or have been, investigated by the national truth commission of another state poses a host of problems. Some are distinct to the tensions inherent in reconciling protective national laws preventing the disclosure of truth commission material with international treaty obligations to provide information to requesting states. This issue may be alleviated in part by the limitation of truth-seeking powers as proposed in Chapter 4. If truth commissions operate without quasi-judicial powers to grant confidentiality and compel self-incriminating information, the need to prevent disclosure of the information obtained through their use under protective national legislation, which may then prevent the flow of information under judicial assistance treaties, will be diminished. This solution will not, however, mitigate the negative impact on truth seeking caused by the inevitable inhibition of perpetrators due to the possibility of prosecution by another state. Vulnerable witnesses may also withhold their testimony if its confidentiality cannot be guaranteed and some information will be lost to the truth-seeking process.

The other problems discussed in this chapter are indicative of a more general problem within the ICC regime, which requires states to place continued reliance on existing international cooperation agreements in carrying out prosecutions of international crimes at national levels. Although the Statute has introduced a framework in which prosecution ought to be the primary response to core crimes at both the national and international level, it provides no guidance on how states ought to cooperate between themselves in pursuing such proceedings. The existing cooperation arrangements on which states will be dependent in order to obtain evidence and custody of suspects are not designed to enable the effective prosecution of such crimes. They include provisions that may make it difficult to gain access to evidence and suspects. Thus, despite the efforts of some states to enact domestic legislation to ensure that they can prosecute ICC crimes wherever they are committed, reliance on existing judicial cooperation treaties, and the grounds for refusal of assistance that they include, may thwart such attempts. It therefore appears that, in an albeit limited number of situations, the impunity gap will remain. This suggests that formulation of new international agreements to facilitate the provision of judicial assistance between states in cases involving serious human rights violations may be necessary if they are to carry out effective prosecutions of ICC crimes wherever they occur.

The proposal of an enhanced cooperation regime in relation to international crimes is not new. The UN General Assembly suggested in the 1970s that there was a 'special need for international action'[198] to ensure the prosecution and punishment of those responsible for war crimes and crimes against humanity. General Assembly Resolution 3074 outlined broad principles of international collaboration in relation to the prosecution of these crimes, stressing the need for inter-state cooperation in tracing, arrest and trial,[199] assistance in the provision of information and evidence[200] and facilitative national laws relating to extradition.[201] However, no special cooperative treaty regime relating to international crimes has ever been concluded. More recently, Akhaven has proposed the formulation of an optional protocol to the ICC Statute enshrining an obligation for the repression of ICC crimes before national courts to combat the inadequacies of the current haphazard scheme.[202] He argues for the negotiation of an *aut dedere aut prosequi* provision between states in relation to ICC crimes[203] and suggests that, as a minimal enforcement mechanism, the ICC should be able to order states to open national investigations and prosecutions.[204]

The argument that proceedings at the national level are essential if the impunity gap is to be closed is compelling. National prosecutions will be necessary where the ICC does not have jurisdiction, where the Court is overstretched and where larger numbers of prosecutions are required than the Court can accommodate. However, the extent to which the proposed scheme would solve the problems associated with lack of inter-state cooperation is questionable. Naturally, an optional protocol would apply only between states that ratify it. Between those states, an enhanced cooperation regime that removes the traditional barriers to assistance in relation to core crimes would be advantageous. However, the scheme would not apply between non-party states to the ICC and it is unlikely that even all states parties would ratify the protocol. A large number of states would likely remain outside the proposed *aut dedere aut prosequi* regime and would continue to provide, and refuse, assistance on the basis

---

[198] General Assembly Resolution 3074 (XXVIII), Principles of International Cooperation in the Detection, Arrest, Extradition and Punishment of Persons Guilty of War Crimes and Crimes against Humanity, 3 December 1973, preamble.

[199] *Ibid.*, para. 1.   [200] *Ibid.*, para. 6.   [201] *Ibid.*, para. 5.

[202] Akhaven, 'Whither National Courts', 1247.

[203] *Ibid.*, 1263–4.   [204] *Ibid.*, 1265.

of existing arrangements. Many of the current problems associated with the provision of judicial assistance would therefore remain.

Akhaven's proposal for the formulation of a new cooperation regime in relation to core crimes therefore leaves many problems unanswered. However, the notion that underpins it, that the creation of a new breed of assistance treaty is necessary to combat impunity at national levels, is undoubtedly correct. Without the creation of new arrangements that remove the traditional barriers to the provision of assistance the impunity gap cannot be closed. Of course, bringing such arrangements to fruition will be dependent on the willingness of states. While there may be an appetite for an optional protocol between some states parties to the ICC, there is unlikely to be widespread international support. It may be that states are more likely to agree assistance arrangements on a regional basis, as they do under many current regional mutual assistance schemes. This would remove some of the problems related to the likely hostility that an arrangement under the auspices of the ICC is likely to invoke in certain states and regions. It may be time for the UN to take up this mantle and draft new model treaties on extradition and mutual assistance in relation to the prosecution of core crimes, which remove traditional barriers to assistance and promote enhanced cooperation between states where these crimes are committed. It can never be ruled out that states will simply refuse to cooperate, regardless of their international treaty obligations, where they consider their sovereignty to be undermined or other interests threatened. However, narrowing the grounds for refusal of assistance would make refusal more difficult for the uncooperative state.

For the time being, rethinking the powers possessed by truth commissions may provide some resolution. For the transitional state where there is a genuine dilemma between providing judicial assistance under international treaties and upholding national provisions that protect truth commissions, departing from what has become the norm and creating a truly 'non-judicial' truth commission may provide a solution. The curtailment of truth-seeking powers would prevent the tension that currently prevails between treaty obligations and protective national provisions. Without their truth-seeking powers, commissions may not be as effective in gaining testimony. On the other hand, neither will they lack credibility by acting as an impediment to the pursuit of criminal justice for ICC crimes. Nevertheless, this solution is only partial. The state that is unwilling to cooperate in prosecutions will doubtless find ways to obstruct proceedings by other states by refusing judicial assistance and may well use its truth commission as a tool in this regard. Truth and amnesty programmes may still prove problematic under existing extradition arrangements and questions remain around the effect of truth commission testimony on the protection of the *ne bis in idem* principle.

7   Conclusion

It must be accepted that despite the accepted logic that truth commissions and trials are complementary in the benefits they deliver to transitional states, there are aspects of their operation that actually conflict. Under current practice, not only does it appear that the operation of truth commissions may have a stultifying effect on bystander state efforts to carry out prosecutions, it seems likely that attempts by bystander states to access information or gain custody of perpetrators from truth commission-holding states may hamper the truth-seeking process. Some of these difficulties have been explored in previous chapters. However, where these institutions operate in different states the problems of coordination are magnified and the resolution options slimmer. In the event of conflict between a truth commission and national prosecutions or ICC proceedings, there is likely to be some method of resolution either at the national level or by recourse to state obligations under the ICC treaty. The situation differs where bystander state prosecutions overlap the operations of a truth commission in the state of territoriality. As can be seen in past experiences with Guatemala and Argentina, where this is the case, existing assistance arrangements may enable a stalemate rather than providing for a means of resolution. It is, therefore, possible that for some transitional states where trials are not pursued at the national level or by the ICC, but by a third state, there will be neither successful prosecutions for past violations or effective truth seeking by the commission. Far from being complementary bodies, in some situations, under current arrangements trials and truth seeking may, in practice, be incompatible initiatives.

6

Conclusion: coordinating truth commissions and trials in the ICC era

1 Truth commissions and trials: complementary or incompatible initiatives?

Within the transitional justice framework, the use of trials and truth commissions has evolved considerably since their initial establishment as opposing alternatives. Contemporary transitional justice theory evidences a belief that these bodies play complementary and mutually reinforcing roles in transitional states. Through their respective abilities to contribute to the delivery of justice, document the truth, respond to the needs of victims, strengthen the rule of law and lay foundations for national reconciliation, their dual operation is understood to provide transitional societies with a range of advantages.[1] This theory is reflected in current practice, which increasingly favours the twin establishment of these institutions as part of a multifaceted response to past violations. Recent studies have added weight to the notion that transitional justice programmes should be multidimensional, demonstrating that human rights protection and democratic governance are more likely to be achieved following the operation of multiple mechanisms, rather than one.[2] The discourse on the merits of trials and truth commissions therefore indicates compatibility. It suggests that together they may deliver a more complete package of benefits to transitional states.

In practice, trials and truth commissions have been utilised as part of a coordinated programme in only a few transitional contexts and have been employed differently in each. Regardless of the relationship basis between them, their contemporaneous operation has given rise to tension. In particular, it has proved difficult to find a means of coordinating

---

[1] See Chapter 1.
[2] Tricia D. Olson, Leigh A. Payne and Andrew G. Reitger, *Transitional Justice in Balance: Comparing Processes, Weighing Efficacy* (Washington DC: US Institute of Peace Press, 2010); Eric Wiebelhaus-Brahm, *Truth Commissions and Transitional Societies: The Impact on Human Rights and Democracy* (London and New York: Routledge, 2010).

their operation without one body functioning at the expense of the other. In large part, this stems from a disharmony between their modes of operation and the powers they possess, which is brought into focus by their overlapping subject matter mandates. While they may deliver a range of complementary benefits to transitional states, coordinating their proceedings poses an array of challenges. At the most general level, where trials and truth commissions operate contemporaneously, some witnesses and former perpetrators will be deterred from offering testimony to the truth commission for fear that their account will be passed to prosecutorial institutions. In addition, there is conflict between the interests of truth commissions to protect from disclosure the information given by some categories of witnesses and those of prosecutorial institutions to have access to all relevant information. The need for prosecutorial institutions to protect the rights of accused persons to a fair trial and against self-incrimination is at odds with the objective of truth commissions to offer to all the opportunity to share, sometimes publicly, their account of the past. The truth-seeking powers commonly possessed by truth commissions exacerbate these difficulties by creating the potential for conflict where two institutions have the ability to exercise judicial powers in relation to the same crimes and individuals. How significantly these issues impact the effective operation of these bodies will depend on the relationship model that exists between them and the level on which interaction takes place.

The prosecutorial climate created by the establishment of the ICC and national efforts to contribute to the fight against impunity could make it easy to overlook truth commissions or sacrifice their efficacy in favour of that of prosecutorial institutions. In many ways, trials and truth commissions are not natural companions. Their differing modes of operation and overlapping mandates have the potential to create tension and conflict. But to conclude from this that they are incompatible seems too quick and simplistic. Such a conclusion, coupled with the international push towards prosecution, risks denying to transitional societies the benefits that national truth seeking seems to bring. If it is accepted that these bodies have different but equally worthwhile benefits to bring to transitional states, attention needs to be focused on ensuring their effective coexistence.

This study suggests that truth commissions and trials are neither truly complementary nor entirely incompatible. Instead, they give rise to operational difficulties, which, if coordinated carefully, can be resolved, or at least reduced, so as to minimise the potential for conflict and ensure, in large part, the delivery of their respective benefits to transitional societies.

This requires detailed consideration of the ways in which they may come into conflict and the levels on which they may interact and the development of targeted solutions at all levels. It requires an abandonment of the 'one size fits all' truth commission and an effort to reconsider how these bodies might be adapted to operate alongside different types of prosecutorial institutions. While past practice arises at the national level, it is increasingly likely that future truth commissions will operate in tandem with the ICC or alongside bystander state prosecutions. Coordination in these circumstances will create additional challenges as there will be an absence of any overarching design in their operation and they will proceed as distinct and autonomous processes. The articulation of transitional justice policy on coordinating trials and truth commissions is a necessity if the dual operation of these bodies is to yield any meaningful result in future practice. This final chapter brings together the findings of the preceding chapters in order to outline proposals on how these bodies might best be coordinated to ensure effective coexistence at different levels.

2   Truth commissions and national level trials: coordination in a broad framework

Coordinating trials and truth commissions at the national level presents an assortment of dilemmas for establishing authorities: should the truth commission and prosecutorial institutions interact and on what basis? Should they share information? Should they have unfettered access to the same persons? Should one be able to exercise powers over the other? These are undoubtedly difficult issues to grapple with and require careful consideration. Nevertheless, national authorities possess a full gamut of possibilities in designing truth commissions and trials and creating a framework for their operation and coexistence. In many situations, prosecution of some past crimes will be required, either as a result of treaty obligations or, where states are party to the ICC Statute, to preclude the assumption of jurisdiction by the ICC under the complementarity regime. Beyond this, states have wide discretion to establish truth commissions and prosecutorial institutions on their preferred basis.

Evaluation of past practice demonstrates that at the national level, following certain guiding criteria may promote effective coexistence between trials and truth commissions. Thus, they should operate:

- as distinct institutions;
- without obligations that link their procedures;

- on the basis of equality;
- under an agreement that regulates their operations;
- with the possibility of recourse to an independent resolution mechanism in the event of dispute.

Analysis of the South African and East Timorese models[3] indicated that creating separate institutions with operational detachment will avoid the role confusion and inter-institutional resentment that can arise where interconnected operational models are established. As part of this, they should not be created with obligations that link their operations. Instituting a multifaceted transitional justice programme to address the past does not require that the mechanisms within it work together. Multifaceted does not mean interwoven. States should be clear about their transitional aims and what they seek to achieve through the establishment and operation of different mechanisms. Trials and truth commissions may produce overlapping benefits through their operation but each should have an overriding objective and should be designed to fulfil that aim. Caution should be exercised in endowing truth commissions with the power to grant amnesty or the responsibility to administer amnesty-related programmes. This risks judicialising the truth-seeking process and opening it to legal challenge, obfuscating the non-judicial character of truth commissions.

Trials and truth commissions should be established on an equality model. Neither should hold powers over the other. The need to ensure effective prosecution of certain crimes need not and should not lead to the conclusion that any truth commission that is also established must be secondary to prosecutorial institutions or serve as a means of furthering criminal proceedings. Neither body should be established as a means of furthering the objectives of the other. This will create a hierarchy from the outset and subordinate the operations of one to the other. Each should be established with a robust mandate aimed at enabling the achievement of its own objectives.

Agreements regulating the relationship between trials and truth commissions ought to be drawn up prior to the commencement of operations. Where two institutions have overlapping subject matter mandates and rely on the same categories of information to fulfil those mandates, it is foreseeable that tension may arise. The Sierra Leonean experience highlights this well.[4] In accordance with the need to maintain distinction between

---

[3] See Chapter 3.   [4] See Chapter 3.

the two, preserve their autonomy and minimise the potential for conflict, information should not be shared. Information gathered through truth seeking should not be available to prosecutorial institutions and those indicted by prosecutorial institutions should not be accessible by truth commissions. Regulating agreements will be particularly important if truth commissions are to possess quasi-judicial truth-seeking powers. There is no reason why, at the national level, truth commissions should not possess these powers, as long as there are clear parameters for their use, which ensure compatibility with contemporaneous prosecutorial proceedings and avoid truth commission encroachment into the prosecutorial domain. The regulating agreement also ought to put in place a means of independent, third party dispute resolution in order to ensure that any disputes are resolved by an impartial body.

These guidelines are not intended to constrain the options for contemporaneous trial and truth commission operation, but to enhance coexistence by maintaining clear boundaries between them, thereby minimising the potential for conflict. Within this broad framework, states have freedom to tailor their transitional programmes to the needs of their particular society. They can decide, in accordance with international legal obligations, which crimes to prosecute, whether or not to grant amnesty for those that do not require prosecution, the nature of the truth commission's mandate, the powers it might be endowed with and which other mechanisms to implement. These are all context-specific variables. As with all transitional justice initiatives, wherever possible trials and truth commissions should be established and operate within the state concerned. National-level operation presents the greatest possibilities for robust truth seeking alongside effective prosecutions, due to the ability of one authority to design and regulate them as part of a tailored and coordinated programme.

3   Truth commissions and the ICC: coordination through policy development

The establishment of the International Criminal Court introduces a new dynamic into the complexities of coordinating trials and truth commissions. The powers of the ICC and the obligations of states parties to cooperate with and provide assistance to the Court have potentially significant implications for truth commission operation. The obligatory cooperative framework of the ICC Statute enables the Court to access truth commission materials, regardless of their status under national law, to further international prosecutorial proceedings. Attempts to access truth commission materials seem likely to prove most problematic where the sought information has been obtained under a truth commission's powers to grant confidentiality or compel the provision of self-incriminating information. This study therefore proposed that where states do not pursue prosecutions at the national level, thereby opening the possibility of prosecution by the ICC, they should limit the powers of any truth commission that they establish to minimise the potential for conflict between the commission and the Court.[5]

The proposal to limit truth-seeking powers is born in large part from the uncertainty that surrounds the status of truth commissions under the ICC regime. Currently, there is no clear understanding of how the Court views truth commissions, whether it will seek to access their materials if they are considered of relevance to prosecution cases or whether it will attempt to support truth seeking by maintaining a clear division between its work and that of national commissions. With the Court now operating contemporaneously with the Kenyan Truth, Justice and Reconciliation Commission, the development of policy guidelines on the interrelationship between truth commissions and the ICC is urgently required. The issues raised by the simultaneous operation of truth commissions and the ICC are unique. No other transitional justice mechanism routinely exercises quasi-judicial powers and the operation of the Court does not have the potential to impact any other mechanism so considerably. The relationship between the two is therefore deserving of special attention.

The ICC Office of the Prosecutor (OTP) *Policy Paper on the Interests of Justice*, in which the OTP states that it 'endorses' the role played by other transitional justice mechanisms and will 'seek to work constructively with them',[6] is overly broad and insufficiently detailed. Explicit consideration of how they will, or will not, interact on a practical, operational level is needed. The Court should clarify the status of truth commissions under the ICC regime and bring to an end the speculation about how commissions may or may not be treated within it. Such clarification will enable the development of wider transitional justice policy on how truth commissions can move forward when their operations have to be coordinated with those of the Court. The Court does not operate in a vacuum, but in the wider transitional justice context, and has a duty to consider how its

---

[5] See Chapter 4.
[6] ICC, Office of the Prosecutor, *Policy Paper on the Interests of Justice*, September 2007, ICC-OTP-2007, 7–8.

proceedings can contribute to and be coordinated with wider goals and other mechanisms.

This study's analysis of truth commission operation within the ICC framework suggests that coordination of truth commissions and the ICC:

- requires clarification through the development of policy guidelines by the Court;
- should be based on the notion that confidential truth commission materials warrant privileged status under the Statute;
- should provide for a consultative process between truth commissions and the Court in order to resolve any disputes over access to information;
- may, depending on policy development by the Court and the content of that policy, require limitation of truth-seeking powers in order to maintain the independence and integrity of truth commissions.

The goal of facilitating effective coexistence should guide the Court in its development of policy in relation to national truth commissions and any interaction with them. The Court's policy on its relationship with truth commissions should be underpinned by the notion that transitional programmes should be multifaceted and enable the contemporaneous operation of multiple mechanisms. This is already implicit within the OTP *Policy Paper on the Interests of Justice*,[7] but should be explicitly enunciated in any policy document on the relationship between truth commissions and the ICC. In contrast to the proposals of some writers,[8] the establishment of a truth commission should not act as an impediment to trials for core crimes or preclude the Court's jurisdiction and should complement prosecution rather than replace it. This accords with the mandate and objectives of the ICC and the wording of the Statute. At the same time, the operation of the Court should not inhibit or undermine truth commission proceedings through the invasive exercise of its information-gathering powers.

Coordination of the operation of truth commissions alongside the ICC requires the development of policy rooted in compromise that seeks to accommodate both positions. The Court should afford protection to confidential truth commission information in accordance with the standards of Rules 73(4) and (6) of the ICC Rules of Procedure and Evidence, in

---

[7] ICC, Office of the Prosecutor, *Policy Paper on the Interests of Justice*, 7–8.
[8] See Chapter 4.

order to strike a balance and promote operational equilibrium. Under this system, confidential truth commission materials would generally be considered privileged and only in the event that information was of great importance to a particular case would the Court seek access to it. This would constitute recognition of both the worthwhile role of truth commissions within transitional societies and the centrality of the ability to maintain the confidentiality of certain categories of information to their work. It would also enable optimal truth seeking by preserving the possibility of truth commissions exercising quasi-judicial powers and protecting the information obtained through their use. At the same time, it would not render confidential truth commission information entirely off limits to the Court in the event that it seemed of real significance to a prosecution case. In line with this arrangement, truth commissions would have to ensure that they provide witnesses with clear explanations of their capacity to preserve confidentiality so that any testimony is given subject to an understanding of its potential use. As is the case with the ICRC under Rules 73(4) and (6), recourse to a consultative process between truth commissions and the Court should be provided for in the event of dispute over access to information or operational dilemma. In order to foster a spirit of cooperation rather than combat, the Court should avoid exercising its treaty powers over states parties in order to resolve conflict with national truth commissions. This will only undermine the possibilities for effective coexistence by creating hostility and resentment.

Thus, access by the Court to confidential truth commission material should be an exception, rather than a rule. Unless such an eventuality is truly exceptional there is no possibility for truth commissions to exercise quasi-judicial powers to obtain information or maintain the confidentiality of testimony. To do so and then be compelled to disclose information to the Court would seriously undermine their credibility. Ultimately, even the slightest possibility that the Court will seek to access confidential materials may prove too great a risk to the integrity of the truth commission for those creating future commissions. Less powerful, but independent and credible commissions may seem a preferable option. However, decisions on how to design truth commissions that may operate alongside the ICC should be informed by a clear understanding of the Court's likely treatment of their operations and the information they hold. In the interim, limiting the powers of truth commissions may provide a means of maintaining the autonomy and integrity of truth commissions where there is potential for overlap with the operations of the ICC and the threat of orders for disclosure of information.

4 Truth commissions and bystander state prosecutions: coordination through cooperation regime development

Coordinating national truth seeking with bystander state prosecutions represents the greatest challenge to the effective coexistence of these bodies. Where trials and truth commissions are undertaken in different states, synchronising their operations will be much more difficult. There will be no single authority controlling their dual operation, nor, as in the case of contemporaneous operation with the ICC, one body with the power to exercise authority over the other. Instead, they are likely to be operating as haphazard and ad hoc responses to past crimes. It also seems likely that in many situations the truth commission-holding state may consider attempts by another to exercise jurisdiction in relation to crimes committed on its territory or by its nationals a violation of its sovereignty. It may therefore refuse to cooperate in the provision of judicial assistance. Bystander state reliance on existing mutual legal assistance treaties in order to obtain the evidence necessary to build prosecution cases creates additional problems. The range of grounds on which assistance can be refused under these treaties may provide uncooperative states with legal means of impeding prosecution by another. Even for cooperative states, there may be an incompatibility between national laws protecting truth commission information and treaty provisions that aim to enable its disclosure. Thus, the lack of joined-up coordination, reliance on existing assistance treaties, traditional grounds for refusal of assistance and the potential hostility of truth commission-holding states, may converge to hamper third state efforts to prosecute. Unlike the other situations considered in this book, where trials and truth commissions operate in different states, it is the pursuit of criminal justice, rather than carrying out truth seeking, that may prove particularly problematic.

Limiting the powers of truth commissions may provide some solution to alleviating the tension where national laws protecting truth commission materials prevent the provision of assistance. If truth commissions cannot grant confidentiality or compel the provision of self-incriminating information, they will not possess those categories of information and there will be no requirement for national laws that prevent their disclosure. The tension between protective domestic provisions and treaty obligations to provide information will be removed. However, this solution is at best partial as it relates only to the situation where the truth commission-holding state is genuine in its desire to cooperate and provide assistance. The real solution in this scenario lies elsewhere. If bystander states are to contribute to the fight against impunity by carrying out effective prosecutions of core crimes, the development of new inter-state cooperation treaties will be required. It is reliance upon existing arrangements and the grounds within them for refusing assistance that constitute the real impediment to bystander state trials by allowing for information to be withheld at the discretion of the requested state. The operation of a truth commission in the requested state may only serve to exacerbate and add another dimension to a problem that already exists.

The development of comprehensive guidelines on the creation of new judicial assistance treaties to facilitate cooperation in the prosecution of core crimes falls outside the scope of this book. However, to enable the effective coexistence of truth commissions and bystander state prosecutions, and eradicate the possibility of truth commissions being manipulated to act as an obstruction to trials, a new cooperation regime is required. Any new regime should:

- be based on a presumption in favour of the provision of assistance where core crimes are concerned;
- eliminate the traditional grounds for refusing assistance in relation to core crimes;
- enable the provision of assistance on the basis of a regime akin to that between states and the ICC;
- make explicit that the operation of a national truth commission in the requested state does not provide grounds for the refusal of assistance;
- afford confidential truth commission materials privileged status;
- make requests for confidential truth commission information subject to a consultative procedure requiring demonstration of its importance to a particular prosecution case and the impossibility of obtaining it elsewhere;
- enable disclosure of confidential truth commission information only upon fulfilment of those criteria and the satisfaction of the truth commission-holding state that disclosure is, on balance, in the wider transitional justice interest.

The unique nature of international crimes requires a distinct inter-state treaty regime to enable their effective prosecution. Existing judicial assistance arrangements were not developed to facilitate cooperation in relation to such violations and as a result, contain provisions that hinder the provision of assistance between states rather than enhancing it. Any new regime will need to radically rethink the grounds on which states can refuse to provide judicial assistance. State sovereignty and national law incompatibility should not be valid concerns where the most serious human rights violations have been committed. The focus of these regimes should divert from the interests of individual states to those of the international community to provide effective redress for the commission of international crimes. New treaties should operate on a basis similar to that between states and international tribunals, where the opportunities for refusing assistance are significantly narrower, in recognition of the shared interest in combating impunity.

A new cooperation regime in respect of core crimes should take note of its likely use in situations where truth commissions, and other transitional justice mechanisms, may be operational. Provisions should be included which state explicitly that the operation of a transitional justice programme in the state of territoriality cannot of itself provide grounds for refusing assistance in relation to the prosecution of international crimes. Truth commissions should be no different. However, the confidential materials held by truth commissions should not be subject to routine requests for disclosure under any new regime but should be afforded privileged status. Prosecutions by bystander states are likely to be prompted by a lack of prosecutorial activity in the state of territoriality, making it essential that any mechanisms operating at the national level are capable of maximum impact. If a truth commission is to be the primary response to past violations in the state of territoriality, it is important to ensure its optimum efficiency. The ability to exercise a range of truth-seeking powers will be required to ensure that truth seeking is a robust and visible process. The commission should have abilities to uncover relevant material to inform national understandings of the past and assign responsibility for the commission of international crimes. If truth commission information is available under judicial assistance treaties, this will constrain the abilities of national truth commissions to exercise powers to compel the provision of information and guarantee confidentiality. Without the ability to exercise truth-seeking powers, the impact made by the commission's operation and final report may be limited. Thus, the efficacy of truth commissions should be protected by excluding the possibility of routine bystander state requests for confidential truth commission information under judicial assistance treaties.

At the same time, it seems overly rigid to preclude absolutely, in all circumstances, the possibility of truth commission information being accessible to prosecutorial institutions in third states. Where prosecutions are undertaken by bystander states, it is likely to prove much more difficult to obtain the necessary information and evidence than it is at the domestic level. It is therefore conceivable that truth commission information may prove of significance in some cases. If the ability to access confidential truth commission information makes the difference between a successful and unsuccessful prosecution, then it would seem sensible to at least maintain the possibility of accessing the information held by a truth commission. As in the case of the ICC, any requests to access truth commission information should be resolved through a consultative process, designated within new judicial assistance treaties, between the requesting and truth commission-holding states. There should be no automatic ability to access confidential materials under judicial assistance treaties. The decision on whether to disclose it should lie ultimately with the truth commission-holding state and should be made upon a balancing of the different interests involved and the consequences of (non) disclosure.

The creation of new inter-state cooperation treaties is not a foolproof means of coordinating truth commissions and third state trials or, more generally, of ensuring the provision of assistance to prosecuting third states. The abilities of third states to obtain the necessary information to support prosecutions will depend on the existence of a relevant treaty between the prosecuting and requested states. Even where such a treaty is in place, their efficacy relies upon the requested state adhering to its treaty obligations and providing assistance. Past practice shows that this does not always occur. However, the current absence of a cooperation regime aimed at facilitating inter-state assistance in the prosecution of core crimes remains a significant deficiency at a time when third state prosecution seems increasingly likely. Without the development of a new treaty regime the valuable role that bystander states might make to ensuring accountability may be thwarted. Under existing arrangements, national truth commissions may become an impediment to bystander state trials, or be used to obstruct them, rather than contributing to a wider sense of accountability. The development of new cooperation regimes is therefore essential to combating impunity and facilitating the effective coexistence of national truth commissions and bystander state trials.

5   Final remarks

Understanding of the roles played by trials and truth commissions in responding to past human rights violations has developed considerably since their initial use as rival paradigms. Current conceptions view them as compatible processes, to be operationalised contemporaneously as part of multifaceted, context-specific transitional justice programmes.

This new utilisation, coupled with the prioritisation of prosecution for core crimes in light of the ICC regime, brings with it novel challenges. National truth commissions may, in future, operate alongside domestic trials, ICC proceedings, bystander state prosecutions or perhaps even all three. Each of these scenarios raises it own set of difficulties. There is no easy or single answer to the dilemmas of how to coordinate the operations of these institutions. This book has developed broad frameworks in order to understand how effective coexistence might be achieved at different levels. However, much policy-making remains to be done to ensure that this becomes a reality rather than an aspiration. Without further development, the legacy of dual operation risks being one of tension and friction rather than the delivery of a range of benefits to transitional societies.

INDEX

KZ
7230
.B57
2012